T0285061

OUT OF THE MELTING POT, INTO THE FIRE

Multiculturalism in the World's Past and America's Future

Jens Kurt Heycke

New York • London

First American edition published in 2023 by Encounter Books, an activity of Encounter for Culture and Education, Inc., a nonprofit, tax-exempt corporation.
Encounter Books website address: www.encounterbooks.com

Manufactured in the United States and printed on acid-free paper. The paper used in this publication meets the minimum requirements of ANSI/NISO Z39.48-1992 (R 1997) (*Permanence of Paper*).

FIRST AMERICAN EDITION

LIBRARY OF CONGRESS CATALOGING-IN-PUBLICATION DATA

Names: Heycke, Jens Kurt, 1961– author.
Title: Out of the melting pot, into the fire: multiculturalism in the world's past and America's future / Jens Kurt Heycke.
Description: First edition. | New York, NY: Encounter Books, 2023.
Includes bibliographical references and index. |
Identifiers: LCCN 2022032761 (print) | LCCN 2022032762 (ebook)
ISBN 9781641773195 (hardcover) | ISBN 9781641773201 (ebook)
Subjects: LCSH: Multiculturalism—History. | Multiculturalism—United States—History. | United States—Race relations—History.
Ethnic relations—Political aspects.
Classification: LCC HM1271 .H49 2023 (print) | LCC HM1271 (ebook)
DDC 305.8—dc23/eng/20220708
LC record available at https://lccn.loc.gov/2022032761
LC ebook record available at https://lccn.loc.gov/2022032762

1 2 3 4 5 6 7 8 9 20 23

TABLE OF CONTENTS

PREFACE

As our van careened around a corner in the rugged Dinaric Alps, the driver gestured toward some people by the roadside:

> They are all Bosniaks [Bosnian Muslims], just like me. Now, count to ten: one, two, three... You see, in that short time, we are in a Serb area. Those people are Serbs. They speak the same language as us and the Croats; we have the same DNA. But they tried to kill us all.

He shook his head: "Only in my country." He described what happened in 1995: men and boys, including some of his own relatives, were shot and bulldozed into mass graves; young girls were raped in front of their families; thousands were burned alive or tortured to death in concentration camps. "Only in my country," he repeated.

Not wanting to question the uniqueness of his country's tragedies, I nodded and remained silent. But I thought about how Bosnia was only one of many multiethnic societies around the world that have suffered similar tragedies. I thought of a woman I met in Rwanda. As a young girl, she went to fetch milk from a nearby village. When she returned, she found her extended family—nineteen people in all—hacked to death with machetes just because they were Tutsis. And I thought of a Sri Lankan pogrom survivor I interviewed. His family managed to slip away from the murderous mobs, while other Tamils nearby were dragged from a bus, dismembered, and disemboweled with broken bottles as bystanders clapped and danced.[1]

Multiethnic societies have a range of possible outcomes, with extreme violence being a tragically frequent one.[2] My Bosniak driver believed the ethnic conflict in his country was horrific and exceptional, but he was only partly right: it was horrific—but utterly unexceptional. Collectively, ethnic conflicts around the world, from Bosnia to Sri Lanka, have killed more than ten million people since World War II.

Many Americans reflexively tune out news of these conflicts. In the words of one satirist, it's just the "unspellables" killing the "unpronounceables"—peoples too distant or inexplicable to pay attention to. But as Americans, we need to pay attention, not just for the sake of the millions around the world suffering from ethnic division, but for our own sake. We must deepen our understanding of what it takes for diverse ethnic groups to get along and share a country, for America is rapidly becoming vastly more multiethnic.

In the last decade alone, America admitted nearly eleven million *legal* immigrants, roughly the combined population of Iowa, Oklahoma, and Oregon. Illegal immigrants may account for an additional, Illinois-sized population of twelve million. The current migrant wave will change America's ethnic composition far more profoundly than previous waves. In the big influx at the turn of the twentieth century, non-European immigrants accounted for only 3 percent of the total; today, they account for over 90 percent.[3]

The United States is unlikely to devolve into another Bosnia or Rwanda overnight. However, the history of other multiethnic countries is instructive: ethnic tension can degenerate into ethnic strife, violence, or outright genocide with ferocious speed. At the end of World War II, Sri Lanka was celebrated as a land of ethnic harmony and rosy prospects. A few years later, divisive affirmative action policies sparked a violent conflict that lasted

Figure P.1. Immigrant population of the United States (millions).[4]

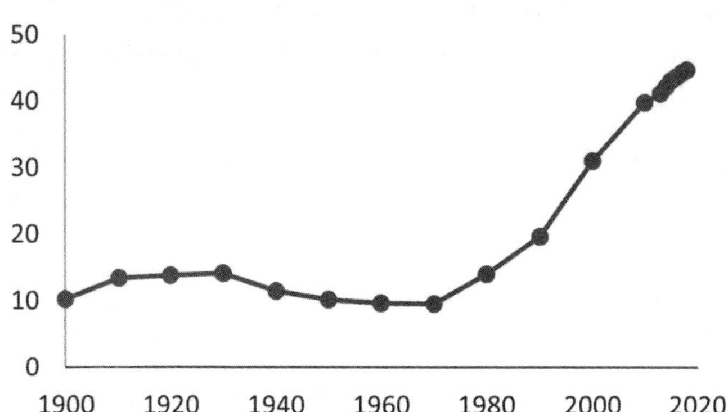

over forty years, killing hundreds of thousands and condemning a once-prosperous island to poverty. Although the United States might not be on quite the same trajectory, that is no cause for insouciance. Group conflict and ethnically motivated attacks have mounted precipitously in recent years.[5] While most Americans conceive of ethnic conflict in white-black terms, it has become increasingly multilateral, involving other groups.[6] The negative consequences of ethnic division also go beyond overt hate crimes and violence. As the social statistics in this book show, ethnically divided societies that simmer in communal tension suffer dire social and economic costs even when that tension is nonviolent.

While the number of immigrants has soared and ethnic tensions have risen, the philosophy for integrating diverse groups into American society has shifted. For most of US history, the "melting pot" was the prevailing ideal, even if it was imperfectly followed much of the time. Beginning in the 1970s, some mainstream leaders suggested abandoning the melting pot and the goal of a shared national identity. This thinking gained popularity while its focus evolved from tolerating or appreciating the cultural differences and distinctions of diverse ethnic groups to actively fostering and promoting them. The underlying philosophy, known as *multiculturalism,* also promoted programs and institutions that distinguish individuals based on inherited characteristics, such as race and ethnic origins, and grant preferences to them on that basis.

Although America's swing from a melting pot to a multicultural model has been vigorously debated, uninformed American exceptionalism has prevailed in this debate. Like my Bosniak van driver, many Americans think their country's challenges are unique. They are oblivious to the fact that countless other societies in history and around the world have grappled with managing diverse ethnicities. For example, *Time* magazine's special issue on American multiculturalism was subtitled: "How Immigrants Are Shaping the World's First Multicultural Society." Apparently, *Time*'s writers were unaware of the existence of the Roman, Ottoman, and Austro-Hungarian empires, as well as a long succession of other multicultural societies that punctuate fifty centuries of history all the way back to predynastic Egypt. This myopia is ironic in the case of multiculturalism's proponents: while they emphasize celebrating other cultures from around the world, they manifest stunning ignorance of these cultures' histories.

Thus, as the United States has veered from melting pot to multiculturalism, there has been little serious discussion about how similar course changes have worked out in other countries. The reality is that both the melting pot and multiculturalist models have been tried many times in history. In some cases, societies have shifted from one to the other. It's worth examining how it has worked out for them; perhaps we can distill some useful lessons from their experiences. That is what this book endeavors to accomplish.

We will begin with a brief introduction to the melting pot concept. Then we will survey examples of societies that have adopted the melting pot or multicultural models. Finally, we will analyze cross-national statistical data to evaluate the social and economic consequences of multiculturalism.

Definitions

The term "multiculturalism" has acquired such a variety of meanings—many of them conflicting—that any coherent discussion of it demands that it be formally defined. For the discussion in this book, multiculturalism is defined as *the doctrine that public policies and institutions should recognize and maintain the ethnic boundaries and distinct cultural practices of multiple ethnic groups within a country; it supports group preferences to achieve diversity or to address past injustices or current disparities.*

This sense of multiculturalism overlaps with what some scholars have called *hard multiculturalism* or *multicultural particularism*—the belief that a shared identity is either impossible or undesirable; in many ways, it is the opposite of the melting pot ideal.[7] It is important not to confuse this sense of multiculturalism with what is sometimes called *soft multiculturalism—the view that the unique contributions of multiple cultures should be valued and appreciated within a society*. Soft multiculturalism is a form of pluralism that is not only consistent with the melting pot ideal but instrumental to it.

1

✳

A BRIEF INTRODUCTION TO THE MELTING POT

Although most Americans are familiar with the term "melting pot," the play that originally popularized it has been mostly forgotten. Written by Israel Zangwill in 1908, it tells the story of David Quixano, a Russian Jewish immigrant. David falls in love with a Russian Christian immigrant whose father turns out to be the commander who directed an antisemitic pogrom that killed David's family back in Russia. The father admits his guilt; David ultimately forgives him and marries his daughter. Throughout the play, David exhorts others to abandon old ethnic and racial prejudices. He envisions an America where diverse ethnic groups reconcile and join in forging a new American identity, which is not based on ethnicity, but on a shared love of ideals like freedom:

> America is God's Crucible, the great Melting-Pot where all the races of Europe are melting and reforming! . . . Germans and Frenchmen, Irishmen and Englishmen, Jews and Russians—into the Crucible with you all! God is making the American . . . Celt and Latin, Slav and Teuton, Greek and Syrian,—black and yellow.[1]

Twenty years ago, when I checked out a library copy of *The Melting Pot*, I was surprised to find a leaflet tucked into the pages: it was a playbill from a 1913 Tacoma, Washington performance of the play. The fact that the play was performed in Tacoma, a small backwater lumber town at the time, suggests how widely popular it was. In fact, when *The Melting Pot* premiered, it was a hit across the country, with President Theodore Roosevelt eagerly attending the opening show in Washington, DC.[2] Over the following decades, the play's popularity declined; my library copy of the book documented this decline with a series of checkout date stamps that were progressively further and further apart, until 1975—the last time someone had checked it out before me.

Although Zangwill's play popularized the term "melting pot," the concept and the metaphor predate it by many years. The French immigrant Hector de Crèvecoeur was one of the first Americans to express the metaphor in writing. In his *Letters from an American Farmer* (1782), he heralds the American who "leaves behind him all his ancient prejudices and manners," and he praises America as a place where "individuals of all nations are melted into a new race of men."[3] A century later, Ralph Waldo Emerson used similar language to extol the ideal of diverse immigrants forging a unified identity:

> In this continent,—asylum of all nations,—the energy of Irish, Germans, Swedes, Poles, and Cossacks, and all the European tribes,—of the Africans, and the Polynesians,—will construct a new race, a new religion, a new state, a new literature ... as vigorous as the new Europe which came out of the smelting pot of the Middle Ages.[4]

The melting pot was only an ideal, one that was never fully realized. In contrast to the vision articulated by Emerson and Zangwill, the actual melting pot excluded black people for most of America's history. Other groups—Germans, Irish, Italians, Jews, Chinese, and many others—suffered periods of exclusion and discrimination before they were eventually accepted and integrated as Americans. But if the melting pot failed some, it became progressively more inclusive and more faithful to the ideal. For example, the rate at which Americans of German ancestry married other Americans went from 2 percent to 90 percent between 1900 and 1990. The intermarriage rate for some other groups had a later starting point but has followed a similar trajectory: it is now 39 percent for Latinos, 46 percent for Asians, and 17 percent for black people.[5]

A list of the origins of top US generals since 1950 illustrates how diverse immigrants could quickly integrate and achieve prominent positions in the American mainstream: Schwarzkopf (Germany); Pagonis (Greece); Powell (Jamaica); Abizaid (Lebanon); Petraeus (Netherlands); Shalikashvili (Georgia); Shinseki (Japan); Luong (Vietnam); Shekerjian (Armenia); and Cavazos (Mexico). Although these individuals are all first- and second-generation immigrants, most of their fellow citizens consider them to be quintessentially American. This reality contrasts starkly with immigrant integration in many other countries. For example, the first Turkish *Gastarbeiter* (guest workers) came to Germany nearly seventy years ago, yet they and their descendants are often still considered Turks rather than Germans; the top soccer player Mesut Özil was born and raised in Germany but complains that he is only considered a German when the national team wins the World Cup. Chinese immigrants first came to the Malay Peninsula over five hundred years ago, yet they are still socially and legally distinguished from the ethnic Malay majority.

Although it is no longer widely acknowledged, the integration of diverse cultures in the American melting pot has always been a two-way street: while immigrants from those cultures have adapted to America, America has adapted to them. The receptiveness to ideas outside the Anglo-Saxon tradition began with America's founders, who drew inspiration not only from Enlightenment Europe but also from Confucian China and the democratic Iroquois Confederacy. This continued through the twentieth century, as mainstream America incorporated minority groups' contributions, from an emphasis on universal education to jazz and rock music.

The melting pot ideal was neither fully realized nor universally accepted, but it was shared by most Americans for nearly two hundred years. Even most black people, after years of being excluded, aspired to take their rightful place in a shared American identity. The mainstream of the black civil rights movement, in particular, focused on integration and a single, shared identity in lieu of ethnic separatism. As Martin Luther King Jr. said in an interview:

> There is always cultural assimilation. This is not an unusual thing; it's a very natural thing. And I think that we've got to come to see this... But I mean as far as the average Negro today, he knows nothing about Africa. And I think he's got to face the fact that he is an American, his culture is basically American, and one becomes adjusted to this when he realizes what, what he is. He's got to know what he is. Our destiny is tied up with the destiny of America.[6]

For most of the twentieth century, the melting pot was celebrated in textbooks and taught to generations of school children. The ABC network's *Schoolhouse Rock!* series, which may have done more than public schools to teach civics to "Boomers," even featured a melting pot song and cartoon.

The Decline of the American Melting Pot

The melting pot did have a few early critics at the beginning of the twentieth century, notably elite intellectuals like Horace Kallen and Randolph Bourne. But it was not until the 1970s that anyone in the American mainstream seriously considered abandoning it. President Jimmy Carter was one of the first prominent politicians to advocate a different ideal, declaring in a speech, "We become not a melting pot but a beautiful mosaic. Different people, different beliefs, different yearnings, different hopes, different dreams."[7] Around the end of Carter's presidency, the idea of multiculturalism gained traction. The term, which was virtually nonexistent before Carter, exploded in use over the following decades.

Figure 1.1. Word prevalence of "Multiculturalism" in American English writing.[8]

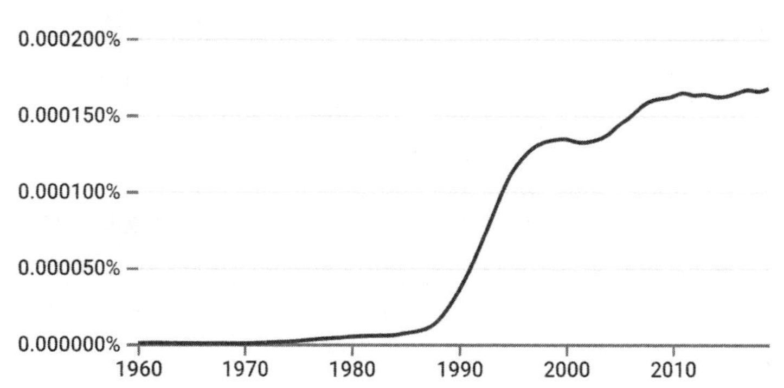

The rise of multiculturalism has been accompanied by various public and private initiatives devised to either compensate for historical disparities or foster diversity by identifying underrepresented groups and granting them preferential treatment. The most prominent of these initiatives has been affirmative action, which awards employment and education preferences to individuals based on which group they are born into. There have been many others, such as college facilities, academic programs, and graduation ceremonies that are limited to members of certain ethnic and racial groups. These measures are manifestly antimelting pot, separating and distinguishing ethnic and racial groups rather than blending and uniting them under a shared identity. In the early twenty-first century, American elites typically deprecate the melting pot ideal; several elite colleges condemn the mere mention of it as a "micro-aggression."[9]

Zangwill and Emerson described the melting pot as a blending process that explicitly included black people, Asians, and Polynesians, with Zangwill writing that it was not a "simple surrender to the dominant type" but an "all-round give-and-take." In a brochure distributed to refugees after World War II, the US government endorsed their vision: "America wants you to share your culture with other Americans. America is the country it is because it has absorbed in its way of life the good of so many varying cultures." Instead of arguing against this inclusive two-way integration, contemporary critics have constructed a straw man version of the melting pot, which they denounce as "little more than Anglo conformity."[10] Some celebrity academics like Ibram X. Kendi have categorically labeled any assimilation as "racist." In a few decades, the melting pot has gone from being celebrated as the key to America's success to being dismissed as destructive and morally repugnant.

The role of elites in the decline of the American melting pot is notable. From early on, the most prominent critics of the melting pot were highly privileged elites like Kallen (Harvard, 1903) and Bourne (Columbia, 1912). This did not change over the years. For example, California Proposition 209, which limited affirmative action by explicitly prohibiting ethnic and racial discrimination, passed by a 9 percent margin statewide but lost by 8 percent in Marin County, the wealthiest county in the state. A similar measure in Washington State (Initiative 200) won by a 15 percent margin overall but lost by 5 percent among voters earning over $100,000 a year. American elites' support for distinguishing people by race and ethnic origins manifests itself regularly in the institutions that the elites run. For example, whenever affirmative action comes before courts, executives of the country's very largest corporations have argued strongly in favor of continuing it.[11] The following chapters in this book show that this continues a pattern that goes far back in history: the political elites or "ruling class" tend to be the most prominent opponents of melting pot integration and the biggest supporters of policies that distinguish and divide people by ethnicity and race. That includes aristocratic Roman senators who opposed Emperor Claudius's effort to assimilate Gauls; Belgian colonialists who instituted racial ID cards in Rwanda; aristocratic Sinhalese who supported affirmative action in Sri Lanka; and elite Slovenian intellectuals who supported ethnic quotas and resisted Tito's aspirations for a Yugoslav melting pot.

The Melting Pot Is Dead, Long Live the Melting Pot(s)

Perhaps the most curious aspect of the shift away from the melting pot in the United States has been the creation of new ethnic categories: *Latinx* and *BIPOC* (Black, Indigenous, and People of Color). These categories do nothing to respect the unique backgrounds of the individuals they include or even give these individuals something new they can take pride in. Ironically, while multiculturalists have rejected the traditional melting pot because people cannot or should not "melt," they have simply replaced it with a set of new melting pots. These new melting pots don't just melt people; they trivialize their unique, diverse origins, pigeonholing them into factitious categories that may be useful to political elites, but which reduce their individual identities to a range of skin tones.

For example, consider the "Latinx" category, which includes the following, along with many others: a Euskadi speaker from the Pyrenees, the heiress to a Spanish duchy, a Miskito native from Nicaragua, and actress Cameron Diaz. These individuals have very little in common: they come from distant lands, don't share a first language, and grew up with different degrees of privilege. All of them presumably take justifiable pride in their distinct individual backgrounds. But under the new multicultural categorization, these diverse backgrounds are denatured and reduced to "Latinx." Unsurprisingly, a 2021 poll found that while the term "Latinx" is popular among elite college administrators, 40 percent of people who are categorized as Latinx said the term bothers or offends them.[12]

The BIPOC category imposes a similar identity reduction. Individuals from Morocco, Ni'iijíhí, and Lesotho, for example, have very different backgrounds. Under the old melting pot paradigm, these individuals would simply be called "Americans," with a focus on what they all share—American citizenship and belief in ideals like freedom and democracy; there is also an aspiration that they might enrich America by adding some of the ideas and energy from their cultural backgrounds to the mix. But under the multicultural model, these individuals are lumped together as BIPOC, downplaying their distinct individual backgrounds and focusing instead on their melanin levels.

The Melting Pot in World History

The melting pot paradigm is commonly associated with the United States. But, as we will see in the following chapters, it has a long history in the rest of the world. Ancient Rome is one of the earliest societies for which there is extensive historical evidence of a melting pot, but it is clear that much earlier societies also followed the model. For example, when the pharaoh Menes united Upper and Lower Egypt five thousand years ago, he initiated a melting pot fusion of the two regions' diverse religions, cultures, and peoples, fostering a successfully integrated society that flourished for centuries.[13]

Although there is ample evidence of the melting pot in ancient societies, record of the ancients deliberating the concept is more elusive. As we will see in chapter 3, Romans like Cicero and Claudius, as well as a Greek (Aelius Aristides), did praise the notion of accepting and assimilating outsiders. But the first person to think and write extensively about ethnic integration was probably the fourteenth-century North African historian and sociologist Ibn Khaldun. Dubbed the "father of modern sociology," Ibn Khaldun generated seminal ideas that have profoundly influenced historians and thinkers over many centuries, from Kâtip Çelebi to Arnold Toynbee.[14] Since Ibn Khaldun's work has been so influential, we will briefly review it here.

Ibn Khaldun introduced a notion he called *asabiyah*.[15] Scholars have translated asabiyah in a variety of ways—"group consciousness," "esprit de corps," "social cohesion," and "group feeling."[16] Ibn Khaldun describes it as the unifying feeling that binds a group together and makes collective action possible. Like an extended sense of kinship, asabiyah inspires individuals to subordinate their own interests to those of a larger community. It's what makes people within a community work together and treat each other nicely, even when there's no consequence for doing otherwise. In its strongest form, it is the "irrational bond" that can give people the "mutual affection and willingness to fight and die for each other." While asabiyah naturally occurs in small groups with actual kinship, like clans and tribes, it is fluid; it can be fostered and cultivated to embrace much larger groups that aren't even distantly related. For example, Ibn Khaldun describes how Persians shared asabiyah with Arabs in the early Islamic period.[17]

Contemplating the ruins of past civilizations that surrounded his hometown in North Africa, Ibn Khaldun speculated about how some civilizations had outlasted others. He asserted that asabiyah is the key: it is both the glue that holds a society together and the engine that makes it work. A society's success and longevity ultimately depend on its ability to forge and maintain a unifying asabiyah that embraces its entire population. History is a repeating cycle of societies rising on the initial strength of their asabiyah and collapsing when they fail to maintain it.[18]

For our purposes, the pivotal part of Ibn Khaldun's social theory deals with societies that comprise diverse groups or ethnicities. Ibn Khaldun is very clear that if these societies are to succeed, they must foster a shared asabiyah that encompasses all their constituent groups. He describes an ideal like the melting pot praised in Israel Zangwill's play. In Ibn Khaldun's version of the melting pot, individual groups merge their asabiyahs into a greater, common asabiyah:

> If a single nation has different houses and multiple asabiyahs, there must be one asabiyah that is stronger than all of them, that subdues and subordinates them, and in which all the asabiyahs become like a single greater asabiyah. Otherwise, divisions occur, leading to discord and strife.[19]

Summary and Conclusions

The melting pot paradigm has enjoyed intellectual support in America that goes back at least to Hector de Crèvecoeur in the eighteenth century. In the rest of the world, it goes back much further than that, to thinkers like Cicero and Ibn Khaldun. The push to abandon the melting pot in favor of a multicultural system is a relatively new development in America, driven primarily by elites in the late twentieth and early twenty-first centuries.

The remainder of this book will examine historical examples and statistical data to evaluate the fundamental claim of those elites: that a society should not strive for a common, shared identity—that it is better served by identifying groups, fostering distinct, separate identities, and granting group preferences to achieve various social goals.

2

LESSONS FROM BYZANTINE RACE RIOTS

Sixth-century Byzantium was a city divided by race hatred, a hatred so intense that people spontaneously attacked each other, not only in the streets but also in the churches. The inscription on an ancient tablet conveys the raw animus that arose from color differences: "Bind them!...Destroy them!...Kill them!"[1] The historian Procopius, who witnessed the race antagonism firsthand, called it a "disease of the soul" and marveled at its irrational intensity:

> They...fight against their opponents knowing not for what end they imperil themselves...So there grows up in them against their fellow men a hostility which has no cause, and at no time does it cease or disappear, for it gives place, neither to the ties of marriage nor of relationship nor of friendship.[2]

This hostility sparked a series of riots across the Byzantine Empire. Most notably, it contributed to the Nika riot of 532 CE, the biggest race riot of all time, in which thirty thousand people perished, and the greatest city of antiquity was reduced to smoldering ruins.[3]

But the Byzantine race riots weren't the sort of race riots you might imagine. The race in question was the chariot race. The color division wasn't between black and white but between blue and green—the colors of the two main chariot-racing teams. The teams' supporters were known as *factions*; the factions wore their team colors and were called "Blues" or "Greens." To help distinguish themselves, the Blues also sported distinctive "mullet" hairstyles, similar to those of 1980s rock stars. Members of both factions were fiercely loyal to the factions and their colors. The chariots and drivers were an incidental concern; it was the colors and the factions that they cared about. The historian Pliny asserted that if the drivers were to swap colors in the middle of a race, the factions would immediately switch their allegiances accordingly.[4]

Although the Byzantine race factions were not based on actual race or ethnicity, their story yields some insight that applies to all group relations, including racial and ethnic relations. It provides useful lessons, confirmed by modern sociological research, which help evaluate the melting pot and multicultural approaches to managing multiethnic societies. These lessons are outlined in the sections below.

Factionalism Is an Innate Human Tendency

One school of anthropology, the Primordialist school, emphasizes how long-standing, "primordial" ethnic distinctions divide people into groups that are reflexively distrustful and hostile toward each other.[5] But, as Blue-Green factionalism demonstrated, people don't even need primordial distinctions to form these divisions; instead, they can seize on something superficial or trivial, like the preference for a sports team.

Modern sociological studies have confirmed the human tendency to divide into cohesive and antagonistic groups, even in the absence of "primordial" or other significant differences.[6]

The earliest and most famous of these studies, the Robbers Cave Experiment, was conducted at a summer camp during the 1950s. The researchers brought boys with identical socioeconomic and ethnic backgrounds to the camp, dividing them randomly into two groups. They initially kept the two groups separate and encouraged them to bond through a variety of group activities. The boys, who had not known each other before, developed strong group cohesion and a sense of shared identity, spontaneously naming themselves "Eagles" and "Rattlers." The researchers then pitted the groups against each other in a series of contests for group privileges and rewards to see if intergroup hostility would arise. The group antagonism escalated far beyond their expectations. The two groups eventually burned each other's flags and clothing, trashed each other's cabins, and collected rocks to hurl at each other. Camp staff had to intervene repeatedly to break up vicious fights. The mounting hostility and risk of violence induced the researchers to abort that phase of the experiment.[7] Subsequent experiments have confirmed how even invented, factitious group distinctions like this can spur not only discrimination but also outright violence.[8] In many of these experiments, researchers have been dumbstruck by the intensity of the violence and how quickly it escalated. For example, in one follow-up study, police had to be called in to avert brutal assaults, and a researcher was so traumatized that he had to be hospitalized.[9]

Experiments like the Robbers Cave study demonstrate that it takes very little to divide people into mutually inimical groups. One psychologist, Henri Tajfel, conducted a landmark series of studies to determine what the minimum is. Tajfel divided his test subjects into groups according to increasingly trivial criteria—for example, whether they preferred Klee or Kandinsky paintings or whether they underestimated or overestimated the number of dots on a page. The results were intriguing: these groupings, as trivial as they were, induced significant discrimination. Individuals adopted a zero-sum outlook; they were willing to sacrifice individual or group well-being as long as their sacrifice hurt the other group even more.[10]

Official Recognition and Group Preferences Exacerbate Group Division

Although the Byzantine race factions had been around for some time before the Nika riot, Procopius noted that the nasty acrimony had arisen only in "comparatively recent times."[11] So what had changed? For most of Byzantine history, emperors had carefully avoided publicly demonstrating a preference for any race faction. But that tradition ended with Marcian, who politicized the factional distinction: he openly favored the Blues and instituted an official policy that favored Blues over Greens for government employment. A few years later, Anastasius favored a third faction—the Reds—and implemented preferential policies that favored them over Blues and Greens.[12] Justinian reverted to Marcian's scheme, reviving official employment preferences for Blues, and denying coveted jobs to Greens.[13] To cast it in modern terms, the emperors had instituted affirmative action for the race factions.

The emperors' official recognition of group distinctions enhanced a sense of difference among the factions. The institution of group preferences turned this sense of difference into bitter antagonism, which finally exploded under Justinian's reign. Procopius placed the blame for the mounting antagonism and the riots squarely on Justinian's endorsement of race identity politics and his enactment of preferences for the Blues.[14] Incredibly, the Byzantine emperors' group preference had not only imbued the two groups with an us-versus-them mindset; it also incited vicious enmity between them, turning a trivial color distinction and a sporting rivalry into a deadly "race war."

As noted above, Tajfel found that minor preferences could induce discrimination between groups. But his most unexpected discovery was that simply telling subjects they belonged to a group induced discrimination, even when the grouping was completely random. On learning they officially belonged to a group, study subjects reflexively adopted an us-versus-them, zero-sum attitude toward members of other groups. Many other researchers have conducted related experiments with similar results: a government or an authority (like a researcher) creating categories for people is, by itself, sufficient to spur group rivalry and strong prejudice.[15]

Considering how policies that recognized group distinctions and instituted group preferences elicited violence from randomly assembled groups like the Blues and Greens, it is easy to imagine how disastrous these policies might be when they are applied to groups that already have some long-standing, historical sense of difference. Indeed, as we will see, there have been numerous instances of this in history, most of them ending tragically. For example, when Belgian colonialists in Rwanda issued identity cards distinguishing Tutsis and Hutus, and granted employment and educational preferences to Tutsis, they ossified an existing (albeit porous) group division and infused it with bitter rivalry, preparing the path to genocide. When Yugoslavia instituted its "nationality key" system, with educational and employment quotas for the country's constituent ethnic groups, it likewise pitted the groups against each other and set the stage for genocide in the Balkans. This is a pattern that has been repeated around the world, from Nigeria to Sri Lanka.

Group Identification Is Fluid and Contextual

Perhaps the most curious aspect of the Byzantine race factions was their indifference to actual race and ethnicity. The Byzantine population was highly diverse, and included Jews, Armenians, Goths, Khazars, Greeks, and Africans, along with many others; there was tremendous potential for ethnic and sectarian division. Yet ethnic affiliation played no role in the greatest conflict of the day.[16] In fact, Blue-Green factionalism overrode racial, ethnic, and sectarian distinctions, with both factions comprising comprehensive cross sections of Byzantine society. Each faction united an ethnically mixed group that got together to don their colors, sport their mullets, and pal it up with each other in the hippodrome and on the street, joining in a cohesive fellowship that overlooked their long-standing ethnic and sectarian differences.

This human ability to overlook "primordial" ties in favor of more current, constructed ones is confirmed in sociological studies. For example, one study replicated the Robbers Cave experiment, but instead of using a homogeneous group of boys, it used a mixed group of Christians and Muslims from war-torn Beirut. If any Primordialist anthropologists had been present, they would have warned that this was an incredibly bad idea, and that violence would quickly break out between the Christians and Muslims because of their bitter and long-held "primordial" differences. The boys, who formed cross-sectarian groups named the "Blue Ghosts" and the "Red Genies," did clash viciously, even using knives at one point. But remarkably, they completely ignored the Christian-Muslim differences that had killed hundreds of thousands of people in their country. Instead, they fought over the newly constructed Blue-Red rivalry.[17]

This behavior is probably unremarkable to anyone who has belonged to a military unit, firefighting squad, or another group that engages in collective enterprise for an extended period: under the right circumstances, completely unrelated humans readily form cohesive groups with bonds that rival or supersede ethnic and even kinship ties. Both theory and field research suggest that the propensity to do this is the product of natural selection; it is built into humans and other primates.[18]

Summary and Conclusions

Although Byzantium's race factions had nothing to do with actual race or ethnicity, they do provide insight into identity politics and thus into racial and ethnic group relations. In particular, the race faction history demonstrates how readily humans can form stark group divisions and how governments can exacerbate these divisions and turn them deadly by recognizing them and by instituting group preferences. It suggests that societies should avoid bolstering group differences and especially refrain from granting different treatment based on group membership. The race faction history also highlights the fluidity of group identification. It hints at how multiethnic societies have the opportunity to promote a greater shared identity that encompasses and unites their constituent ethnic groups. The following chapters will examine some societies that have seized that opportunity.

3

THE ROMAN MELTING POT

Nearly two thousand years ago, the Roman emperor Gaius assembled a massive invasion force and marched it across Europe to the English Channel. The elite of the greatest army in the world, along with a massive array of siege engines, drew up in battle formation along the shore, awaiting orders. Mounting a platform, Gaius commanded the trumpets to sound and then issued the orders: "Gather shells!" The soldiers frantically scrambled around the beach to fill their helmets with seashells. Gaius then erected a monument to celebrate this "victory against the sea" and transported the "booty" a thousand miles back to Rome for a triumphal march.[1]

Gaius, or *Caligula*, as he is more commonly known, was crazy. According to Roman chroniclers, this was only one example of his crazy behavior. He also nominated his horse to the consulship, capriciously threw law-abiding citizens into the arena, and depleted the treasury with lavish spending on orgies. Unfortunately for Rome, Caligula was just the first of many lunatic emperors. Nero, Commodus, and many others would rival him in both lunacy and incompetence. Although the chroniclers probably exaggerated the malfeasance of these emperors, the record of the imperial succession by itself evinces the instability of Rome's leadership. Of the fifty emperors preceding Diocletian, only a handful died naturally, and several lasted only a few weeks. A gladiator had better odds of avoiding violent death than an emperor.[2]

For all the attention devoted to the "fall" of Rome, the real wonder is not that Rome fell, but that it lasted as long as it did. For it lasted a very, very long time—nearly a thousand years—or two thousand years if we include the Eastern Empire. This was a fabulous and enigmatic success, given the challenges it confronted. History is littered with regimes destroyed by a few bad rulers. Yet Rome managed to endure dozens of them. From the time of Caligula, it not only survived, but actually thrived—for another four hundred years.

So, what was the secret sauce that accounted for Rome's spectacular and enigmatic longevity? It is actually not secret at all. In fact, the Romans obligingly hammered out the recipe for us on a bronze tablet, which now resides in a Lyon museum. The tablet records a speech in which Emperor Claudius explains Rome's ethnic policy and how it enabled Rome to succeed where others had failed:

> Is it regretted that the Cornelii Balbi immigrated from Spain and other equally distinguished men from southern Gaul? Their descendants are with us; and they love Rome as much as we do. What proved fatal to Sparta and Athens for their military strength was their segregation of conquered subjects as aliens. Our founder Romulus, on the other hand, had the wisdom—more than once—to transform whole enemy peoples into Roman citizens within the course of a single day.[3]

Claudius's speech is not the only place we find this explanation of Rome's success. Over the centuries, numerous other Romans were also very clear about it. For example, Cicero wrote:

> without any dispute, that has been the most solid foundation of our empire, and the thing which has above all others increased the renown of the Roman name, that that first man, the creator of this city, Romulus, taught by the treaty which he made with the Sabines, that it was expedient to increase the population of this city by the adoption of even enemies as citizens.[4]

A more detailed analysis of Roman ethnic policies comes from an outsider, the Greek orator Aelius Aristides. Aristides surveyed empires of the past and noted how each had fallen because it failed to sufficiently assimilate the different ethnic groups within its domain. Rulers of unassimilated populations had to continually scramble about to quell uprisings, whereas the Roman emperor could "stay where he is and manage the entire civilized world by letters." Rome achieved this unique success by assimilating disparate groups, granting them both citizenship and a shared identity:

> You have everywhere appointed to your citizenship, or even to kinship with you, the better part of the world's talent, courage, and leadership... Neither sea nor intervening continent are bars to citizenship, nor are Asia and Europe divided in their treatment. In your empire all paths are open to all. No one worthy of trust remains an alien... You have caused the word Roman to be the label, not of membership in a city, but of some common nationality...[5]

As Claudius and Cicero noted, Rome faced the challenge of incorporating diverse ethnic groups into its realm from the very beginning. Even in the early days of the republic, Rome comprised a mixed population of Latins, Sabines, Volscians, Etruscans, and others. Later, it embraced numerous other groups: Gauls, Spaniards, Britons, Africans, and so on. The Roman policy for handling this challenge was remarkably consistent for nearly a thousand years: progressively extend citizenship to the people under its control and assimilate them. From early on, Romans were very clear about this policy and its rationale. Even if we dismiss Cicero's claim that it goes back to the legendary Romulus, it was established at least by the fourth century BCE, when the consul Camillus reminded the senate that the only way to manage their fractious Latin neighbors was to "follow the example of your ancestors and extend the State of Rome by admitting your defeated enemies as citizens."[6]

In chapter 1, we reviewed Ibn Khaldun's notion of asabiyah—the sense of group cohesion and shared identity that makes societies work. Although they lived one thousand years before Ibn Khaldun's time, the Romans had a good sense of the concept and strove to spread it wherever they went so that diverse peoples who originated thousands of miles from Rome were assimilated and came to identify themselves as Roman. When Rome annexed a region, it typically granted citizenship to the local leaders quickly, appointing them as magistrates answerable directly to Rome. Other residents often qualified for Latin rights (that is, citizenship without voting privileges). After the region had firmed its bond with Rome over time, all the free residents might qualify for full citizenship.[7] Until then, it would provide auxiliaries to serve alongside the Roman legions. The auxiliaries normally earned full citizenship on retirement. But an individual who demonstrated exemplary valor might receive it before then and might even be promoted to a command or to the privileged equestrian class.[8] The genius of this system was that it configured incentives around building an affiliation with Rome. The rewards for serving Rome were themselves progressive degrees of Roman "team membership": first Latin rights, then full citizenship, and then elevation to the equestrian class. So an individual's and a province's aspirations and ambitions were channeled into joining the Roman team.

This system enabled the Roman Republic to effectively consolidate most of the Italian Peninsula under its control. The peoples of Italy were not subjugated but rather assimilated and allowed to improve their status so that they ultimately accounted for many of Rome's most prestigious and powerful families. The Julii and Servilii were Alban; the Aurelii and Claudii were Sabine; and Cicero's family and the Marii were Volscian.[9]

From the very beginning, Roman assimilation of diverse ethnic groups was not a one-way process; much from these societies was adopted into a common culture. For example, the toga and the fasces—now viewed as quintessentially Roman symbols—were originally Etruscan; and Rome's legal structure and many of its popular deities came from the Sabines. Prominent Romans appreciated the importance of this heritage: Emperor Claudius wrote a twenty-volume Etruscan history, and Varro wrote extensively on the Sabines. Today, Rome's culture is often viewed as monolithic. However, at the dawn of the empire, it was widely recognized that *Romanitas* was a fusion of Latin, Sabine, Etruscan, and many other cultures.

The Roman Republic's policy of integrating rather than subjugating its neighbors provided it with cohesive support both to defend itself and to expand its domain. This was well demonstrated in the Second Punic War, in which the Carthaginian general Hannibal led one hundred thousand men and thirty-seven elephants across the Alps to attack Rome. Hannibal was one of the greatest generals of all time; his canny stratagems are still studied in military colleges.[10] The Roman leadership, by contrast, was weak, with two concurrent commanders pursuing misguided and incompatible strategies. The leadership failure cost Rome several key battles, and Rome itself might have perished, but for one thing: Hannibal had counted on winning the cities of Italy to his side. The cohesion that Rome had forged with the rest of Italy, and particularly Latium, made that impossible. Hannibal averred that he came to fight "on behalf of the Italians against Rome," and he offered the Italian cities great advantages to join him. But their affiliation with Rome was so strong that most decided to fight and die for Rome, even though it appeared that Hannibal would prevail.[11] Without Italian support, Hannibal's manpower and provisions were inadequate. Supply lines across the mountains to Spain and across the sea to Carthage were untenable. Rome eventually crushed Hannibal's army and Carthage. The Greek historian Polybius credited Hannibal's ultimate defeat to the cohesion and commitment of the Roman forces: they were loyal and spoke with "one voice."[12]

As Rome transitioned from republic to empire, it continued its successful policy of liberal enfranchisement and integration outside Italy. By 49 BCE, the republic had granted full citizenship to Cisalpine Gaul and Latin rights to Transalpine Gaul. The emperors quickly extended this, with Julius Caesar bestowing full citizenship on Transalpine Gaul, Vespasian giving Latin rights to Spain, and Caracalla enfranchising free-born residents of all the provinces. In the Roman world, a province or a country could greatly improve its lot by demonstrating its loyalty to Rome and by Romanizing. The prospect of integrating as a Roman province was so appealing that the rulers of Bithynia, Pergamum, and Mauritania all voluntarily bequeathed their countries to Rome.

The incentives for individuals to integrate themselves as Romans were also clear. A Gaul or a Spaniard did not get ahead by being a Gaul or a Spaniard but by becoming Roman. When Emperor Claudius elevated a number of Gauls to the senate, he emphasized that this was part of Rome's tradition of rewarding outsiders who integrated and Romanized.[13] Although new citizens typically kept their religions, they were expected to adopt some of the shared culture, particularly the language. When a Lycian appearing before the senate failed to answer questions in Latin, Claudius summarily revoked his citizenship, saying it was "not proper for a man to be a Roman who had no knowledge of the Romans' language."[14]

Ambitious and capable provincials who did assimilate and attain citizenship enjoyed tremendous possibilities. Neither ethnic origin nor race precluded an individual's ascent in the imperial administration. Over two thousand years before the United States elected its first minority president, Rome had already elevated minorities to the consulship. Even the imperial throne was an equal-opportunity possibility. Emperor Trajan was from Spain, and several of his successors also had Spanish roots. Septimius Severus, Geta, and Caracalla were part African, and Marcus Philippus's ancestry was probably Arab. Other emperors hailed from areas now in Bulgaria, Hungary, Serbia, Syria, and Turkey. This equal-opportunity environment extended beyond the political realm to the rest of society. While many of Rome's most prominent writers and artists had Greek origins, many came from other regions. For example, the playwright Terence and the historian Suetonius came from Africa.

Rome's greatest tool for integration was its military. The military was a compelling opportunity for a provincial who wanted to get ahead. If he served in an auxiliary unit, he could become a full citizen by the end of his tour of duty. If he managed to join a legion, his citizenship was confirmed immediately. Although citizenship was theoretically required before one joined a legion, inscriptions and Roman historians recount numerous instances of noncitizens being admitted and thereby being made citizens.[15] Whether a provincial joined an auxiliary unit or a legion, he would enjoy privileges unavailable to his compatriots, such as Roman legal rights and exemption from various taxes. His descendants would be recognized as full citizens, giving them a tremendous advantage over other provincials.

Figure 3.1. Bronze diploma granting citizenship to retired soldier.[16]

In modern movies, the Roman army is typically depicted as a homogeneous collection of white guys, all presumably originating from Rome or Italy. This could hardly be further from reality. Roman soldiers were Roman by virtue of Romanization, not birth. Most were not from Rome or even Italy. For example, in the first century, the Legion III Augusta was only 19 percent Italian; by the third century, it had no Italians at all.[17] Beholding a Roman army during the imperial era, you were more likely to see Spaniards, Africans, and Pannonians than Italians. Soldiers with exceptional courage and ability could quickly ascend to the highest ranks regardless of their race or ethnic origin. The writings of Roman historians, as well as various inscriptions, describe countless high-ranking leaders of barbarian stock. For example, Lusius Quietus, who came from an African tribe, joined as an auxiliary, and achieved not only citizenship but privileged equestrian status for his valiant service. Quietus eventually became a senator, a consul, and a provincial governor.[18] To this day, Quietus's image occupies a prestigious spot on Rome's Quirinal hill. If you scrutinize Trajan's column, you can identify him, sporting what appear to be dreadlocks, leading his cavalry against the Dacians.

While some soldiers did serve in their home provinces, Rome was careful to relocate units whose local ethnic affiliation might pose a risk. For example, Britons were normally stationed on the continent, and it was typical for Gauls to serve in Africa and Syrians to serve in Egypt. This helped sever soldiers' old ethnic ties and cement their identification with Rome. As Aristides observed:

> You released them from their fatherland and gave them your own city, so that they became reluctant henceforth to call themselves by their original ethnics. Having made them fellow-citizens, you made them also soldiers . . . who together with their enrollment in the army had lost their own cities but from that very day had become your fellow-citizens and defenders.[19]

Though some auxiliary units had ethnic names, they often integrated individuals from different tribes and distant regions, as well as some soldiers who were already Roman citizens. There was a clear effort to blend groups from very distant areas. For example, there were units named "Ligurians and Spanish" and "Gauls and Pannonians."

While in the military, soldiers had to learn to speak Latin and might also be required to read and write it. They were immersed in Roman culture. The cognomina (or nicknames) they adopted were predominantly Latin, and many also gave their children names from Latin literary classics.[20] While diverse private religious practices were permitted, Roman military tradition focused on devotion to Rome, the princeps, the unit, and its standard.[21] Surviving inscriptions from all around the Mediterranean evince the powerful integrative influence of the Roman military. Epitaphs written by soldiers for their fallen comrades were often written in Latin verse, suggesting competence, if not fluency, in the language. These inscriptions describe men who, regardless of their race or origins, trained and fought alongside each other, often for many decades, all the while absorbing the shared culture of Rome. For example, one epitaph celebrates a centurion born in Pannonia, who served for forty years in areas that are now Hungary, Egypt, France, Germany, Austria, Serbia, and Spain.[22]

On retiring from the legions, soldiers often received grants of farmland in the provinces. Emperor Augustus alone settled over one hundred thousand veterans outside Italy.[23] Thus, a powerful lattice of respected citizens, steeped in Roman culture and bearing a passionate attachment to Rome, was spread across the provinces.

Supplementing the military's influence, the provincial administration helped Romanize the provinces. While Rome incorporated many cultural practices from the provinces, it diligently spread the shared Roman culture along with its citizenship. As Pliny wrote, Rome's mission was:

> to unite the discordant and uncouth dialects of so many different nations by the powerful ties of one common language, to confer

> the enjoyments of discourse and of civilization upon mankind, to become, in short, the mother-country of all nations of the Earth.[24]

Seneca joked about trying to dress the "whole world in the toga"—the toga being one of the most powerful symbols of Roman-ness.[25] Even if Seneca did not take this mission seriously, the provincial governors did. For example, Agricola reconfigured Britain's cities in the Roman style, taught Latin to the locals, and encouraged them to adopt Roman dress.[26] Charters from cities around the empire also manifest the effort to create miniature replicas of the Roman municipality.[27] Still extant Roman amphitheaters from Britain to Jordan and Romance languages from Portugal to Romania attest to the tremendous success of Rome's Romanization efforts. As one contemporary poet wrote: "Thou hast made of alien realms one fatherland... Thou hast made one city of the once wide world."[28]

Like republican Rome, imperial Rome did not eradicate the cultures it embraced but integrated many of their elements into the shared sense of Romanitas. It was a true melting pot, incorporating not only the highly esteemed contributions of Greek civilization but also of Near Eastern and North African cultures. This was particularly evident when it came to religion. Near Eastern deities were widely worshipped, alongside the traditional pantheon, which was already stocked with Greek Olympians and Etruscan *lares* and *penates*. In the well-preserved ruins of Ostia Antica, we can still get a feel for Rome's integration of diverse faiths. The small port city features not only temples to Roman gods and borrowed Greek deities like Heracles but also shrines to the Egyptian Isis and the Phrygian Attis, no less than seventeen *mithraea* devoted to the Persian Mithras, and a vast Jewish synagogue.

Rome's melting pot ethnic policy, combined with its liberal enfranchisement, helped make it incredibly resilient to both internal and external threats. From Britain to the Middle East, Rome enjoyed support from vast numbers of people who identified with it and had a stake in its success, even though their ancestors were not originally Roman or even Italian. As the poet Claudian wrote, Rome "protected the human race with a common name ... drawing together distant races with bonds of affection."[29] Even as Rome's ancient families faded, there arose a set of Gauls, Pannonians, and others said to be "more Roman than Romans themselves," who invigorated Rome with fresh energy and resolutely defended it. As late as the fourth century, Rome still fostered individuals like the great general Flavius Stilicho, who, despite his Vandal pedigree, steadfastly identified himself as Roman, devoting his life to defending Rome against barbarian invaders.

With so many people in the provinces identifying with Rome, there was little incentive to rebel, even when there was discord or anarchy at the top. Outsiders were likewise reluctant to attack a polity that was so unified and powerful. The result was an unprecedented, long era of peace—capped by the two-century period known as the Pax Romana. This peace fostered widespread prosperity that would remain unrivaled for more than a thousand years after Rome's fall. With the entire Mediterranean basin living peaceably under a single regime, beneficial commerce and trade flourished.

Beyond fostering peace, Rome's asabiyah increased prosperity in another way: it bolstered the provision of public goods—particularly infrastructure. As we will see in chapter 10, societies with a sense of shared, common identity tend to provide far more public goods than do divided societies. A society is much more inclined to build roads and bridges for the benefit of "its own kind" rather than for the benefit of outsiders. The Greek city-states, for example, cooperated in maintaining Delphi and a few other sites but otherwise did little to provide public goods outside their city walls.[30] By contrast, Rome, which had "made one city of the once wide world," built a staggering number of aqueducts, roads, baths, and other infrastructure all the way from Britain to the Red Sea. The Roman road network, for example, was more extensive than the current US interstate highway system. It is unlikely that Rome would have built so vastly without the sense that all this area and its inhabitants were Roman.

By modern standards, Rome was hardly a kind and gentle empire. Its tremendous legacy in law, literature, and engineering was darkened by practices of gruesome brutality: gladiatorial games, crucifixions, and slavery. Some groups, like Jews and Christians, were persecuted at times, and women had very limited rights. Nevertheless, Rome contrasted starkly with other classical civilizations in the degree of opportunity, meritocratic social mobility, and material comfort that it afforded people from very diverse racial and ethnic backgrounds. In other classical civilizations, citizenship was a jealously guarded tribal entitlement, seldom granted to other ethnic groups. In Athens, for example, nearly a third of the population were *metics*—foreigners who had few rights and a vastly inferior status to ethnic Athenians. Unlike provincials in the Roman Empire, metics in Athens had no hope of ever becoming Athenian citizens, even after living there for generations. We find in Demosthenes's speeches, for example, how jealously Athens restricted its citizenship. Unless an individual's Athenian pedigree was unassailable, his citizenship rights could be challenged in court.[31] In Rome, by contrast, even barbarians from beyond the limes could quickly become full citizens.[32]

Those who did become citizens had a good chance of enjoying a standard of living that was unmatched for a millennium after Rome fell. Artifacts from former Roman sites from Britain to Egypt suggest that many people enjoyed a high level of comfort;

it was not limited to the patrician elite. Ordinary household articles from even the lower social strata often reflect a high level of artistry and luxury. A look at the well-preserved layout of Ostia Antica is instructive. With a population of roughly twenty thousand, Ostia had eighteen lavishly decorated public baths, with the largest covering over thirty-four thousand square feet. The still extant public amphitheater could accommodate up to five thousand people. The capacity of these facilities relative to Ostia's size suggests that many of the benefits of Roman civilization were enjoyed by much of the population, not just a tiny minority.

So why did Rome finally "fall?" Although a complete examination of the question is beyond the scope of this book, we will briefly consider one key factor here: Rome's shift from a "melting pot" to a "multicultural" system of managing its ethnic diversity. This shift accompanied the mass immigration of entire communities of Goths and other barbarians into Roman territory, starting in the fourth century and culminating with the massive flood of refugees fleeing the Huns in the fifth century. Unlike communities that the Romans had absorbed in the past, these refugees were neither integrated nor granted citizenship. Instead, they were allowed to settle in enclaves, maintaining their own languages, loyalties, and leadership. Rome was abandoning its mission to spread its asabiyah and shared identity over all the people in its dominion.

For example, in just one instance, Emperor Valens agreed to allow a group of two hundred thousand Thervingi to cross the Danube and settle on Roman lands. One of our Roman sources cynically writes that Valens took the greatest care that "none of those destined to overthrow the Roman Empire should be left behind." Another describes the Thervingi and other Goths as being "sown in the Roman Empire like teeth."[33] Both may have had a point: the Thervingi never assimilated and eventually became a big problem for Rome, ravaging Thrace and virtually destroying Rome's army in the Battle of Adrianople.

As unintegrated immigrant enclaves proliferated, the emperors also took a more multicultural approach to Rome's military. As we have seen, the military was the core of Rome's melting pot, smelting barbarians into loyal Romans and defenders of the empire. But the last few emperors abandoned the melting pot approach, staffing the army with unintegrated barbarian units, known as *foederati.* The traditional arrangement that encouraged barbarian soldiers to Romanize and identify with Rome did not apply to the foederati. In earlier days, barbarians were integrated into auxiliary units (or legions) with Roman leadership and enough Roman recruits to provide a critical mass of Roman cultural influence. By contrast, the foederati were not integrated at all. Their units comprised only barbarians who swore oaths of allegiance to their own tribal leaders. They were not required to learn Latin or practice the customary Roman military devotions. Unlike earlier barbarian units, who were often relocated to loosen their original ethnic ties, the foederati remained with their ethnic communities and settled in ethnic enclaves on assigned areas of land. During the fourth century, the emperors rapidly expanded the foederati, enlisting Alans, Attacotti, Franks, Vandals, Goths, Sarmatians, and others so that they ultimately constituted the majority of Rome's military power.

Thus, Rome increasingly relied on people who did not identify as Roman—who did not share in Rome's asabiyah. Three centuries after Aristides praised Rome for effectively assimilating barbarians as Romans and turning them into stalwart defenders of the Empire, a Gothic leader would scoff at the ethnically fractionalized assemblage that defended Rome:

> The vast number of the enemy is worthy only to be despised, seeing that they present a collection of men from the greatest possible number of nations. For an alliance which is patched together from many sources gives no firm assurance of either loyalty or power, but being split up in nationality it is naturally divided likewise in purpose.[34]

According to the sixth-century historian Jordanes, Attila similarly derided the ethnic fractionalization of Roman forces.[35]

In earlier Roman history, as we have seen, a barbarian could greatly improve his lot by Romanizing and serving Rome. For example, a black African like Lusius Quietus could integrate, rise through the ranks, and achieve the top job of consul. For the foederati in the late imperial period, the traditional incentive structure was turned on its head. Instead of a system where individuals from different backgrounds strived together to support Rome and thereby earn rights and privileges as Romans, there were distinct ethnic groups vying against each other to advance their group status at Rome's expense. Under the multicultural organization, which allowed, or even sanctioned, ethnic separation in lieu of shared identity, the rewards were for serving one's own ethnic group. The foederati did not get ahead by being faithful Romans but by cleaving to their own ethnic groups—by being faithful Goths, Franks, or Alans. There was little motivation for a barbarian to devote his life to the defense of Rome. To put it in modern terms, "identity politics" became the order of the day.

So individuals like Lusius Quietus became increasingly rare. In their place, there arose a series of powerful foederati leaders whose affiliation with Rome was evanescent and conditional—individuals like Firmus, Gildo, and Alaric. Not identifying with Rome or seeing a promising future as Romans, these leaders might fight for Rome, but only while it remained dominant and there were no other options. By the fifth century, with Roman dominance depending on the foederati themselves, there were other options. Thus, the emperors found themselves having to quash successive foederati rebellions. They often suppressed these rebellions by enlisting even more foederati. A eulogy for one of these emperors, Julian, praised him for the strategy of "employing barbarians against barbarians."[36] The eulogist did not foresee the catastrophic effects it would have over the following century.

The ethnic separateness of the refugee enclaves and the foederati spurred distrust between them and the Romans, who came to see the unassimilated foreigners as a menacing fifth column. There was a backlash—one that has been echoed in modern times by anti-immigrant and "National Front" type groups in response to the flood of immigrants and refugees into Europe and the United States. Synesius, for example, suspected that the foederati might try to seize control and hoped to replace them with "true" Romans:

> Before matters have come to this pass, one to which they are now tending, we should recover courage worthy of Romans, and accustom ourselves to winning our own victories, admitting no fellowship with these foreigners, but disowning their participation in any rank.[37]

Distrust of the barbarians led to widespread antibarbarian discrimination. Thousands of the wives and children of foederati were killed in a series of purges. Not even loyal, assimilated Romans of barbarian ancestry were spared. Most notably, Stilicho, the last great Romanized barbarian leader, was targeted. Despite his stellar record of defending Rome against barbarians, the identity politics of the day made his own barbarian ancestry fodder for court intrigues. Rumors spread that he had invited

Goths to invade and that he had colluded with the rebellious leader Alaric. In response, the emperor had Stilicho apprehended. A loyal Roman to the end, Stilicho willingly submitted and was executed. If the foederati ever had any doubts about where their ethnic loyalties belonged, the purges and Stilicho's execution must have dispelled them. Thirty thousand of Stilicho's former soldiers joined Alaric in rebellion.

Alaric was himself emblematic of barbarian leaders during the late imperial period. Born a Visigoth, Alaric served as a foederati leader under Emperor Theodosius. In an earlier era, his capabilities and ambition might have been channeled into achieving status as a Roman and devoting his life to Rome's defense. He might have had a career like Lucius Balbus, a first-century barbarian who Romanized and fought valiantly for the republic, earning citizenship and the very pinnacle of Roman honors—a triumph. However, in the multiculturalist organization of the late empire, Alaric's identity and destiny lay with his own ethnic group and not with Rome. Alaric and his compatriots were never Romanized: they would remove their animal skins briefly when they entered the senate house but scoffed at the Roman toga.[38] After Theodosius's death in 395 CE, Alaric had hoped to be promoted from the foederati to a high command in the regular Roman army.[39] This must have posed a dilemma for the leadership at the time. With Alaric's affiliation to Rome already doubtful, increasing his power probably seemed risky. So, they chose to deny him the post. This spurred him to rebel and eventually to invade Italy with his Visigoths. In 410, he besieged Rome, demanding everything the Romans owned to lift his siege—their gold, silver, and all their household goods. Responding to an envoy who asked him what he proposed to leave for the Romans, he answered: "their souls." When he finally sacked the city, he took most of those too.[40]

It would be too much to say that Rome's abandonment of its melting pot policy and the attendant deterioration of its asabiyah were the sole causes of its decline and fall. However, it is clear that Rome's ethnic policy of liberal enfranchisement and ethnic integration helped strengthen and sustain it against numerous internal and external challenges for a thousand years; Romans of many different generations frankly acknowledged this. It is also clear that something had changed by the fifth century: barbarians were not being integrated as they had been in earlier centuries. It was those unassimilated barbarians who ultimately sacked Rome and dismembered its empire.

Summary and Conclusions

Rome's melting pot system of assimilation and liberal enfranchisement helped foster a shared sense of identity across its domain, giving it tremendous resilience for most of its history—from monarchy to republic to empire. No matter what their race or ethnic origins were, many people had the opportunity to Romanize, become citizens, and ascend to the highest levels of the military and the government. So, millions of people with tremendous diversity—Gauls, Spaniards, Britons, Africans, Arabs—came to share in Rome's melting pot, bringing the energy and strengths of their own cultures, but identifying themselves as members of the Roman "team," with a stake in its success. Getting this one thing so very right helped Rome survive terrible leadership and countless other problems for over a thousand years.

The beneficial effects of Rome's melting pot went far beyond simply allowing it to survive. They also contributed to the quality of life. People lived relatively well under Rome because it embraced an expansive community of people who viewed themselves as sharing an identity and who enjoyed the benefits of that: long periods of peaceful coexistence; mutually beneficial commerce and trade that vastly improved living standards; support for public goods like roads and baths; and so on.

By modern Western standards, Rome was a brutal regime: it expanded its domain by violent conquest, violated human rights, and was never fully democratic. So one might doubt that modern democracies can learn anything from it. However, when we compare Rome with other polities that took a melting pot approach and contrast it with those that took a multicultural approach, as we shall do in the following chapters, consistent patterns emerge. It is also instructive to look at Rome in its historical context, comparing its achievement with those of contemporary civilizations. When it came to providing peace, freedom, and material comfort to the most people, Rome outshone all the civilizations of its day. Indeed, many historians claim that it outshone those of the following millennium as well. The historian Edward Gibbon knew ancient Rome better than anyone living in the eighteenth century; he doubted that Rome had been surpassed even by his own time, writing that it had fostered the era "during which the condition of the human race was most happy and prosperous." Rome's adoption of the melting pot model helped make that possible.

4

✷

THE MULTICULTURALIST MEXICA

Six centuries ago, a cluster of Spanish soldiers stood in front of a catapult they had just constructed in Tlatelolco, Mexico. They were jabbing their fingers in the air, making threatening gestures toward the ranks of their Aztec opponents, indicating how the Spanish catapult was going to demolish their fortifications. The Spaniards' native allies piled on, taunting the Aztecs in their Nahua dialect, warning them they would die in a "marvelous manner." When the catapult was finally fired, it unexpectedly launched its payload straight into the air. As it plummeted straight back down, its operators had to scramble for their lives. The weapon had turned out to be more dangerous to the Spanish than to their Aztec opponents. Contemporary Aztec sources recount the whole event with great amusement, describing how the catapult's failure provoked an altercation among the Spanish, who began to point fingers and make threatening gestures at each other instead of at their Aztec foes.[1]

The Spanish soldiers' incompetence was exceeded only by their cowardice and greed. After they landed on Mexico's Yucatan Peninsula, their leader had to destroy their ships to prevent them from fleeing. In the battle over Tenochtitlan, many of them drowned in Lake Texcoco, weighed down by the gold they were trying to run away with.[2] Their leader was equally feckless: his secretary and biographer described him as a sickly youngster and a "source of trouble to his parents as well as to himself." As a young adult, he was a wastrel who flunked out of law school. He was trained not as a military leader but as a humble notary, better suited to commanding piles of documents than ranks of soldiers.[3]

The contrast between the Aztec and Spanish forces could hardly have been more striking. Like the ancient Spartans, the Aztecs rigorously trained their men as warriors from early childhood. The top Aztec warriors vowed on pain of death never to take a single step backward during battle. The Aztecs had a clear leadership advantage, as well. Their emperor, Montezuma, was a seasoned warrior who had personally led his men to victory in several wars.[4] But the Aztecs' greatest advantage lay in their numbers: their vast empire fielded a force of more than one hundred and fifty thousand men—against the Spanish force of five hundred.[5]

The quest of a feckless notary leading what sounds like a sixteenth-century Iberian version of the Keystone cops against a force that was highly disciplined and 30,000 percent larger seems absurd and quixotic. Yet, in one of history's greatest upsets, the notary—Hernan Cortes—would lead his handful of men to thoroughly crush the Aztecs. Few exploits in history match Cortes's "conquest" of Mexico in its success against overwhelming odds.

Improbable Conquest; Improbable Theories

Scholars have advanced numerous theories to explain Cortes's wildly improbable success. Most of them are soundly refuted by the facts. One theory is that the Aztecs thought that Cortes and his contingent were gods and therefore yielded to them out of piety. This is based mostly on second and thirdhand accounts of a speech that Montezuma delivered when he first met Cortes. According to Cortes's own firsthand account, Montezuma's speech was extremely deferential, even submissive, but Montezuma did not recognize him as a god.[6]

The "conquistadors as gods" theory overlooks the fact that indigenous Mexicans had encountered Europeans several times before. Rather than venerating them as gods, they fought and enslaved them.[7] Moreover, Cortes proselytized relentlessly among the Mexican natives, encouraging them to replace their idols with crosses. He even asked Montezuma to abandon the Aztec religion and erect Christian crosses in the capital.[8] It is hard to imagine that the Aztecs believed Cortez belonged in the pantheon of a religion he was trying to abolish. Indeed, the actions of the Aztecs and other natives suggest they did not believe this at all. They attacked Cortes and his men within days of their arrival. Even some of Cortes's eventual allies, like the Tlaxcalans, had attacked him before they joined him. As Cortes traversed Mexico, Montezuma sent several delegations, not to encourage Cortes's visit but to persuade him to return home.[9] From the start, the Aztecs saw the Spanish as threatening rivals, not as revered gods whose return they were eagerly awaiting.

Another theory is that the technological superiority of the Spanish enabled them to subdue the Aztecs. This theory fails because the Spanish would have needed an enormous technological edge to overcome the three thousand-to-one numerical advantage the Aztecs enjoyed, and the edge they actually had was minimal. Cortes had a few small cannons, which initially impressed the Aztecs. However, after the Aztecs ascertained that the shot only came out in a straight line, they modified their tactics to minimize the cannons' effect.[10] Moreover, the Spanish were chronically short of powder for the cannons, which is why they attempted to build catapults to replace them. The Spanish had a few primitive muskets or arquebuses. These took several minutes to load and were not very accurate. They had some crossbows, which were powerful and accurate but also slow to load. Neither projectile weapon offered any meaningful advantage over the Aztec longbows.[11] The Spanish armor must have been more of an impediment than an advantage in the tropical heat because many of the Spanish abandoned it in favor of the fortified cotton armor the Aztec fighters wore.[12] Although the famous Toledo steel swords were effective weapons, they hardly outmatched the Aztec *maquahuitl*, which the Spanish claimed could behead a horse in a single blow.[13] The Spanish cavalry was effective, but Cortes started with only sixteen horses and never had more than seventy. The natives did not fear the cavalry as a pack of divine centaurs, as some European sources suggest. They actually thought the horses were just oversized domesticated deer. When they managed to capture a few, they concluded the poor beasts would serve them better on the dinner table than on the battlefield.[14]

Some historians assert that European diseases devastated the native population of Mexico, making it an easy target for conquest. While smallpox did ultimately decimate the indigenous population of the Americas, it could not possibly have accounted for Cortes's success. The disease was carried by members of the Narvaez expedition, which arrived a full year after Cortes. Whatever diseases the Spanish brought, in the final siege of Tenochtitlan, Aztec warriors still outnumbered Spaniards by more than a hundred to one.

Another theory is that the Aztecs lost because they were accustomed to a different style of warfare than the Spaniards. Before the Spanish conquest, the Aztecs often fought "flower wars" with their neighbors. In these peculiar wars, which were scheduled like sporting matches, they tried to capture as many of their opponents as possible, rather than killing them. According to the theory, this style of warfare severely handicapped the Aztecs against the Spanish, who fought an all-out war, simply killing as many of the enemy as possible.[15] It is odd that this theory is favored by historians who are sympathetic to the Aztecs because it patronizes the latter as noble but dim-witted savages. But even according to Spanish accounts, the Aztecs were extremely clever and resourceful. It is clear that the Aztecs knew better than to employ *flower war* tactics against their European adversaries.[16] Although the Aztecs did capture and sacrifice some Spaniards, most Spanish deaths were on the battlefield. Cortes and Diaz only mention a handful who were taken as captives.[17]

The Multicultural Triple Alliance

If the Mexican natives did not believe that Cortes was a god, and European diseases, technology, and battle tactics did not defeat the Aztecs, what did? To answer this, we need to examine the organization of the Aztec Empire and how Cortes exploited it. The term "Aztec Empire" is actually a European misnomer. What we call the Aztec Empire was the Triple Alliance, a multicultural coalition of Texcoco, Tlacopan, and Tenochtitlan, founded in the early 1400s. What we call Aztecs were the ethnic groups who anchored the coalition—the Acolhuas, Tepanecs, and Mexica-Tenochca. The Mexica-Tenochca had come to dominate the Triple Alliance by Montezuma's time; the Tenochca leader (or *tlatoani*) was effectively the Aztec emperor. However, stark ethnic distinctions persisted among the three groups, with each group identifying themselves as separate, maintaining separate temples and gods. In joint conquests, they often contested whose gods would get the spoils.

Through aggressive conquest, the Triple Alliance expanded its control from the Valley of Mexico to the Pacific Ocean, the

Gulf coast, and present-day Guatemala, ultimately comprehending forty provinces. When the Aztecs conquered an area, they left the local culture and political organization intact. For many towns, they assigned a *calpixque*, or tax gatherer. For a province that embraced a dozen or more towns, they might also assign a governor, though many distant provinces did not have governors. The primary duties of the calpixques and governors were to gather tribute to deliver to Tenochtitlan. In provinces beyond the very core of the empire, extracting tribute appears to be all that the Aztec administration did.[18] They did nothing to integrate the provinces politically or culturally as Roman governors like Agricola did. They did place garrisons in some areas where they feared rebellion. However, these garrisons were only temporary, so interaction with the local populations was limited. In contrast to the Romans and many other empires, they did not colonize extensively. The Duran Codex describes only a few colonies, and these were only established in areas that had been completely depopulated. The colony in Guaxaca exemplified the Aztecs' predilection for ethnic distinction and separation: each of the Triple Alliance's ethnic groups settled in a completely separate *barrio*.[19]

At the Aztec Empire's peak, it reigned over a vast array of ethnic groups who spoke as many as eighty different languages.[20] Cortes discerned that the Aztecs, in stark contrast to the Romans, made no effort to spread their language or forge a common culture in their domain. After he landed near Vera Cruz, Cortes communicated with the local Mayan speakers through a Spaniard who had been shipwrecked years earlier and had lived among them. But only the fortunate discovery of the bilingual slave, Malintzin, allowed him to communicate with the Aztecs. Malintzin, who had been taken from a town closer to the Aztec heartland, was one of the few people in the area who could speak the Nahua dialect of the Aztecs.

The practice of maintaining ethnically separate subject populations was explicit policy from the beginning of the Aztec Triple Alliance. Its founder, Tlacaelel, decreed that conquered towns should be neither assimilated nor destroyed.[21] Tlacaelel's nonassimilation policy continued with his successors, including Montezuma, who decided not to integrate nearby Tlaxcala.[22] The Tlaxcalans, along with other unassimilated groups, would play a key role in the Aztecs' destruction.

With an empire of unintegrated ethnic groups who had no stake in their success, the Aztecs had to continually suppress rebellions, even in areas near the very core of their domain. In Aztec codices that tout the victories of each leader, it is striking how many times they had to reconquer the same areas.[23] The lack of ethnic cohesion also weakened the army that was used to suppress these rebellious areas. As one native leader told Cortes, the army had many warriors conscripted from the provinces who "did not fight with good will." They even secretly warned the Aztecs' foes of impending attacks.[24] They did not want to fight or die for an empire they did not identify with.

Discerning the ethnic fractionalization in the Aztec Empire, Cortes resolved to exploit it to his advantage.[25] His first opportunity came with the Totonacs of Cempoala, who lived near the coast where he originally landed. The Totonacs were a recent addition to the Aztec Empire and were unhappy with their status. Cortes was able to persuade them to capture and flog Aztec notables who had come to collect taxes. He secretly freed two of the Aztecs, allowing them to return to Tenochtitlan. This ploy widened the rift between the Aztecs and Totonacs. The Totonacs, who Cortes estimated had fifty thousand warriors, became a tremendous asset for the Spanish. Having gone from simmering resentment to outright rebellion against the Aztecs, they provided a large contingent to assist Cortes in his march on Tenochtitlan.

On his way to Tenochtitlan, Cortes easily peeled constituent ethnic groups away from the Triple Alliance, including large numbers from Xocotlan and Huexotzinco. By the time Cortes reached Tenochtitlan, he was heading a force of many thousands, of which the Spanish contingent was only a small part.[26] If the natives joined Cortes as allies, it was not because they worshipped, or even liked, the Spanish. Many of Cortes's eventual allies, like the Tlaxcalans and Cholulans, had initially fought against him. Even after native allies had joined them, the Spanish occasionally antagonized these allies by entering their temples and destroying their idols.

Unlike Hannibal, however, who fruitlessly scoured Latium for rebel allies against Rome, Cortes had little difficulty finding allies for his assault on Tenochtitlan. There was a vast population, even at the very heart of the Aztec Empire, who were happy to part with it. Even Texcoco, originally part of the Aztec Triple Alliance, provided thirty thousand men.[27] One group after another joined to fight the Mexica-Tenochca so that by the final siege of Tenochtitlan, Cortes had assembled a massive force of both Aztec defectors and rivals.[28] We might expect the Spanish sources to exaggerate their own role in toppling the Aztec Empire. However, even by their accounts, it is obvious that the multitude of Aztec defectors, not the handful of Spanish, really won the war. For example, in the Battle of Chalco, the Chalcoans and Huexotzincans crushed an army of twenty thousand Aztecs before the Spanish even reached the battlefield.[29] The constituent tribes of the Aztec Empire were so eager to annihilate the Mexica-Tenochca that Cortes complained he was "more engaged in preventing our allies from slaughter and insensate cruelty than in fighting against the enemy."[30]

Spanish sources effusively praise the Mexica-Tenochca's bravery and martial skill. Cortes was amazed at how they continued to fight ferociously even when defeat was inevitable. But in the end, they were a relatively small number out of the Aztec Empire's millions. *Ultimately, the Aztec Empire fell because there were no Aztecs.* Nobody ever became an Aztec in the way that so many Gauls, Britons, Jews, and Africans became Romans. So, instead of Aztecs, there were only Acolhuas, Tepanecs, Mexica-Tenochca, Totonacs, and a fractious multicultural salad of hundreds of other groups, who lacked what Ibn Khaldun called a "single greater asabiyah." Very few of these people felt any affinity for the Aztec Empire. That so much of the population would stand by or even join forces with foreign strangers who had insulted their gods demonstrated the empire's failure to spread any sense of shared identity. The Aztecs contrasted starkly with the Romans, who united their empire with citizenship and a sense of Romanitas. For many centuries, whenever barbarians beset Roman frontiers, men from Britain, Spain, Gaul, Asia Minor, and Africa sacrificed their lives to defend an empire that had made them citizens and Romans. When a handful of strangers challenged the Aztec Empire, few besides the core Mexica-Tenochca were willing to lay down their lives in its defense.

Summary and Conclusions

The Aztecs were brilliant in so many ways—they had excellent leaders, a sophisticated bureaucracy, and a formidable army. But they got one thing very wrong: they pursued an explicit policy of multicultural particularism, of keeping ethnic groups distinct and separate. They never attempted to cultivate any sense of shared identity or unity among their empire's ethnic groups. Only a small contingent of the population identified themselves with the empire. In fact, members of the core Triple Alliance barely perceived themselves to be on the same team. So the empire was continually embroiled in rivalry among its anchoring ethnic groups and in suppressing rebellion from subordinate groups. As a result, the Aztec reign was nasty, brutish, and short. Life for the Aztecs and the people in their dominion was generally miserable, and the Aztec Empire crumbled before the end of its second century.

The Aztec Empire was so different from modern democracies that one might doubt that its history can teach us anything. Yet, we can abstract its ethnic policies and their effects from the historical context, especially by contrasting them with those of other societies in history. In particular, it is useful to consider how different ancient societies expended their energies. With an ethnically fractionalized population and a multicultural organization rather than a sense of shared identity, the Aztec Empire was continually distracted by wrangling among its constituent groups. It devoted much energy to internecine struggles, expending relatively little to improving life. The Roman Empire, by contrast, with a sense of shared identity that it spread over two million square miles, fostered a relatively peaceful coexistence, culminating in the Pax Romana; this gave it the ability to provide abundant public goods and to nurture quantum advances in arts and sciences, vastly improving the quality of life for millions. The fragility of the Aztec Empire is also striking when contrasted with the resilience of the Roman Empire. Rome was continuously challenged by other great empires (Carthage and Parthia) and vast barbarian hordes, yet it managed to survive for over one thousand years; the Aztec Empire was toppled by a notary and a few hundred Spanish freebooters in less than two years.

5

✷

ISLAM, FROM MELTING POT TO MILLET

Imagine walking the entire length of Manhattan, from the George Washington Bridge to the Battery. It is not a vast distance, but if you left after breakfast, you would have to walk briskly to finish the trip in time for lunch. Now consider that, on average, the early Islamic state expanded by an area equal to Manhattan every four hours, every single day, 365 days a year, every single year, for its first hundred years. Islam began with only the Prophet Muhammad and a handful of believers. Yet, in just a century, it blossomed into a flourishing civilization with footholds on three continents. This explosive expansion is unparalleled in the history of the world.[1]

One explanation for the Islamic expansion is that it was driven by religious fervor: ruthless jihadis surged across the Near East with a Qur'an in one hand and a sword in the other, commanding everyone in their path to convert or die. This explanation is popular not only with anti-Muslim polemicists, who want to portray Muslims as fanatical and intolerant but also with eighth- and ninth-century Muslim historians who seek to emphasize the religious devotion of the first Muslims.[2] Yet archaeological evidence—or to be more precise, the lack of archaeological evidence—suggests that the earliest phase of the Islamic expansion was not so calamitous. Big battles leave traces: charred ruins, arrowheads, bones, and so on. We can still find evidence of wars that happened over a millennium before the Islamic era, everywhere from Bronze Age battlefields in Germany to ancient Troy. Yet, given the size of the territory absorbed by the early Islamic state, there is surprisingly little physical evidence of cities being razed or Christian churches being torched. That is not to say there was no violent conflict: Byzantine and Muslim armies did fight a number of large battles that sources from both sides agree took place.[3] But it is likely that the early Islamic expansion was achieved with much less fighting than later sources suggest. As one contemporary Christian chronicler wrote, the Islamic state grew, not so much "with war or battle, but in a menial fashion."[4]

The role of jihadi fervor in the early Islamic expansion, like the level of violence, has been overstated. For most of the first Islamic century, contemporary Christian sources did not even distinguish the newcomers as Muslims but referred to them as "Hagarenes" or "Saracens" and observed that they included Christians and Jews.[5] Churches were still constructed in areas controlled by the early Islamic state, including at least one built by the Muslim governor himself.[6] Some churches were even shared by worshipping Christians and Muslims.[7] There is other intriguing archaeological evidence that hints at Muslim-Christian comity. For example, in 2005, the wreck of a late seventh-century merchant ship was discovered off the coast of Israel. The ship sailed during an era in which Muslims and Christians were supposedly at each other's throats, and trade was at a standstill, yet the ship's contents reflect extensive trade between Muslim and Christian regions. Writing on the ship's timbers and its cargo of amphorae indicate that its crew was a mixed group of Christians and Muslims.[8]

How Early Islam Succeeded

Early Islam's phenomenal success derived not from unleashing militant religious zealotry but from fostering a sense of shared identity and communal cohesion that superseded existing tribal and ethnic ties—that is, by instituting a melting pot system. In Arabia, where Islam began, this was a revolutionary innovation. Before Islam, the region was riven by fractious tribalism. Intertribal enmity was both reflected and sustained by the prevailing religious cults, which were based on tribe-specific gods: each tribe honored its own gods by attacking tribes who served other gods.[9] Islam departed from this paradigm by proclaiming a single universal god for all tribes and all peoples. It thus laid the groundwork for uniting disparate tribes—and, ultimately, diverse ethnicities—into a single community.

In contrast to the pre-Islamic deities, the God of Islam does not care about tribes or races, and he doesn't want people to either; those categories exist merely so humans can easily identify each other. Instead, God focuses on behavior, favoring those "who act righteously" and chastising those who are "hypocrites." As the Qur'an asserts:

> A people should not ridicule another people…And do not insult one another and call each other epithets…And do not spy on or backbite each other…We have…made you into peoples and tribes that you may recognize one another. Verily, the noblest of you in the sight of God is the most righteous of you.[10]

This is echoed in *ahadith* (sayings attributed to Muhammad). In one, for example, Muhammad deprecates ethnic and racial differentiation:

> O people, your Lord is one and your father is one. There is no preference of an Arab over a non-Arab, nor of a non-Arab over an Arab, nor red [skin] over black, nor black over red, except by righteousness.[11]

Early narrative accounts tell us that Muhammad and his first followers did not just preach these antitribalist and antiracist ideals; they practiced them as well. Among the first adherents they welcomed were people of Greek, Persian, Jewish, and African descent. One of the most celebrated among these was Bilal, a freed black slave who became Islam's first *muezzin* (the person who makes the call to prayer—a highly prestigious role).

The "Believers' Movement" and the Ummah

Just as the nascent Islamic community welcomed people of different tribes, ethnicities, and races, it also accepted members of the other major religions. This was an uncomfortable reality that Islamic historians would omit from history in subsequent centuries. But when we look past these historians, who were at least three or four generations removed from the events they describe, and scrutinize contemporary sources, we find ample evidence of early Islamic ecumenism. One example of that evidence is provided by early Islamic coins (shown in figure 5.1).

Figure 5.1. Islamic coins from the late seventh and early eighth centuries.[12]

The coins in figure 5.1 were minted fifty to a hundred years after the beginning of the Islamic era (672–722 CE). The most striking thing about them is that, although they bear Islamic legends written in Arabic, they also feature symbols from other religions: crucifixes, menorahs, and Zoroastrian fire temples. In the first millennium, coins were not just a medium of exchange; they were an essential medium of propaganda—an ancient version of "Twitter" with similar message-length constraints. The fact that the early Islamic state allowed symbols from non-Islamic religions to occupy some of that valuable propaganda bandwidth is noteworthy. Modern Iranian leaders never wear ties with their suits because they think they resemble Christian crosses. Yet seventh-century Muslims stamped crosses and other "infidel" symbols all over their coinage.[13] While they might not have been endorsing these symbols or the associated faiths, they were at least demonstrating a level of tolerance and inclusion that no other major faith practiced at the time.

More evidence of early Islam's ecumenical tendencies comes from seventh-century Christians, who, unlike the eighth- and ninth-century Muslim historians, witnessed the early Islamic expansion firsthand. As one Christian archbishop wrote:

> For also these Arabs . . . are no enemy to Christianity, but they are even praisers of our faith, honorers of our Lord's priests and holy ones, and supporters of churches and monasteries.[14]

Other missives describe the caliph Mu'awiya praying at the tomb of Mary and appointing a Jewish governor. They also describe Jews and Christians fighting alongside Muslims against the Byzantine forces.[15]

Islamic tolerance of other faiths has a clear basis in the Qur'an, which famously declares: "There is no compulsion in religion."[16] But the Qur'an goes beyond mere tolerance, implicitly endorsing fellowship between Muslims and members of other monotheistic faiths. It mentions the term "Muslim" less than one hundred times but uses the terms "believer" (*mu'min*) and "those who believe" over a thousand times. Several verses suggest that righteous members of non-Muslim denominations are affiliated with this category of "believers:"

> Verily, those who believe, those who are Jews, Christians, and Sabians—whoever believes in God and the Last Day and does good—they shall have their reward from their Lord and they shall have no fear, nor shall they grieve.[17]

This is not to say that the Qur'an wholly endorses the other denominations' practices; many verses sternly chastise Jews and Christians—mostly for corrupting or ignoring the revelations previously sent to them. But it does allow for the different denominations to share a measure of fellowship and common cause. When we put it all together with the other historical evidence, the outlines of a cohesive "big-tent" community emerge, one that included both early Muslims and "believers" from non-Muslim denominations. For this reason, some historians now refer to the early Islamic community as a "believers' movement."[18]

The foundation of this believers' movement was codified in the "Constitution of Medina," which was drafted when Muhammad and his followers went to the city of Medina to escape persecution in Mecca. A translation of this remarkable document is provided in appendix A.[19] The constitution declared that Muhammad's Meccan followers and all the tribes in Medina, which included many Jews (and possibly other non-Muslims), formed a single unified *ummah*—a cohesive community. The term "ummah," which in modern Arabic translates as "nation," derives from the same root as the word for mother, so it hints at metaphorical kinship. The constitution asserts that "the Jews have their religious observance and the Muslims have theirs," but they all nevertheless constitute a single unified "ummah of believers."

The Islamic Melting Pot

The early Islamic ummah shared many characteristics with the Roman melting pot. Claudius and Cicero asserted that Rome's continual assimilation of diverse populations and "adoption of even enemies as citizens" was one of the keys to its success. The early Islamic state embraced and followed this paradigm assiduously. Both the Qur'an and Muhammad's policies established that it is best to welcome even former opponents into the ummah:

> Repel the evil deed with one which is better, and the one with whom you had enmity will become your loyal friend.[20]

So, beginning with the tribes in the Arabian Peninsula, former foes of Islam were quickly assimilated into the ummah, becoming its most stalwart supporters.[21] This policy continued as Islam expanded outside the peninsula so that a variety of formerly adversarial tribal and ethnic groups quickly became key participants in the Islamic enterprise: Levantine Christians, Berbers, Persians, Turks, and so on.

Early Islam, like Rome, fostered a sense of asabiyah and shared identity, which people of diverse origins could readily join and become part of. It did not matter what your race, ethnic origins, and, at least initially, your religion were; you could join the ummah. Although the ummah was founded in religion, its ecumenism made it open to most of the peoples of the Mediterranean region. Like the Roman system, the Islamic system contrasted starkly with its contemporary rivals, which were more exclusionary and far less integrative. This made "conquest" an easier, and often bloodless, enterprise. Byzantine territories were teeming with a variety of denominations that the Byzantine government persecuted for their heterodoxy: Copts, Nestorians, Monophysites, and Jews. Many of the adherents of these denominations eagerly opened their gates to, and joined forces with, the Islamic regime, which treated them as believers and did not persecute them over doctrinal niceties.[22]

Like Rome, the early Islamic state was open to ambitious individuals from diverse backgrounds, enticing them with great opportunities. As already noted, Mu'awiya granted a key governorship to a Jew, which would have been unthinkable under the Byzantine administration. Many other Levantine Jews and Christians rose to positions of influence under Islam: a Berber leader, Tariq bin Ziyad, was entrusted with one of early Islam's greatest projects, the annexation of al-Andalus; the Barmakids, a Buddhist family originating from Afghanistan, rose to top government positions, which they held over three generations; and highly educated Zoroastrian Persians who had formerly served the Sasanian dynasty formed the core of the Islamic administration in Iraq.[23]

Like Rome, Islam assertively spread its asabiyah and sense of shared identity. And like Rome, it assimilated much from other cultures to forge that identity. This was epitomized in the regnant notion of *adab*, an ideal of syncretic cultural sophistication, which reached its apogee during the Abbasid era. Adab melded literature, science, and philosophy from a variety of cultures into a uniquely Islamic synthesis. Adab and the Islamic melting pot are probably best exemplified by the ninth-century polymath al-Jahiz: though his own heritage was African, he incorporated Indian and Persian stories and aesthetics, along with Greek science and philosophy, into some of the finest Arabic prose ever written.[24] We get a sense of the Islamic melting pot, not just from Jahiz's writing itself, but from the occasional glimpses he provides of the society in which he lived. In one letter, for example, he praises a prominent military commander who chastised an orator for merely mentioning the different ethnic backgrounds of soldiers:

> You challenged this ... affected orator, who had set up these subdivisions and distinguished these groups, contrasting their racial origins, differentiating between them on ethnic grounds and emphasizing the disparity of their antecedents. You upbraided him severely for his words and heaped abuse on him, saying the Imperial army ought to be described as united, or virtually so, and that you did not approve of the introduction of racial distinctions between its various groups, or any loosening of the ties that bound them together.[25]

Just as it did for Rome, the melting pot model gave Islam tremendous vigor, creativity, and resilience. Islam's openness to different ethnic, racial, and religious groups enabled it to attract adherents with talent and energy; its notion of ummah, like Rome's citizenship, helped assimilate these adherents into a cohesive community with a sense of shared enterprise. Thus, during an era in which Christian Europe was mostly stagnating, Islamicate civilization flourished economically, culturally, and technologically. It not only preserved Greek and Roman science and mathematics; it improved on them. It also originated or enhanced many technological innovations, from the astrolabe to the papermill, and fostered wealth-generating trade both within its own domain and with far-flung regions, from China to sub-Saharan Africa.

The assimilation of different groups into the ummah was by no means seamless; the tribalism of seventh-century Arab society would not change overnight. Early on, the rivalry between northern and southern tribal coalitions occasionally flared. The Islamic state, like Rome, sought to diminish this sort of division and to foster unity by organizing military units across tribal and ethnic lines.[26] The process for assimilating non-Arabs was also imperfect: when they joined the ummah, they were incorporated in the only way the Arabs knew—they were made into "clients" (*mawali*) of existing Arab tribes. In many ways, this helped integrate them into the ummah: they assumed the adopting tribe's name and received its support and protection. However, their status was normally subordinate, and they typically did not enjoy the full privileges that Arab Muslims had. Discontent among non-Arab mawali ultimately contributed to the overthrow of the first Islamic dynasty.[27]

While the melting pot process did encounter hitches like these along the way, it proved inexorable. Joining in the melting pot—participating in the shared identity and cultivating adab—was key to status in the new regime, while having Arab genealogy became progressively less so. For example, Islam's most esteemed early scholars came from a wide variety of non-Arab backgrounds.[28] Only seventy years into the Islamic era, one caliph noted that the top religious authorities in all the key regions were non-Arabs.

Abu Muslim, a Persian who helped launch the Abbasid caliphate, was perhaps representative when he proclaimed a new shared identity that superseded all ethnic and racial origins:

> I do not trace my descent to any one group to the exclusion of another . . . My only ancestry is Islam.[29]

Early Islam, like Rome, would be invigorated and strengthened by countless individuals like this—people who had remarkably diverse ethnic and religious origins but came to share in the unifying identity that it promoted.

From Believers to Dhimmis

Around the beginning of the eighth century, the Islamic state began to shift away from its earlier ecumenism and to emphasize confessional distinctions within the believers' movement. A medieval Arabic "tweet"—that is, another Islamic coin—exemplifies this shift (figure 5.2).

Figure 5.2. Islamic dirham from the mid-eighth century.[30]

This coin was minted roughly fifty years after the coins in figure 5.1. The most obvious difference is that the "infidel" symbols are gone, replaced with verses from the Qur'an. The key verse in the center of the coin is: "[God] neither begat nor was

He begotten"—a clear jab at Christianity. To ensure this message got sufficient exposure, Muslims also embossed it, along with some other jibes at Christianity, on the Dome of the Rock, the distinctive gold-domed building in the center of Jerusalem.[31] If the coins were like "tweets," the inscriptions on the Dome of the Rock were like Times Square billboards. A while after these Christian-taunting messages first appeared, Islamic historians would write histories that omitted the ecumenism described by Christian writers who actually witnessed the early Islamic expansion. According to these Muslim historians, Islam was, from its inception, clearly distinct from, and mostly inimical toward, Christianity and Judaism. Although the Qur'an contains many verses that endorse religious tolerance and suggest that non-Muslims could be part of the ummah, it also contains some that can be used to justify subordinating non-Muslims. From the eighth century onward, Islamic regimes tended to emphasize the latter set of verses over the former.

There are many possible reasons for the shift toward confessional differentiation of the believers. For example, it may have been that rulers found that distinguishing Christian and Jewish subjects and imposing special taxes on them helped public finances; taxes on non-Muslims would constitute the single largest revenue source for many later Islamic regimes.[32] Whatever its underlying motivation, the confessional differentiation of the believers became the basis for differential treatment: Jews, Christians, and members of other faiths were eventually relegated to a distinct subordinate status outside the ummah, designated as dhimmis, rather than believers. As dhimmis, they received protection and enjoyed substantial religious freedom. However, under most later Islamic regimes, they had considerable legal and social disadvantages. They had to pay a special tax, known as the *jizya,* and obey a set of rules that distinguished them from Muslims and subordinated and humiliated them. For example, they were required to wear outfits that identified their religions and were prohibited from adopting Muslim names, styles of dress, and manners.[33]

Although the initial ecumenical approach of the first Islamic state was discarded, the melting pot paradigm was not abandoned altogether. It usually still applied to individuals who converted to the state-approved brand of Islam. And a few regimes also maintained the more inclusive, integrative approach toward non-Muslims practiced in Islam's first few decades. For example, Spain's Umayyad rulers integrated Christians and Jews, allowing them to share in cultural and technological innovation and to attain the very highest government posts.[34] One ninth-century Christian theologian complained that young Christians were so devoted to pursuing careers in the Umayyad administration and perfecting their Arabic that they could barely write letters in Latin.[35] Mirroring the ecumenical spirit that prevailed in the early Islamic State, Muslims and Christians across Umayyad Spain often celebrated festivals in honor of the Virgin Mary together.

In Mughal India, Emperor Akbar revoked the jizya, hired thousands of Hindu officials, and inaugurated an era that revived early Islam's ecumenism and syncretism. As Akbar's successor wrote:

> This was different from the practice in other realms, for in Iran there is room for Shias only, and in Turkey, India, and Turan there is room for Sunnis only . . . in [Akbar's] dominions . . . the road to altercation was closed. Sunnis and Shias met in one mosque, and Franks and Jews in one church, and observed their own forms of worship. He associated with the good of every race and creed . . .[36]

Like the early Islamic State, these more inclusive melting pot regimes were fabulously successful. Umayyad Spain became the economic, intellectual, and cultural capital of the western Mediterranean. It preserved and translated countless works from the classical era and fostered innovation in everything from mathematics to pharmacology. Mughal India under Akbar and his immediate successors was not only a cultural marvel, producing magnificent Perso-Indian melting pot art, literature, and architecture; it also became an economic powerhouse, accounting for 25 percent of the world's industrial production by the year 1700—eight times greater than France's share.

Unfortunately, these success stories would end when subsequent rulers reverted to multicultural particularism. In Spain, the Umayyads' successors, the Almoravids and Almohads, distinguished starkly between Muslim and non-Muslim subjects, progressively instituting discrimination against Christians and Jews, spurring many of them to flee the Iberian Peninsula. In India, Akbar's great-grandson Aurangzeb reversed policies of religious and ethnic syncretism, reintroducing measures that distinguished between different ethnoreligious groups. The sectarian and ethnic conflict this unleashed would ultimately fracture the Mughal regime; India's share of world GDP would plummet to less than 7 percent of the global total.[37]

Aside from exceptions like Umayyad Spain and Mughal India, later Islamic regimes tended to adopt a hybrid approach to integrating diverse denominations and ethnicities—typically a melting pot for those who converted to the state-approved brand of Islam and subordinate status for everyone else. The following sections focus on the Ottoman Empire because it was the largest and most enduring of these regimes.

Ottoman Millet: Seeds of Division

In 1453, when the victorious Ottoman sultan Mehmed II entered Constantinople, he did something few people expected after a long and brutal siege: he asked the defeated Orthodox Christians to nominate their own leader. Then, as a contemporary chronicler wrote, he granted that leader "the rule of the church and all its power and authority, no less than that enjoyed previously under the [Christian] emperors." Mehmed also returned captured churches and other properties to the Christians.[38] Ten years later, Mehmed similarly accommodated Franciscan Catholics in Bosnia, drafting a pact that guaranteed them protection.

Figure 5.3. Mehmed II's pact granting protection to Catholics.[39]

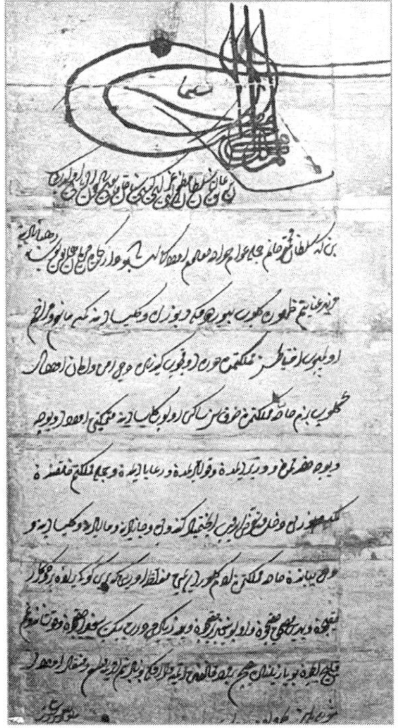

This was how Mehmed and the Ottomans observed the dhimmi status of the defeated Christians. It was the foundation of what would later be known as the "millet system."

The term "millet" derives from the Arabic word for religious denomination. However, the millet system was not based solely on religion. Nor, for that matter, was it truly a system. It was more of a model or paradigm that encompassed a variety of arrangements under which various subjugated groups could maintain their group identities and enjoy a large measure of autonomy.[40] The Ottomans initially designated the empire's major religious denominations (Greek Orthodox, Jews, and Armenian Gregorians) as millets. Over time, they also granted millet (or millet-like) status to a variety of minor denominations and ethnic groups, such as Vlachs and Kurds.[41] These groups administered their own religious affairs as well as many communal institutions. The Ottomans' principal requirements of the millets were that they provide tax revenue to the Ottoman government and refer any legal issues involving Muslims to the Muslim courts. Beyond that, they were permitted to use their own languages and follow their own cultural and religious practices. Many contemporary proponents of multiculturalism cite the millet system as an excellent model for multicultural governance. It was the sort of arrangement that advocates of multiculturalism laud as an ideal for modern societies.[42]

In addition to autonomy, millets in the Ottoman Empire enjoyed a large measure of tolerance—far more than most contemporary religious minorities in Europe. For example, while Jews suffered from pogroms and harsh persecution in some European countries, they were treated relatively well under the Ottomans; they were not only allowed to practice their religion but to become quite prosperous.[43] The situation was similar for Christian denominations under Ottoman rule. While Catholics were being hanged in England, Huguenots massacred in France, and Anabaptists burned at the stake in Switzerland, diverse Christian denominations could all safely practice their faiths in Ottoman lands.[44]

The Ottoman approach to integrating diverse peoples shared some aspects with the Roman approach. The Ottomans, like the

Romans, allowed individuals from a vast array of backgrounds to ascend to the highest levels of government. Conversion to Islam was generally a prerequisite, but once converted, individuals enjoyed tremendous opportunities, regardless of their original ethnicity or religion. Of the eighty-two grand viziers who took office between the conquest of Constantinople and the Köprülü era, only a dozen were ethnically Turkish. The rest were Abkhazian, Armenian, Bosnian, Bulgarian, Circassian, Georgian, Greek, Hungarian, and Italian.[45] The Ottomans also cultivated a unifying syncretic cultural ideal comparable to Romanitas. Converts, including many from Western Europe, participated in this ideal, coming to see themselves as "true Ottomans."[46]

But Ottoman comparisons to Rome end with the Muslim ruling elite. Non-Muslims who did not convert faced a communal order that was more like that of the Aztecs than the Romans. Although the masses of non-Muslims in the millets enjoyed relative autonomy and tolerance, they were not entitled to anything like Roman citizenship; their status was both separate and unequal. For most of the Ottoman period, they had to pay the jizya tax, as well as adhere to onerous and humiliating limitations on dress and public behavior. Christians and Jews had to wear special tokens, like yellow badges, and were restricted to clothing of certain colors. Individuals who adopted dress or behavior designated for a millet other than their own faced harsh penalties.[47]

Thus, while the millet system allowed minorities to follow their own religions and cultural practices, it fostered a sense of distinction and separateness, not only between the Muslim overlords and the millets, but also among the millets themselves. This was reflected in the stark segregation of the different millets in many Ottoman cities and towns.[48] One sixteenth-century emissary to the Ottoman Empire observed that every sizeable town needed a detachment of Janissaries to protect Christians and Jews from "the violence of the mob," suggesting there was significant animus between Muslims and non-Muslims.[49]

The Ottoman government granted rights, privileges, and responsibilities to the millets rather than to individuals. So, a competitive tension festered among the millets, with them vying for status at each other's expense. As an early traveler to the Ottoman Empire wrote:

> The Armenian regards the Greek with jealousy, and the Greek in turn regards the Armenian with distrust, each watching lest the other acquire undue influence at the Porte [the Ottoman government], and both unite in cursing the Turk; while he hates them as Christian dogs who may eventually oust him from his dominion over them.[50]

The Ottomans divided subject populations, not only with the millet system but also with preferences (known as *istimalet*), which were granted to various groups.[51] For example, the Ottomans granted tax exemptions and other special privileges to Christian Vlachs in exchange for their help in conquering the western Balkans.[52] While the millet system fostered a sense of group distinction, istimalet enhanced that sense and fueled it with envy and rivalry. It was a clever arrangement that worked well for the Ottoman administration. A subject population of distinct, mutually antagonistic groups is far less likely to revolt successfully than a more unified, homogeneous population. As the British diplomat Charles Eliot observed:

> Greeks, Serbs, and Bulgarians, to say nothing of Vlachs and Albanians, have each their peculiar aspirations, and by playing off one against another and consistently supporting whatever may happen to be the weaker party, the central authority maintains its power.[53]

The "conquer, divide, and tolerate" paradigm of the millet system and istimalet enabled the Ottoman Empire to quickly incorporate vast, diverse territories into its domain while minimizing conflict with, and among, the subject populations. The Ottomans would successfully govern an overwhelming non-Muslim majority for over two hundred years.[54]

The Ottoman Empire's unassimilated millet populations did pose a threat to stability, just as unassimilated groups like the Totonacs and the Tlaxcalans threatened the Aztecs' stability. But the Ottomans partially mitigated this threat by allowing assimilation into the ruling class through both voluntary and compulsory (i.e., *devşirme*) conversion to Islam. Talented and ambitious members of the millets could get ahead by converting, and some did just that.

In this way, the Ottoman polity was a hybrid of the Roman and Aztec systems: for those who converted to Islam, there was melting pot integration into the Ottoman ranks; for the rest, there was subordination, tempered by a measure of tolerance. Thus, while the Ottoman regime was not as resilient as Rome, it was not as fragile as the Aztec Empire. It all worked pretty well... until it didn't.

As long as the iron fist of Ottoman power was poised to suppress strife between millets and rebellion against the central government, things held together. When that power began to falter, all the religious and ethnic divisions that the millet system had diligently fostered emerged as threatening fissures in the body politic. As a traveler to the Ottoman Empire nearly a century before its dissolution presciently observed:

> With so many evils to combat, so many races and creeds to conciliate, the Turkish Empire requires an able hand at the helm to steer its course with safety... The evil passions—fanaticism and

> rivalry—of so many races and creeds, must, on the dissolution of Osmanli rule in these provinces of Turkey in Europe, lead to a fearful state of anarchy.[55]

The decline and collapse of the Ottoman Empire, like many major historical events, was caused by a confluence of many factors. But it is clear that the ethnoreligious fractionalization fostered by the multicultural millet system contributed materially, expediting the decline and making the ultimate collapse more calamitous. Centuries of rigorously maintaining group distinctions, along with the failure to instill any sense of shared identity across the vast array of peoples in the Ottoman domain, made it impossible to either maintain or divide the empire simply and peacefully. Ultimately, the divisive legacy of the millet system helped set the stage for five genocides (of the Armenians, the Assyrians, the Bosnians, the Greeks, and the Serbians) as well as the toxic division of multiple successor states (Cyprus, Lebanon, and the Balkan states). These catastrophes cost millions of innocent lives and displaced millions more.

Two episodes, in particular, illustrate the inherent hazard of systems like the millet system and of multicultural particularism in general, demonstrating that maintaining ethnic divisions and a sense of difference, even in the spirit of tolerance and protection, creates a latent Damoclean danger. The first occurred when southern Greeks revolted in 1821. False rumors spread that the Greeks had massacred Muslims, which incited widespread attacks against all Greeks, most of whom were uninvolved in the revolt. Even Phanariot Greeks in Istanbul, powerful and loyal supporters of the Ottoman regime, were targeted. Although the Greek patriarch had excommunicated the Greek rebels, the Ottoman authorities, asserting a principle of collective responsibility, hanged him. In a characteristically invidious move, they instructed Jews to cut down and dispose of his body—which helped pit Greeks against Jews. Before its eventual collapse, the Ottoman Empire had murdered hundreds of thousands of Greeks.[56]

The second episode, the Armenian genocide, is similarly instructive. The Ottomans had long honored Armenians as the *millet-i sadıka*—"the loyal millet." But being loyal did nothing to assure a group's safety, so long as that group was perceived to be separate and distinct. In a very short time, Armenians went from being cherished members of the "loyal millet" to being victims of a genocide. Because of the long-standing divisions maintained in the millet system, Ottoman Turks, along with the Armenians' rival minorities (Circassians and Kurds), had always perceived the Armenians to be very distinct from themselves. Difference and distinction make fertile ground for the seeds of distrust. So, when an Ottoman commander blamed Armenians for his loss of a World War I battle to Russia, few questioned it and one of the twentieth century's worst genocides was initiated. Ultimately 1.5 million innocent Armenians would be deported or murdered.[57]

As terrible as the Greek and Armenian genocides were, they were only part of Ottoman multiculturalism's baleful legacy. In chapter 6, we will take a more detailed look at how this legacy played out with other peoples in another region—the Balkans.

Summary and Conclusions

Like Rome, the early Islamic state offered a shared identity that vast populations, regardless of their race or ethnic origins, could adopt and become part of. And like Rome, the early Islamic state formed that identity by melding the contributions and the genius of its diverse populations in a melting pot. This melting pot paradigm was as compelling for early Islam as it was for Rome, drawing enthusiastic adherents from a vast array of cultures and races, infusing it with tremendous energy, and allowing it to expand at a spectacular pace.

Although the early Islamic state was religious at its core, it was not denominationally exclusive: not only did it tolerate the other major faiths; it embraced them as cousins, including them in its ummah of believers. This inclusive and unifying approach was a key factor in the Islamic melting pot's success. It allowed the early Islamic state to quickly gain support from many non-Muslims, particularly the numerous religious minorities that were persecuted under Byzantine and Sasanian rule. Highly educated scribes, artisans, scientists, and many others who had served Byzantium or the Sasanian Empire quickly joined the Islamic enterprise. This helped drive a cultural and scientific efflorescence that stands out as one of the greatest in history.

Sometime after the early Islamic expansion, Muslim leaders abandoned the notion enshrined in the Constitution of Medina that non-Muslims could be part of a unified community—an ummah—with Muslims. They began distinguishing between Muslims and non-Muslims, relegating the latter to subordinate, dhimmi status outside the ummah. This diminished the Islamic melting pot and opened the door to a variety of official group distinctions in later Islamic societies, distinctions that may have made governance easier in the short term, but which ultimately weakened these societies.

The Ottoman millet system exemplified this best: Ottoman rulers governed vast non-Muslim subject populations by dividing them into millets and granting those millets some limited rights and toleration. Although the millet was originally a religious conception, it transitioned into an ethnoreligious one: by the end of the Ottoman reign, there was a vast array of ethnoreligious group divisions, Albanians, Greeks, Serbs, Croats, Vlachs, Armenians, Kurds, and others. Despite its initial advantages, the millet system had a terrible cost. Because of state-enforced distinctions and preferential policies, not only did each group perceive that it was in a zero-sum competition with the others, it also lacked affinity or loyalty to the larger polity. With little besides the Sublime Porte's iron fist holding things together, the Ottoman Empire quickly collapsed as soon as that iron fist faltered. Multicultural particularism ultimately proved to be as disastrous for the Ottomans as it was for the Aztecs and the late imperial Romans. The Ottoman reign, the world's longest-lasting multicultural experiment, would ultimately cost millions of innocent lives and leave a legacy of division and rancor that lingers to this day.

6

*

THE BALKANS—MILLET, MULTICULTURALISM, AND MURDER

In 1998, the psyops staff of NATO's Bosnia Stabilisation Force devised a secret weapon. They hoped that dropping half a million of these weapons from bombers would help end conflict in the region. The secret weapon was a Serbo-Croatian translation of *The Sneetches* by Dr. Seuss. *The Sneetches* is a children's book about mythical creatures called Sneetches, who appeared nearly identical, except that some had stars on their bellies; the Sneetches discriminated against each other based on these stars. After an entrepreneur devised a machine that enabled the Sneetches to apply and remove stars at will, they determined that they would do best to ignore superficial differences and just be nice to each other. Apparently, some optimistic NATO officers hoped the book could convince the Bosnian population to do the same.[1]

It is understandable that these officers might think former Yugoslavs were akin to Sneetches. Although Yugoslavia has been described as a country of "five nationalities, four languages, three religions, and two alphabets," most former Yugoslavs have a great deal in common. The majority have South Slavic ancestry, with DNA studies showing no significant differences among the groups.[2] The local languages, with the exception of Albanian, are all closely related. In fact, Bosnian, Croatian, Serbian, and Montenegrin were all considered to be the same language (Serbo-Croatian) until the 1990s.[3] People of the region listen to the same pop music and share the same cuisine: *cevap*, *burek*, and *rakija*.

Through personal experience, I discovered that Balkan coffee is perhaps emblematic of ethnic distinctions in the region. In Skopje, a Macedonian served me what most Americans would call Turkish coffee, asserting that it was Macedonian coffee and that it was vastly superior to other Balkan coffees, whether Turkish, Greek, Albanian, Serbian, or Bosnian. In Sarajevo, I had a similar experience with Bosnian coffee: I was assured that though it might seem similar, it was different and superior to all the others. It was the same with Albanian coffee in Kosovo, and so on. In the end, it was clear to me that Balkan coffees, like Sneetches, are far more alike than they are different.

The most prominent distinction in the Balkans is religion, with the population divided among Catholic, Muslim, and Eastern Orthodox denominations. It does not seem like that should matter, though, because the Balkan population is not that religious. Less than a quarter of Bosnians and Croatians attend religious services weekly; only 7 percent of Serbians do, making Serbia one of the least observant Christian countries in the world.[4] Yet, people in the former Yugoslavia, like Sneetches, are starkly divided along the lines of this seemingly minor distinction. Rather than stars, they bear crescents and a few different types of crosses.

The divisions in the Balkans have been so persistent and bitter that the region is inextricably associated with conflict and terms like *balkanization* and *ethnic cleansing*. Governments in the region have entire departments devoted to documenting unidentified human remains from past ethnic conflicts; construction companies call them in when an excavation exposes piles of bodies (typically with wire-bound wrists and bullet holes in the backs of their skulls).[5] While the ethnic cleansing of the 1990s stands out in the collective memory, it was only the most recent chapter in a terrible history of conflict. To get a sense of the depth and intensity of that history, we will consider just one of the earlier chapters: the genocide of Serbs in the "Independent State of Croatia" (NDH) during World War II.

When the Nazis invaded Yugoslavia in World War II, they chose a Croatian group, known as the Ustaše, to run things. The Ustaše, staking claims to a greater Croatia, sought to "cleanse" Serbs from the region, murdering three hundred and fifty thousand of them and expelling another three hundred thousand.[6] It is hard to imagine the extremes of barbarity it would take to horrify Nazis, but the Ustaše actually managed it. They committed atrocities so heinous that many of their allies—not only Nazi SS officers but also hardened Spanish and Italian fascists—begged to be reassigned rather than witness any more. Incredibly, one Nazi general wrote to Himmler that he feared that Ustaše atrocities would ruin the Nazis' reputation. In his memoir, he described women impaled through the genitalia and piles of dead children in a concentration camp, writing that "these places of horror here in Croatia have climbed the summit of abomination."[7]

The genocide of the Serbs underscores both the multilateral nature and the pervasiveness of Balkan conflict. Because of the Serbs' role in the 1994 Bosnian genocide and the conflict in Kosovo, there has been a perception in the West that they have been the perennial "bad guys." But in the past, other groups were the bad guys, and Serbs were the victims. Indeed, over the last century, few groups in the Balkans have not perpetrated ethnic violence at some point. Not only have most groups participated in ethnic violence; participation within the groups has been widespread. Killings were sometimes orchestrated by extremists. Ultimately, however, mass ethnic cleansing did not occur because of a few bad people acting normally, but because of lots of normal people acting badly. The scale of the slaughter was so immense that it could only have occurred with widespread participation. This raises the question: what has elicited so much ethnic antagonism from so many ordinary people in this region? The answer lies in the legacy of the vast multicultural experiment that began with the Ottoman millet system and ended with the Yugoslav "nations and nationalities" policy.

Millets and Multiculturalism in the Balkans

The Ottomans began their conquest of the Balkans in the fourteenth century, incorporating local populations into the millet system.[8] As discussed in chapter 5, this system was an early form of multiculturalism, one that many modern-day advocates of multiculturalism would approve of. Under the millet system, Orthodox Christians, Catholics, Jews, and other groups did, in fact, enjoy a level of tolerance far beyond what religious and ethnic minorities could have hoped for in Western Europe at the time. Each group, as a millet, was allowed to maintain its own cultural practices and distinct identity. The system allowed the millets considerable autonomy, with the Sublime Porte granting rights to the millets rather than directly to individuals. A pivotal consequence of this arrangement was that it bolstered ethnic boundaries, fostering a sense of distinction and separateness, not only between the Muslim overlords and the millets but also among the millets themselves.

The effects of the Ottomans' invidious millet policies on ethnic groups in the Balkans were such that an early seventeenth-century traveler observed:

> I noted them so desperate malicious towards one another, as each loves the Turke better than they doe either of the other, and serve him for informers, and instruments against one another: the hatred...is at this day so implacable, as...in any Christian warre upon the Turke.[9]

Until the day the Ottomans left the Balkans, each of the groups in the region complained that the other groups were treacherously assisting the Ottomans against them. In modern sociology parlance, the millet system was wildly successful at "othering" the different groups.

As Ottoman rule neared its end in the Balkans, the balkanizing effect of the millet system on the region's ethnic groups was clearly established.[10] For centuries, relations were defined in terms of the Ottoman government and groups rather than the government and individuals. So, individuals came to see everything through a group lens and to view their interactions with other groups as a ruthless zero-sum game. Writing during the Tanzimat Reform era, the British captain, Edmund Spencer, observed:

> In Bosnia, Croatia and Herzegowina, where we find Servian Mussulmen [Serbian Muslims], Servian schismatic Greeks, and Servian Roman Catholics, this intolerance prevails to such a deplorable extent, that...each in their turn make common cause with the infidel Mussulman, in the hope of exterminating their detested rival.[11]

Because individual groups in the Balkans had this sense of pugnacious communal identity fostered by the millet system but no shared asabiyah with each other or with the Ottoman Empire, they were only waiting for an opportunity to seek independence. And so, as the Ottoman Empire weakened in the nineteenth and twentieth centuries, the Balkans attempted to throw off the Ottoman yoke, an effort that culminated in the Balkan Wars of 1912 and 1913. These wars recapitulated the legacy of Ottoman multiculturalism in the region: in the first war, the nascent Balkan states fought the Ottomans; in the second war, they fought each other.

Brotherhood and Unity—For a While

During World War I, representatives of Balkan groups living in exile met to organize a new Southern Slavic nation from former territories of the Habsburg and Ottoman empires. It would be a constitutional monarchy called the "Kingdom of the Serbs, Croats, and Slovenes," with Alexander I of Serbia's Karađorđević dynasty as head of state. The new nation would grant equal rights and status to the "Orthodox, Roman Catholic, and Mussulman religions."[12] An enigmatic and taciturn figure, Alexander was also bright and perceptive. He was keenly aware of the threat ethnic factionalism posed to the country. So, he renamed it Yugoslavia and reorganized it with a centralized government and *banovinas* (states) with borders deliberately drawn to abrogate ethnoreligious boundaries. But the divisions and communal distinctions the Ottomans had maintained and reinforced over centuries could not be erased so easily. Many Croats and Serbs resisted Alexander's effort to create a unitary nation; a Macedonian radical ended it altogether by assassinating him. A few years later, when the Nazis invaded the country, it was already on the verge of collapse.

The disruption from the Nazi invasion spurred Yugoslavia's ethnic factionalism to explode.[13] By the end of the war, internecine ethnic conflict had killed more Yugoslavs than the Nazis had.[14] The militias of the two principal factions (the Croatian Ustaše and the Serbian Četniks) ultimately alienated most Yugoslavs with their Nazi collaboration and gratuitous attacks on civilians. So popular support swung to the Communist-led Partisan Army. By 1945, the Partisans comprised over eight hundred thousand fighters, almost evenly drawn from the country's various regions and ethnic groups.[15] The Partisans were extremely effective, defeating both the Četniks and the Ustaše and driving the Axis powers out of the country.

With broad support among all the constituent ethnic groups, the Partisans were well positioned to construct a unified polity after World War II. Their leader, Josip Broz (better known as "Tito"), was the perfect candidate to orchestrate the effort. With a Slovene mother, a Croat father, and a Serb wife, he was one of a few leaders who could claim to be a true Yugoslav; moreover, he was a canny and ruthless politician. Tito and his Communist Party devised the Federal People's Republic of Yugoslavia, which comprised six republics and two autonomous provinces carved out of Serbia.

Although the republics were partly self-governing, Tito would exercise firm control through the federal government. Like Alexander I, Tito recognized the need for Yugoslav unity, claiming that the borders between the republics would be like the "white lines in a marble column." He made "Brotherhood and Unity" a national slogan; before long, nearly every village in the country had a "Brotherhood and Unity" bridge or square. Even the national highway was named "Brotherhood and Unity." Tito articulated a clear vision of a unifying Yugoslavism, invoking America's "melting pot:"

> I would like to live to see the day when Yugoslavia would become . . . a single Yugoslav nation, in which our five peoples

> would become a single nation…This is my greatest aspiration. You had a similar process of establishing a single nation in America, where a single nation was created from English and other nations.[16]

To support this melting pot ideal, the government launched programs to sponsor film and literature that featured unifying "all-Yugoslav" content. For example, the 1947 film *This People Will Live* centered on a Serbian girl who joined the Partisans and fell in love with a Croatian fighter. The state-controlled press also vigorously promoted the idea that "Yugoslavism" had prevailed over ethnic jingoism in defeating the fascists.[17]

Initially, some intellectuals agreed that Yugoslavia needed to forge a common culture and shared identity. In 1954, prominent intellectuals signed the Novi Sad Agreement to standardize the vernaculars of Serbs, Croats, Bosnians, and Montenegrins as a single language. The goal was to create a new, unifying Communist Yugoslav identity that would renounce the Ustaše and Četnik legacy of ethnic division and antagonism. Old-time Yugoslavs reminisce about those years when Yugoslavs were beginning to see themselves as a unitary nation. Older Bosnians still recount heartwarming stories from that era of Christians and Muslims paying each other cheerful social visits on holidays like Christmas and the Muslim Eid al Fitr. Stories abound of Croats, Serbs, Slovenes, and others working together in the "youth brigades" right after the war, developing a sense that they were one people with a shared mission and purpose. Over a million young Yugoslavs volunteered to build the country's infrastructure and would begin constructing a shared identity in the process.[18] The brigades were deliberately organized to mingle youth of different ethnic origins, and there are many accounts of individuals discarding prejudices and ethnic grudges in favor of a new, shared Yugoslav camaraderie.[19]

Another Affirmative Action Empire

But the ideal of national identity and unity was short-lived, with Communist Party members increasingly challenging it on theoretical grounds. Because traditional Marxism is preoccupied with class and class struggle and mostly ignores ethnicity and nationalism as irrelevant, it provides no coherent ideology for managing them.[20] So some Yugoslav Communists looked to the Soviets, who had preceded them in establishing a multiethnic state, for ideas. The Soviets' enigmatic and disastrous multicultural policies merit a thorough exposition and perhaps a separate chapter in this book. However, they have been so exhaustively and capably covered by Terry Martin that I will not seek to recreate that effort and will only summarize it briefly here.[21]

Marx provided no roadmap to negotiate ethnicity and nationalism, so Lenin and Stalin had to develop a homegrown ideology for it. They asserted that national consciousness was a necessary phase that societies had to pass through to reach the ideal of Communist internationalism. Therefore, Communist states should vigorously promote national consciousness until it burns itself out. Summarizing the policy that he and Lenin developed, Stalin said:

> We are undertaking the maximum development of national culture, so that it will exhaust itself completely and thereby create the base for the organization of international socialist culture.[22]

To that end, the Soviet government aggressively encouraged distinct ethnonational identities (which it printed in passports), established dozens of official regional languages, and strongly discouraged assimilation. It also set numerous political, occupational, and educational quotas for ethnic groups, inspiring Martin to call the Soviet Union the "Affirmative Action Empire."[23] Of course, the results were disastrous and deadly. Stalin came to suspect disloyalty from many of the nationalities that the Soviet government had encouraged to foster distinct identities. So, the government "ethnically cleansed" no less than nine of these nationalities; the public also attacked some of them in spontaneous outbursts of ethnic antagonism. Ironically, nationalities that had been urged to nurture their own distinct identities were then persecuted precisely because of those identities. The malign effects of the Soviet "affirmative action" policy linger on and continue to plague the former Soviet republics today.[24] Probably unaware of the Soviet policy's calamitous outcome, Yugoslav Communists sought to implement a similar policy in their own country.

Yugoslavism and ethnic integration also came under attack from leading Slovenian intellectuals because they had long feared that their ethnic identity would be subsumed and lost in a Yugoslav identity that had too much of a Serbian tinge. This group included Edvard Kardelj, who, as draftsman of the Yugoslav constitutions and presumed successor to Tito, was extremely influential. The Slovenian intellectuals thus joined in a push to abandon Yugoslavism and replace it with a Soviet-style "affirmative action empire" that fostered distinct ethnonational identities. This push had enough impetus that even Tito could not resist it.[25]

From 1946 to 1974, Yugoslavia underwent multiple constitutional changes. With each one, it moved closer to a Soviet-style multicultural system. This culminated in the 1974 Yugoslav Constitution, which not only granted the republics considerable independence but also explicitly gave "nations and nationalities" the right to foster their own separate cultural identities. The nations and nationalities were extraterritorial, with their members having linguistic and cultural rights regardless of where they lived. For example, an ethnic Albanian had the right to be educated in

Albanian, whether he lived in Bosnia, Kosovo, or Macedonia.[26] This was what Aleksandar Pavković has called the "new communist policy of segregationist multiculturalism:"

> Every nation and every (larger) nationality was to be enabled to promote its separate culture, without any fear of "contamination" from the others, through an appropriate set of cultural and educational institutions established in each of the six republics and two provinces. The federal institutions for promotion of the Yugoslav culture were disbanded... Instead of them, institutions and organizations for the promotion of separate national cultures proliferated in each republic and province. Each of the six republics and two provinces established separate school curricula at each educational level...[27]

The 1974 constitution also introduced the "nationality key" system, an affirmative action program that apportioned national military and political positions to the different ethnic groups.[28] The system was adopted by the republics, which also applied it to education and nonpolitical employment. To give one example: in 1981, the University of Priština established that precisely 3.8 Albanian students must be enrolled for each student of another ethnic group. Education preferences like this, along with employment preferences, encouraged many non-Albanians (mostly Serbs and Montenegrins) to leave Kosovo, with 5 percent of them moving away just in the first six months after the policy was introduced.[29] Thus, this policy increased the segregation of groups, enhanced feelings of group distinction, and fueled group rivalry.

Curiously, Yugoslav Communist rule came to resemble Ottoman rule in many ways. For starters, the Communists had discarded Alexander's transethnic Banovinas and adopted borders that largely followed the Ottomans' ethnically oriented borders.

But more significantly, the Communists' management of Yugoslavia's ethnic components mirrored the millet paradigm: they granted the individual ethnic groups the ability to foster their own identities and cultural practices; the ethnic groups were partly extraterritorial; and each had its own power structure, ultimately answering to the central authority. In both cases, the central authority benefited from the group division; the separate (and mutually distrustful) groups balanced against each other, diminishing the threat to central control. Both regimes also periodically implemented preferential policies that favored one group over others, fomenting group separation and rivalry. The Communists did not have a sultan keeping the groups from fighting with a poised iron fist, but they did have Tito and his cadres in the federal government performing the same function. Ultimately, the Yugoslav multicultural system, like the Ottoman millet system, worked well... until it didn't.

The Yugoslav Breakup

For decades, Tito had masterfully played East and West against each other, procuring large amounts of aid and favorable economic deals from both sides. His death in 1980 (along with the collapse of Eastern Bloc Communist countries) ended that, exposing the weaknesses of Yugoslavia's "market socialist" economy, with the resulting stresses magnifying tension among ethnic groups. But more importantly, the iron fist that had held things together was now gone. It did not take long for the country's ethnic groups to clash. It began in Kosovo, where a dwindling Serb population protested the affirmative action programs that discriminated against them, complaining that they were oppressed. Even though Serbs constituted only 10 percent of the population, Serbs all over Yugoslavia considered Kosovo their heartland and part of their ethnic inheritance—it was, after all, the site of the Battle of Kosovo, the Serb Alamo.

As ethnic conflict expert Donald Horowitz has observed, when clear ethnic fault lines emerge in a society, the political dynamic tends to favor leaders who take the most extreme stands against other ethnic groups; leaders who take more moderate stands tend to be outflanked by extremists who can effectively label them as "traitors to their own kind." Often, the extremists are *ethnic opportunists* who engage in strident rhetoric and ethnically divisive actions, more out of cold political calculation than heartfelt ideology; they foment ethnic division and animus mostly because they perceive that it will bolster their political fortunes and help them get ahead.

The Serb leader Slobodan Milošević was an archetypal ethnic opportunist. Starting in 1987, he delivered inflammatory speeches condemning Kosovo's pro-Albanian affirmative action programs and the discrimination against Serbs, hinting at violent solutions.[30] He was a profoundly mediocre and odious character—a fact that many Serbs recognized. But his appeal to Serb ethnic solidarity nevertheless helped propel him to the Serbian presidency. As president, he peremptorily annexed Kosovo. His belligerent posturing appalled several of the other Yugoslav republics, which began plans for secession from the country, initiating a terrible cycle of violence: the Ten-Day War, the Croatian War of Independence, the Bosnian War, and the Kosovo War.

Milošević was not the only ethnic opportunist; others, like Radovan Karadžić in Bosnia and Franjo Tuđman in Croatia, stepped forward to both exploit and foment ethnic division. Decades of Yugoslav policies that had divided ethnic groups and accorded them differential treatment made it easy for them. Collectively, these men instigated inhuman cruelty on a scale that we associate mostly with the Nazi era: tens of thousands executed and dumped in mass graves; people tortured or burned alive; concentration camps; and so on. Perhaps most horrifying were the "rape camps," where Bosniak women were raped and held captive until they came to term; they were tortured and then released to care for the babies of their Serb rapists.

Beyond the staggering body count and terrible stories of torture and rape, one reality underscores the depth and bitterness of the ethnic antagonism in the Yugoslav breakup: no side was blameless. After the conflict had ended, international tribunals convicted numerous individuals from all sides of war crimes.

The Aftermath and the Future

Every day, my Bosniak friend's son walks to school with Croats in his town. When they arrive, he and other Bosniaks enter one door, and the Croats enter another. Inside the school, the Croats and Bosniaks take different classes with different curricula—and especially, with different histories. During breaks, they all exit to the same schoolyard, but it has a fence down the middle: Bosniaks on one side; Croats on the other. This school is one of Bosnia's many examples of "two schools under one roof."

In the Republika Srpska portion of Bosnia, politicians still honor convicted war criminals who orchestrated the Bosnian genocide; dozens of streets, parks, and squares bear their names. In Croatia, the governing HDZ party has held events honoring Ustaše war dead and continues to adopt incendiary Ustaše slogans and symbols; genocide denial is widespread.[31] In Kosovo, Serbs and Bosniaks continue to face persecution.[32]

The prospects for the former Yugoslav republics are not auspicious. Secession and ethnic cleansing have made some of them fairly homogeneous, so they might avoid the internecine ethnic conflict that remains an ever-present risk in the others. But the specter of pernicious irredentism lingers nearly everywhere. The ominous, persistent tensions across former Yugoslavia are instructive: the division and enmity that arise when governments foster ethnic distinctions and reinforce them with group preferences do not fade quickly.

Summary and Conclusions

A popular cliché among Western writers is that ancient, "primordial" tribalism has been the source of enduring ethnic conflict in the Balkans.[33] They claim that this tribalism is so deep-rooted (and imply the region is so backward and beholden to primitive tribal instincts) that conflict is inevitable. But this view overlooks that the area's stark group divisions were largely a political creation, first constructed and fostered in the Ottoman system of millets and istimalet, and then revived and enhanced in the Yugoslav implementation of a Soviet-style "affirmative action empire."

Although both the Ottoman millet system and the Yugoslav "nations and nationalities" policies were founded on multiculturalist notions of tolerance, they ultimately worked against those notions by "othering" the different groups. Under the Ottoman and Yugoslav multicultural systems, ethnic distinctions were officially encouraged and given political standing, so people came to perceive social and political relations in terms of their own group versus the "other." By granting preferential treatment based on group membership, both the Ottoman and Yugoslav governments bolstered that perception and infused it with envy and antagonism. Individuals interacted with the government and each other, not as individuals, but as members of groups—which were pitted against each other in a zero-sum game. This ultimately created a ripe climate for a series of murderous ethnic opportunists: Pavelić, Milošević, Tuđman, and Karadžić. These men all gained stature and political advantage by appealing to their groups' sense of grievance at the hands of the "other"—and, of course, by taking revenge for it.

King Alexander and Tito, who were both astute leaders, perceived the danger of perpetuating disparate and mutually antagonistic ethnic identities. They recognized the imperative of unifying Yugoslavia under a shared identity, with Tito specifically invoking America's melting pot. Although both leaders were ultimately thwarted in their efforts, there was a glimpse of possibility near the beginning of Tito's tenure, with the emphasis on "brotherhood and unity" and programs like the youth brigades, which attempted to build a common asabiyah among Yugoslavs. For a brief hopeful moment, it looked like Serbs and Croats might begin to forgive past offenses, and Muslims and Christians might celebrate the common ground of their Abrahamic faiths. Many people in the region still look back on that era as a brief "golden age." But that would fade to darkness when Communist ideologues steered the country toward a system of multicultural particularism that mirrored that of the Soviets' "affirmative action empire." Just as it had in the Soviet Union, the practice of encouraging group distinctions and enhancing them with group preferences led inexorably to violent conflict and ethnic cleansing.

7

ETHNIC IDENTITY CARDS AND GENOCIDE IN RWANDA

"Hutus this side and Tutsis this side," barked a Kalashnikov-toting thug at a group of terrified schoolchildren. He and twenty other militants from the Interahamwe militia had infiltrated Rwanda from a neighboring country and stormed the Nyange School, intent on killing all the Tutsis and restarting the genocide that had ended three years earlier. One girl defiantly declared:

We are all Rwandans.

The militants shot her through the head at point-blank range and continued to hector the students to separate into Hutus and Tutsis.[1] The students stood fast, refusing to be divided. Some more murmured:

There are no Hutus and Tutsis. We are all Rwandans.

So the militants decided to kill them all. Over twenty years later, Rwandans still mourn these children and draw inspiration from their courage.[2]

Fortunately, the Nyange School attack was one of the last major instances of ethnic violence in a country that had suffered terribly. The Rwandan genocide stands out for its scope, its savage speed, and its hand-to-hand, intimate cruelty: genocidaires murdered one million of the country's inhabitants in only a hundred days.[3] In percentage terms, that would be comparable to killing forty-seven million Americans. In absolute terms, the genocidaires surpassed even the Nazis in the pace of their butchery. That is particularly incredible given the Nazis' technological advantages: efficient railways, automatic weapons, and Zyklon gas. The Rwandan genocidaires were mostly limited to farm implements like machetes and hoes—and walls that infants' heads could be smashed against. The high-speed but low-tech slaughter required hands-on participation by many thousands of individuals, often killing people they knew: neighbors, soccer teammates, and former drinking buddies.[4]

Twenty-two years after the Nyange School attack, a pack of bicycles whirrs by on the main road near the school: it is the 2019 Tour du Rwanda. As a spectator, one could almost mistake it for the Tour de Suisse or the Tour de Luxembourg. The streets are beautifully paved and microscopically clean. The race organization is impeccable, with each stage run with clockwork precision. The terrain is verdant and undulating; the final stage features seven Category One climbs.

Comparisons to Switzerland and Luxembourg go beyond the annual bicycle race. Since the genocide, Rwanda has amassed a number of distinctions to challenge those countries: the world's second-fastest economic growth; the cleanest city in the world; the safest country on the continent; the least corruption in the region; and the most female legislators in the world. Although Rwanda has a long way to catch up when it comes to overall public health, it surpasses the European countries in some narrower categories: for example, the Swiss smoke fifteen times as many cigarettes per capita; Luxembourgers smoke sixty-seven times as many.[5] Expatriates I have talked with say they have lived in Rwanda for years without ever spotting a cigarette butt on the ground.

In only two decades, Rwanda went from genocidal hell to a 500 percent increase in GDP, hosting world-class bicycle races and competing with the world's richest countries in categories like "cleanest city" and "most women in politics." The account of how Rwanda accomplished this is as instructive and inspiring as it is incredible. As we will see, it provides both useful lessons and hope for other multiethnic countries.

The Rwandan People

Rwanda's population comprises three groups: Hutus (85 percent); Tutsis (14 percent); and Twa (1 percent). These groups have been variously described as races, tribes, castes, classes, and ethnic groups. Each description contains some small element of truth, but none is very accurate. The Twa, who are descended from indigenous pygmies, might be a different race, but the differences between Hutus and Tutsis in both appearance and DNA are minimal and inconsistent.[6] The traditional stereotype has been that Tutsis are taller, thinner, and lighter-skinned. But anyone who relies on these traits to distinguish Rwandans is likely to be wrong much of the time. The Nyange School attackers, for example, could not discern which students were Tutsis and Hutus—that is why they asked them to separate. During the genocide, genocidaires faced the same difficulty: many Tutsis used fake Hutu IDs to elude death and the genocidaires sometimes killed Hutus whom they mistook for Tutsis.[7]

Historically, Tutsis raised cattle and occupied the upper rungs of the social ladder, whereas Hutus raised crops and occupied the lower rungs. But the boundaries between the two were quite porous, with intermarriage taking place fairly frequently. In pre-colonial times, Hutus who acquired cattle could become Tutsis; Tutsis who lost their cattle might likewise transition to Hutu status.[8] Because of this social mobility, the Hutu-Tutsi distinction was on a long-term decline. Since it was largely based on an agrarian-pastoralist divide, it is very likely that twentieth-century modernization and the shift away from a purely agricultural economy would have accelerated this decline—that is, if there had been no outside intervention. People working in factories or office buildings do not usually concern themselves with differences between cassava growers and cattle herders.

When colonialists first arrived in the late 1800s, all Rwandans spoke the same language, sang the same songs, and ate the same food. They were culturally indistinguishable. Despite the sociopolitical stratification along Hutu-Tutsi lines, all the people had a strong sense of common identity, referring to themselves as *Banyarwanda* ("people of Rwanda").[9] In most wars, they fought as a unified nation against outsiders rather than among themselves. The internecine struggles that did occur were along factional lines orthogonal to the Hutu-Tutsi division.[10] When the Europeans arrived, Rwanda, unlike most other African regions, was a fairly cohesive nation. The colonialists would change that dramatically.

How Colonialists Set the Stage for Genocide

Belgians were the primary colonizers of Rwanda, taking over in 1918 after a brief period of German control. By the time the Belgians took over, English explorers and German colonialists had already developed pseudoscientific racial theories about Rwandan society, asserting that Tutsi were a variety of dark-skinned Caucasians ("Hamites") who came from the north of Africa and were racially superior to the "negroid" Hutus.[11] The Belgians enthusiastically adopted and promoted this racist claptrap. For example, one Belgian priest claimed that a Tutsi was "a European under a black skin."[12] Whether or not the Belgians actually believed this, it served them in two ways: it allowed them to justify their own control over the country and it divided Rwandans so that administering and controlling them was much easier. To formalize the racial distinction, they conducted a census and issued mandatory identity cards that specified each individual's "race."

The Kigali Genocide Memorial displays some unsettling photos from the early 1900s showing colonialists using calipers to measure Rwandans' facial features to establish their race. That was, of course, a pointless exercise since the Hutu-Tutsi distinction often did not align with differences in physical traits. Indeed, the fact that the Belgians perceived a need for racial identity cards was an inadvertent admission that the different "races" were not really identifiable as such.[13] Nevertheless, under what they called a "race policy," the Belgian administration instituted a system of affirmative action for the Tutsi minority. They replaced Hutu chiefs, who were once common, with Tutsis; and they excluded Hutus from administrative jobs in general. Abetted by the Church and the "White Fathers," they also reserved higher-quality and higher-level education for Tutsis.[14]

This had several effects on the Rwandan population. Some of the Tutsis embraced the notion that they were superior and better suited to run things; when authorities give you power and status, it's hard to tell them they're wrong. *Petit-Tutsis*, who had inferior status to many Hutus, probably rejoiced at being permanently elevated on the social ladder. The effect on Hutus was twofold. First, some internalized the Belgian-imposed distinction, acquiring an inferiority complex. Second, many came to view the situation just as the Belgian racial fantasies portrayed it: the Hutus were the downtrodden indigenous people, and the Tutsis were a race of imperious overlords who came from somewhere else.[15] Both groups acquired the sense that they were locked in a zero-sum game: advantages for one group could only come at the other's expense.

By themselves, the racist views and the ethnic preferences Belgians propagated were toxically divisive to Rwandan society. But the imposition of race-designating identity cards greatly amplified the effect. In the precolonial period, the Hutus generally enjoyed less political power, but if that was ever irksome, it was ameliorated by the opportunity of becoming Tutsis. It was not necessary for that many people to actually do it (though many did); the mere possibility of mobility between the groups confirmed to everyone that they were ultimately part of the same unified country. The strict division established by the identity cards removed that possibility. The colonialists had not just divided Hutus and Tutsis with a spurious racial distinction; they had made that division both profound and permanent.

The Belgians maintained that division throughout their administration. However, in the final years leading up to Rwanda's independence, they completely reversed the affirmative action system, from favoring Tutsis to favoring Hutus. This was partly because they were concerned about Tutsi elites agitating for independence, and they wanted to suppress that agitation; but it was also because of an influx of left-leaning Belgian bureaucrats who viewed the Hutus as an oppressed proletariat who should benefit from affirmative action rather than suffer from it. Colonel Guy Logiest exemplified the new sort of bureaucrat. After his appointment as "Special Military Resident," he reversed the prior ethnic preferences, instituting a new preference system that favored Hutus rather than Tutsis. His administration quickly replaced Tutsi chiefs and administrators with Hutus to check Tutsi privilege, or what he termed "arrogance" and "oppressive aristocracy."[16] Ironically, that privilege had gained the Tutsis little financial advantage: a 1959 survey found their average annual income was only 4.5 percent higher than that of the Hutus.[17]

In summary, if the Belgian colonialists had taken lessons from sociological experiments in creating group conflict and had determined to pit Rwanda's groups against each other in a death struggle, they could hardly have done a better job of it. They nailed all the key elements of the recipe: separate individuals into distinct groups; assign labels to them; implement group preferences that favor one group; then reverse the preferences to favor the other. When the colonialists first arrived, Rwandans were completely indistinguishable culturally and virtually indistinguishable physically; they had previously enjoyed a long, relatively peaceful coexistence and they had similar average incomes. But, like the Robbers Cave experiment described in chapter 1, the Rwandan colonial period demonstrated the ease with which ethnic labels and ethnic preference programs can divide such populations, creating starkly divided antagonistic groups and eliciting murderous hatred from them. It would have been impressive if it had not been so evil.

From Independence to Genocide

In the 1950s, with the encouragement of Belgian clergy and some left-leaning colonial administrators, a Hutu movement emerged to assert Hutu rights and nationalistic aspirations. A document drafted by the leaders of the movement, the *Hutu Manifesto*, captured its spirit. It was designed to sound reasonable, but it contained troubling indications of the movement's real inclinations. Although there were feel-good clauses about education, free press, and elections, the language was divisive, beginning with the title, which was emphatically not *The Rwandan Manifesto*. The document invoked colonialist notions of the Tutsis as overlords who had oppressed the indigenous Hutus for "nine hundred years." It even referred to Tutsis as "Hamites." Most ominously, it advocated retaining the racial identity cards to counter the Hamitic "race monopoly."[18] It was clear that Hutu leaders wanted reparation for the forty years of "privilege" the Belgians had granted the Tutsis. They would not wait long for it.

In 1962 Rwanda gained independence; national elections followed in 1965. With the Hutus constituting a solid majority of the electorate, the Hutu leader Gregoire Kayibanda won. Kayibanda, like Yugoslavia's Milošević, was an ethnic opportunist—a politician who profited by magnifying ethnic antagonism. Although he may have believed he was correcting past injustices, he clearly exploited ethnic division to bolster his political standing; his rhetoric and attacks against the Tutsis tended to ebb and flow inversely with his political fortunes. Whenever his position began to look precarious, his regime would inevitably generate more propaganda about the Tutsi "cockroaches," which would then be followed by attacks on unfortunate Tutsis.

In accord with the *Hutu Manifesto*, Kayibanda had instituted an ethnic quota system that severely limited the numbers of Tutsis allowed in government jobs and higher education. In 1972, as he became fearful of political discontent, he initiated vigilante committees to further "purify" educational and government institutions of Tutsis (and, of course, to distract from internal dissension). The vigilantes purged and killed many Tutsis, but they exceeded their original mission, settling personal scores against fellow Hutus. The resulting chaos provided a pretext for General Juvenal Habyarimana to remove Kayibanda in a coup.

Initially, Habyarimana was poised to limit the system of ethnic preferences against Tutsis, but that system had already acquired a tremendous momentum of its own. A common characteristic of racial and ethnic preference (i.e., "affirmative action") programs is that they quickly become entitlements whose beneficiaries will defend them ferociously; they are consequently extremely difficult to rescind. Around the world, nearly all these programs have been proposed as short-term solutions to correct past inequity. But the beneficiaries tend to perpetually argue that the inequity remains so that they can continue to enjoy preferential treatment. Thus, many of these programs have persisted decades after they were supposed to have achieved their goals. For example, Sri Lanka's has lasted fifty years, Malaysia's has lasted sixty-three years, and India's has lasted seventy years. Rwanda followed this pattern: faced with vociferous Hutu support for the ethnic quota system, Habyarimana had no choice but to maintain it.[19]

Although the group preference system under Kayibanda and Habyarimana was the precise reverse of what it had been in the colonial days, it had many of the same effects. Most importantly, it continually inculcated both Hutus and Tutsis with the sense that they were distinct groups whose interests were at odds. The education system exacerbated that sense: teachers would call out the ethnicity of all the students on the first day of school, so everyone would know which group everyone belonged to.[20] History lessons often focused on Tutsis' "privilege" and their historical oppression of Hutus. As one student recounted:

> So the way the teacher could teach a history, was not really a history, but hatred history. You know, what they [Hutu and Tutsi]

> did. The kingdom belongs to Tutsi and they did this. And the Hutu, they were slaves to the Tutsi...And then they were seeing the teacher getting angry. Hating those Tutsi who were there [in the classroom].[21]

Even though the quotas benefited Hutus at the expense of Tutsis, they did nothing to warm Hutu feelings toward Tutsis. On the contrary, at a subconscious level, they probably perpetuated the inferiority complex that the colonialists had originally imbued in the Hutus. In my interviews with genocidaires, they sometimes said they hated the Tutsis because the Tutsis acted "privileged," yet they were at a loss to recount actual firsthand experiences of such behavior.[22] The invidious quota system helped promote this sort of baseless stereotyping by maintaining the old colonialist fiction that hapless indigenous Hutus were dominated by alien Hamite overlords. Beyond that, the quotas instilled a sense of political insecurity among Hutus: if they ceded any power at all to Tutsis (or even moderate Hutus), the cherished quotas might be at risk.

There is a critical and underappreciated aspect of affirmative action programs, one that manifests itself nearly everywhere affirmative action is implemented. In the inevitable quest to maintain affirmative action benefits for perpetuity, the beneficiaries often claim the nonpreferred group continues to enjoy "privilege"—demonizing that group in the process. Thus, affirmative action around the world has typically deepened ethnic divisions rather than diminishing them. In Malaysia, for example, even after ethnic Malays have benefited from sixty-three years of affirmative action, they support political parties and politicians that focus on ethnic group power and spread racist conspiracy theories about nefarious ethnic Chinese plots to maintain their ill-deserved privilege. These conspiracy theories continue to proliferate and are more prevalent than ever today.[23] As we will see in chapter 9, decades of affirmative action in Sri Lanka had even more dire results.

The Hutus' sense of insecurity about the affirmative action they benefited from put Habyarimana in a bind. For a long time, the Tutsis in exile had been more of an irritation than a threat. But by the 1990s, a group of Tutsis who had trained in the Ugandan army formed a formidable guerilla army, the Rwandan Patriotic Front (RPF), that could challenge the Rwandan government's own army; in 1990, the RPF launched a major incursion into northern Rwanda. Habyarimana had to negotiate with them, but at the same time placate the Hutus who did not want to risk their ethnic preferences by relinquishing any power to Tutsis. In 1993, Habyarimana signed the Arusha Accords, ceding substantial power to the RPF. The power-sharing provisions in the Arusha Accords would have greatly diminished the status and influence of many Hutu leaders. So, many of them chose the old fallback of ethnic opportunism to preserve their positions, stirring up hatred against Tutsis by bolstering the "Hutu Power" movement. They backed both the Hutu Power radio station, Radio Télévision Libre des Mille Collines (RTLM), and a murderous Hutu militia known as the Interahamwe.

Before the Arusha Accords were implemented, Habyarimana was assassinated, probably by extremist Hutus.[24] His plane was shot down on approach to the Kigali airport, crashing by strange coincidence in his own backyard. Within hours of the plane crash, the military and the Interahamwe set up roadblocks and one of the most brutal mass murders in human history began. RTLM claimed the "cockroaches" had killed the president, and it instructed loyal Hutus to "cut down the tall trees"—code for "kill all the Tutsis." In the next hundred days, roughly a million Tutsis and moderate Hutus would be murdered.

A Grassroots Genocide

A hallmark of violent conflicts and genocides that arise from ethnic division (and ethnically divisive policies) is that they garner widespread participation from ordinary people. We have already seen that in the case of the former Yugoslavia. There is something about ethnic antagonism that motivates very ordinary people to commit terrible acts. Rwanda was no exception to this. According to one researcher, one in four Hutus committed violence during the genocide.[25] No sector of society was left out, and no category of social trust was left unviolated: teachers killed their students, doctors killed their patients, and soccer players killed their former teammates. Even priests and nuns killed parishioners.[26]

While interviewing genocidaires, I was struck by their ordinariness. Because they constituted such a large proportion of the population, perhaps they had to be ordinary by definition. One man I interviewed had killed over twenty people (he had stopped counting at twenty), putting him in league with the most prolific serial killers in US history. Yet he was clearly no Ted Bundy or John Wayne Gacy; he was a simple farmer, more concerned with avocado prices and when the next rain was coming than ethnic politics. He projected a kind, grandfatherly manner and deeply regretted his crimes. He was representative of many of the genocidaires. Prior to the genocide, they were generally ordinary people who were swept up quite suddenly in what many called a "tumult." As one survivor described it, the atrocities were "the abnormal actions of perfectly normal people."[27]

The fact that a crime is committed by vast numbers of normal people just doing their jobs or "following along" in no way exculpates or absolves them from responsibility; the genocidaires I talked with recognized that themselves. But it does raise the imperative to explicate the causes and understand: what could have made so many ordinary people take up machetes and hack their neighbors to death?

The Genocide's Causes

Many genocidaires say that the Hutu Power movement and RTLM "hate radio" incited them to attack Tutsis. Starting in 1993, RTLM broadcasted frequent diatribes against Tutsis, referring to them as *inyenzi* ("cockroaches") or *inzoka* ("snakes") who enjoyed unfair privilege.[28] Perhaps most importantly, as noted above, schools had long made a point of distinguishing Hutus and Tutsis. They also taught lessons that cultivated a powerful sense of ethnic grievance among the Hutus, focusing on Tutsis' historical "privilege." As one genocidaire noted:

> They taught us that the Tutsi lived better than the Hutu and that the Tutsi had come to colonise them. . . . So we grew up thinking that the Hutu were oppressed.[29]

The average income of Tutsis was only slightly higher than that of Hutus in 1959, and that was before thirty-five years of official discrimination against Tutsis in the form of educational and job preferences. Yet schools continued to drill into children the notion that Tutsis were privileged oppressors. This indoctrination, along with the ethnic quota system, made Hutus feel insecure and convinced them that relations with Tutsis could only be a zero-sum game; it made fertile ground for seeds that ethnic-opportunist leaders and RTLM would plant.

In addition to the motivations identified by individual genocidaires, some scholars have cited a variety of contributing factors in the Rwandan genocide: population pressure, falling prices for crops, and avarice for Tutsi cattle. These factors may have contributed, but they were all present before the colonial period; there were droughts, famines, population pressure, and many other problems that might have spurred conflict. But there were no genocides. There weren't even large-scale clashes between Hutus and Tutsis. It was only after the construction of distinct racial identities, reinforced with identity cards, school doctrine, and group preferences, that the first mass killings occurred.

Focusing on ancillary factors, which already existed when there were no mass killings, distracts from the reality that there was a single factor that was an absolutely essential precondition for the genocide—that is, the existence of a group distinction in the first place. It is an inescapable truism: *without groups, there can be no group conflict.* If the colonialists had not constructed "racial" groups from a porous and fading sociopolitical distinction, and the identity card, education, and group preference systems had not maintained group boundaries, there would have been no genocide. One exhaustive study found that the handful of Rwandan districts that had extensive integration and intermarriage between Hutus and Tutsis experienced no ethnic violence before 1994 and also avoided killings after Habyarimana's assassination. The fuzzier the line between Tutsis and Hutus was, the more reluctant Hutus were to kill their neighbors.[30]

As an example of how the conflict depended on an artificial and arbitrary distinction, consider Robert Kajuga, president of the murderous Interahamwe, which played a pivotal role in the genocide. Kajuga's mother was half Tutsi; his father was entirely Tutsi but somehow managed to have "Hutu" marked on his identity card. If not for that card, Kajuga would likely have been a victim of the genocide rather than one of its most prominent perpetrators. More broadly speaking, if not for all the identity cards and the spurious division they represented, there would have been neither victims nor perpetrators.

As we saw in chapter 2, even when group distinctions are constructed from nothing, they can quickly assume lives of their own. The Robbers Cave experiment and numerous follow-up experiments demonstrated that the mere existence of a group distinction, no matter how factitious, can spawn animus. Creating an environment in which groups compete for group spoils (like job and education preferences) amplifies the effect. The Belgian colonialists began this process; once it was in motion, the incentives all naturally lined up in favor of maintaining or enlarging the group division rather than diminishing it. In a vicious circle, division spawned divisiveness, which spawned more division. For example, although Hutus earned only a little less on average than Tutsis, they insisted on maintaining group preferences for jobs and education; their insecurity and defensiveness over losing those preferences deepened the divide. To justify continuing preferences favoring Hutus, school curricula dwelled on the historical privilege enjoyed by the Tutsis, further expanding the divide. When Hutu politicians wanted to strengthen their support, they often became ethnic opportunists, consolidating their ranks by stoking Hutu hatred against the Tutsi "cockroaches"; this helped make the divide much deadlier.

The Rwandan experience highlights the dangers of allowing ethnic division to get started and the importance of attentively healing it once it does. Fortunately, the postgenocide government took lessons from this experience and resolved to change Rwanda's course dramatically.

Reconciliation and Recovery

In 1994, sixteen-year-old Jacqueline left her village in Bugasera to get milk. When she returned, she found the corpses of nineteen family members, hacked to death with machetes. Just a few hours earlier, they had been living people—people she ate with, talked with, and held in her arms. Now, almost everyone she knew lay dead: her mother, father, brothers, sisters, and uncles. By chance, one uncle survived and rejoined her. Together, they hid in the woods and fields during the day and made their way at night across the border to Burundi.

Today, Jacqueline lives in another village, where she works in the fields and weaves sisal bowls and mats of exceptional craftsmanship and elegance. She lives near some genocide survivors like herself, and also several genocidaires, including Mathias, a childhood neighbor who helped kill her family. Jacqueline and Mathias both told me that they were terrified when they first reencountered each other after he was released from prison: she thought he might try to kill her, and he thought she would rally fellow Tutsis to kill him. But Matthias begged for forgiveness, and she granted it. After years of rebuilding trust, they now work side-by-side in the fields, and she sometimes asks him to look after her children when she goes into town. When asked how she could possibly forgive someone who helped kill her family, Jacqueline responded: "If I did not forgive, I would always carry a burden. I let go of that burden." She and Mathias are emblematic of the incredible strides Rwanda has made toward reconciliation and recovery.

Following the genocide, Rwanda confronted a litany of conditions that are horrific individually and unthinkable in combination: four hundred thousand children like Jacqueline were orphaned; agricultural output was cut in half; annual GDP was slashed to $126 per person; and infrastructure was completely demolished. Rwanda's living standards ranked dead last in the world for both 1994 and 1995.[31] On top of these appalling circumstances, Rwandans were menaced by stray dogs that had acquired a taste for human flesh because corpses were the only thing they had eaten since their owners had been killed.[32]

The RPF, whose forces took over Kigali and ended the genocide in July 1994, faced a seemingly impossible challenge: not only was the country in shambles; two million Hutus, who feared reprisals, had fled to surrounding countries. Massive refugee camps in these countries were both humanitarian disasters and staging grounds for unrepentant genocidaires to launch attacks into Rwanda.

The RPF began by concentrating on reconciliation and justice. Although its ranks were primarily Tutsis, it formed a transition government with Hutus as both president and prime minister; only the vice president was a Tutsi. The transition government strongly encouraged hundreds of thousands of Hutus who had fled the country to return. Most would be reintegrated into Rwandan society; if they had committed crimes, they would be treated fairly. The government quickly established a system for trying the staggering volume of genocide perpetrators, making it clear that it would show leniency to those who turned themselves in and confessed their crimes. Over fifty-five thousand people convicted of genocide crimes were sentenced only to community service.[33]

The new government focused relentlessly on ending ethnic division and promoting national unity. It began by eliminating the ethnic ID cards and stipulating that it would not tolerate any racial or ethnic distinctions whatsoever in politics or public life. Distinguishing people as Hutu, Tutsi, or Twa would no longer be permitted; the new motto was "We are all Rwandans now." A new constitution was drafted in this spirit, forbidding "propagation of ethnic, regional, racial discrimination or any other form of division" and committing the government to the "promotion of national unity." It also prohibited political organizations that are based on "race, ethnic group, tribe, lineage, region, sex, religion or any other division which may lead to discrimination."[34] To this day, the government continues to zealously promote the theme: "There are no groups; we are all Rwandans." To even speak of someone as a Tutsi or Hutu is considered unacceptable.

The Rwandan government has effectively promoted the goal of a race- and ethnicity-blind society not only in government institutions but also in the private sector. As one expatriate businessman told me, when he reviews job applications, he can only see the applicant's job-related qualifications; any details that might reveal race, gender, ethnicity, or religion are carefully masked.

Anyone who has lived in Rwanda since the genocide has likely observed shadows of the old group divisions. After such a brutal conflict, it is hard to imagine that every trace of division would vanish. The official approach has been to act as if the differences are gone with the hope that this will eventually become a reality. By the best measures, it is working, albeit gradually. The fact that the country has passed the inflection point, where a majority of the population was born after the genocide, has certainly helped; an entire generation has only experienced an environment in which group distinctions are publicly discouraged. In a 2015 survey, 93 percent of Rwandans agreed that "Rwandans trust each other without discrimination," and 95.6 percent agreed with the statement, "I can leave my child in the family of somebody with whom we do not share the same social category (like ethnic, regional, religious)." These and other indications of equality and social trust have continued to improve, even over the last five years.[35]

Since the genocide, the Rwandan government has had to deal with vast numbers of displaced people: Tutsi refugees who lived in neighboring countries for decades; Hutus who fled immediately after the genocide; genocide survivors; and genocidaires who have been released from prison. One of the ways it has addressed this challenge is with "reconciliation villages," communities that bring together individuals from all these groups with the goal of fostering a sense of shared purpose and unity. The reconciliation villages, which are supported by several international organizations, have not only helped individual residents like Jacqueline and Mathias; they have showcased the potential for other people with histories of conflict to put aside their differences and unify. The message is clear: if genocidaires and their former victims can reconcile and be neighbors, all Rwandans should be able to live together in peace.

To continue erasing past differences and fostering unity, the Rwandan government established the National Unity and Reconciliation Commission (NURC). Instead of relying on nostrums from international organizations, NURC has revived homegrown Rwandan traditions to rebuild communities; these have been so effective that other countries are now copying them. Among these traditions, *umuganda* is perhaps the most prominent. Umuganda takes place for three hours on the last Saturday of each month: the entire country turns out to work on community improvement projects such as planting trees, clearing out drainage ditches, and constructing schools. The event often has a festive atmosphere, with competing work groups vying to outperform each other. News outlets make a point of showing the president, his wife, and prominent business leaders working alongside ordinary citizens. Although there is a small fine for not participating, no one I spoke with had ever heard of anybody actually being fined: umuganda is just something all Rwandans do. Rwandans say that umuganda has not only given them a sense of pride and national unity, but it has also made them protective of its public spaces. Even when they are not participating in umuganda, they tend to instinctively pick up any rubbish they see. This has helped Rwanda achieve a level of cleanliness and tidiness that challenges countries like Switzerland and Singapore.[36]

In another key departure from the past, the Rwandan government steered the economy toward free market capitalism. As we will discuss further in chapter 10, the more the government controls the allocation of resources in ethnically divided countries, the greater the incentives are to seize or maintain a monopoly on government power. Under the Kayibanda and Habyarimana regimes, not only did the government preside over a system of ethnic preferences, it also managed and allocated a large proportion of the country's resources. This constrained the economy so that it failed to grow for three decades; it also contributed greatly to Hutu-Tutsi tensions. The Hutu elites, not wanting to cede control of any resources, had a powerful motivation to suppress Tutsis or eliminate them altogether.

The new Rwandan government decided to relinquish as much of the economy as it could to free markets. Not only did this diminish the incentives for group contention over government control, it also vastly increased the efficiency of capital allocation and Rwanda's economy in general. When the RPF took control, Rwanda's level of economic freedom was among the worst in the world; the Fraser Institute ranked it 119 out of the 123 countries it covered that year. Today the Fraser Institute ranks it the third freest in Africa. The Heritage Foundation ranks it even higher: first on the African continent and thirty-third in the world.[37] As statistics in chapter 10 show, the combination of national unity and economic freedom is extremely potent. In Rwanda's case, it has yielded tremendous dividends. For thirty-five years, the economy languished under ethnically divisive, big-government policies, with per capita GDP growing less than 1 percent per year. When those policies were abandoned, the economy exploded. For twenty-five years, it has consistently ranked as one of the fastest-growing economies in the world.[38]

Figure 7.1. Rwanda GDP (constant 2010 US$).[39]

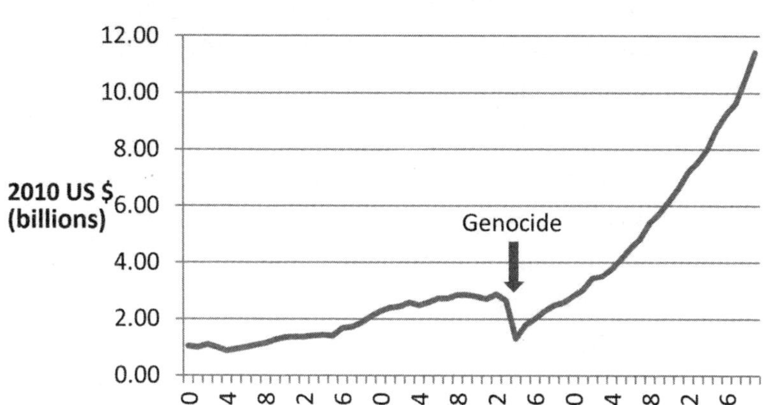

Rwanda's economic success has translated to an enormous improvement in living standards, with huge gains in infant mortality (down 70 percent since the pregenocide low) and life expectancy (up 32 percent). Since 2000, the percentage of Rwandans living below the poverty line has dropped from 70 to 39 percent.[40]

Not Perfect

Despite its tremendous success in turning "Hell on Earth" into one of the nicest places in Africa in only twenty-five years, Rwanda has faced some international criticism. Many have denounced Rwanda's conviction of Paul Rusesabagina, who was lionized as a life-saving hero in the Hollywood film *Hotel Rwanda*. The government is dominated by a single party and there is well-founded concern about human rights and freedoms. Not only is there evidence that RPF forces conducted reprisals right after the genocide, but several prominent government opponents have also disappeared or died under suspicious circumstances.

Although these criticisms have some validity, they must be considered in context. The movie's portrayal of Rusesabagina was wildly inaccurate; the leader of the UN peacekeeping force during the genocide has called *Hotel Rwanda* "pure Hollywood crap." Survivors of the hotel say that Rusesabagina extorted money from them and cooperated with the genocidaires. Moreover, until his arrest, he backed terrorist organizations.[41] RPF misbehavior also deserves explanation: many individuals joined the RPF military force after seeing their entire families murdered; it is hard to imagine even the best-disciplined army preventing all reprisals under those circumstances.[42] The fact that there is no death penalty and that the government has released thousands of former genocidaires from prison attests to the overall policy of leniency and forgiveness. Most countries in Africa have not suffered anything close to the upheaval that Rwanda has undergone; the country still faces the threat of incursions by genocidaires from neighboring countries. Given these conditions, it is impressive that it still ranks fifth on the continent for human freedom.[43]

Summary and Conclusions

Aside from clinical experiments conducted by sociologists, Rwanda stands out as one of the purest examples of authorities dividing a relatively peaceful population into bitterly antagonistic groups. Although precolonial Rwanda had some conflict, it was comparatively small-scale and almost never occurred along Hutu-Tutsi lines. Colonialists ossified the Hutu-Tutsi distinction with ethnic labels, identity cards, and affirmative action, setting the stage for one of the worst genocides in human history.

The Rwandan experience evinces the hazard of having any group distinctions at all and the extreme danger of setting groups against each other in a competition for ethnic preferences and affirmative action. Rather than ameliorating ethnic divisions and antipathy, group distinctions and affirmative action exacerbated them. The Hutu beneficiaries of affirmative action were perpetually defensive about their benefits, seeking to justify and maintain them by demonizing Tutsis as oppressors. Schools and media played along with this, continually emphasizing Tutsi privilege and the historical exploitation of Hutus. Elites saw tremendous incentives to becoming ethnic opportunists, continually bolstering group division. The ultimate result was the destructive power of ethnic antagonism was unleashed. If there is any doubt about how ineluctable this power can be, we need only consider how many ordinary Hutus participated in the genocide: it was not just a handful of criminals, but a quarter of the entire population—hundreds of thousands of ordinary and otherwise law-abiding Rwandans—that participated to some degree, with many taking up machetes to hack their neighbors and co-workers to death.

If Belgian colonialists did a near-perfect job positioning Rwanda for genocide, the new Rwandan government did a near-perfect job in recovering from it. By eliminating the invidious system of group distinctions and affirmative action and insisting that there are only Rwandans—and no separate groups—the government has enabled Rwandans to live and work together as a peaceful and united nation. Its promotion of institutions like umuganda has helped foster a shared identity and asabiyah for all Rwandans. That, combined with policies of forgiveness, reconciliation, and free markets, has driven Rwanda's phenomenal social and economic recovery.

Rwanda's commitment to reconciliation and its new asabiyah, the asabiyah that the Nyange School children gave their lives for, are a model for the world: "There are no Hutus and Tutsis. We are all Rwandans." Today, over 92 percent of Rwandans say that they, like the Nyange students, would rather die than participate in ethnic division.[44]

8

FROM SERENDIPITY TO CALAMITY IN SRI LANKA

One of the most remarkable sights in Sri Lanka is Sri Pada, a 7,300-foot mountain, which is also known as Adam's Peak. If you wake up at 2:00 a.m. and start the steep, arduous climb to the summit in the dark, you can reach it in time to see what might be the most magnificent sunrise in the world. In doing so, you will be joining an esteemed succession of Sri Pada visitors that stretches far back in history. This includes luminaries like the explorer Ibn Battuta, who visited in the fourteenth century. Never one to eschew comfort, Ibn Battuta got a ride to the top in a palanquin. The ultimate ascent has three times as many steps as the Empire State Building, so we can forgive his indulgence—and pity the poor souls who had to carry him.

The sunrise is not the only reason to endure the climb. You might do it for the same reason Buddhists, Hindus, Jews, Muslims, and Christians have done it for over a thousand years: to view a shrine near the peak that contains a five-foot-long "footprint" in a rock formation. For Buddhists, the footprint is Buddha's; for Hindus, it is Shiva's; for Jews and Muslims, it is Adam's; and for some Christians, it belongs to Saint Thomas. The shrine is emblematic of Sri Lanka's pluralist and syncretic past: it was amicably shared by all these faiths for a very long time.[1] When Ibn Battuta—a devout Muslim—visited, the local Buddhist ruler expedited his trip to the shrine by providing him with an ecumenical escort of Buddhists and Hindus. Ibn Battuta was duly impressed at how well Sri Lanka's religious communities got along:

> Its [Buddhist and Hindu] people still live in idolatry yet they show respect for Muslim darwishes[:]... they honour the Muslims, allow them to enter their houses and have no suspicions regarding their dealings with their wives and children.[2]

This irenic environment prevailed over the following centuries: in the 1600s, a marooned Briton, Robert Knox, observed how the Buddhist king and his people supported the local Muslim mosque and at the same time demonstrated great respect for the Christian faith.[3]

Tamils, Sinhalese, and Muslims certainly had clashes, both with each other and within their own groups. But these clashes took the form of political power struggles, rather than one group seeking to completely exterminate the other on the basis of religion or ethnicity. In some instances, Hindu Tamils even fought on behalf of Sinhalese Buddhist kings or helped protect sacred Buddhist shrines against invaders.[4]

As Sri Lanka entered the modern era, the relative toleration and comity that Ibn Battuta had observed among the island's ethnic and religious communities persisted. Before Sri Lanka's independence in 1948, a British governor observed the "large measure of fellowship and understanding" that prevailed among the ethnic groups, and a British soldiers' guide noted that "there has never been any real conflict between the Sinhalese and Tamils... and no historic antagonisms to overcome."[5] With quiescent communal relations, abundant natural resources, and one of the highest literacy rates in the developing world, newly independent Sri Lanka was poised to flourish and prosper. The British governor called it "the best bet in Asia."[6]

It turned out to be a very poor bet. A few years after Sri Lanka's independence, violent communal conflict erupted, culminating in an on-again, off-again civil war spanning twenty-six years. By the time it ended, hundreds of thousands of people were displaced, killed, or unaccounted for. Sri Lanka's per capita GDP, which was on par with that of South Korea in 1960, was only one-tenth of it by 2009. Shiva Naipaul provides a horrifying vignette of ethnic relations in the country three decades after independence:

> The mob was stopping cars and mini-buses, dragging out their occupants for interrogation, demanding that all Tamils declare themselves...a man, axe in hand, hack[ed] to limbless death a young boy...A group of men pushed their way into the bus. They ordered the driver to choose them a Tamil. He picked out one of the women passengers...[H]er belly was ripped open with a broken bottle...Petrol was poured over her and she was set ablaze...The spectators clapped and danced.[7]

What caused "the best bet in Asia" to turn out so abysmally? Ultimately, it was an unserendipitous confluence of geohistorical happenstance and divisive ethnic policies. We'll discuss these in turn.

The Land and the People

Sri Lanka is a teardrop-shaped island located twenty miles off the southeast coast of India. It has roughly the population of New York State but half the land area. Over a millennium of immigration from neighboring lands, along with centuries of Portuguese,

Dutch, and British colonialism, have given the island a complex ethnic and religious mix. Table 8.1 lists the country's main ethnic groups. The population percentages reflect 2019 data; the Tamil percentages were somewhat higher in the past, but many were killed and many more fled the country during the civil war.

Table 8.1 Sri Lanka's principal ethnic groups

Group	Population share (%)	Origins (first presence in Sri Lanka)	Religion	Principal language
Sinhalese	75	Northern India (500 BCE)	Buddhism	Sinhala
Sri Lankan Tamils	11	Southern India (200 BCE)	Hinduism	Tamil
Moors (or Muslims)	9	Arabia; Malaysia; Southern India (900 CE)	Islam	Tamil
Indian Tamils	4	Southern India (1820)	Hinduism	Tamil
Burghers	<1	Europe; Sri Lanka (1600)	Christianity	English; Sinhala

The Moors are descendants of Muslim traders who arrived from many different regions over many centuries. Indian Tamils are descendants of Indian plantation workers whom the British imported in the late nineteenth and early twentieth centuries. Burghers are descendants of European colonialists who married locals.

For most of Sri Lanka's history, the different ethnic groups have been geographically concentrated. There has nevertheless been at least some cultural integration and intermarriage among them over the centuries. Sri Lankan Buddhism and Hinduism have borrowed extensively from each other, and DNA studies show that Sinhalese and Sri Lankan Tamils are genetically closer to each other than they are to inhabitants of the regions from which they originated.[8] Even locals cannot always guess by sight which group an individual belongs to. This reality sometimes confounded participants in anti-Tamil riots. Before they tried to douse hapless Tamils with petrol and burn them alive, rioters sometimes checked electoral registers to ensure they would not inadvertently torch their fellow Sinhalese; sometimes, they forced potential victims to read difficult passages in Sinhala. They nevertheless killed numerous Sinhalese whom they mistook for Tamils.[9]

The Origins of Disparity

When Sri Lanka became independent, there was considerable educational and income disparity among the different ethnic groups. This arose from happenstance rather than explicit policy. Individuals who inhabited the more Westernized coastal areas benefited from the European colonialists' trade, technology, and education, and were, therefore, typically better off. People who lived farther inland had less access to those benefits and were usually worse off. Beyond that, Sri Lankan Tamils were generally better educated than Sinhalese, Moors, or Indian Tamils. The north of the island where Sri Lankan Tamils predominate is arid and poor in resources. Because of this, the Tamils devoted their productive energy toward developing human capital, focusing on education and professional skills development. This focus was abetted by American missionaries, who set up schools in the north, providing top-notch English-language education, particularly in math and the physical sciences. As a result, Sri Lankan Tamils accounted for an outsized proportion of the better-educated people on the island, particularly in higher-paying fields like engineering and medicine. Their intellectual capital became an inheritance: one generation of well-educated doctors and engineers tended to beget another.[10]

Because of the Sri Lankan Tamils' superior education, the British colonial administration hired them disproportionately compared to the Sinhalese and Moors. In 1948, Sri Lankan

Tamils accounted for 32 percent of the doctors and 40 percent of the clerical workers employed by Sri Lanka's colonial government, greatly outstripping their 11 percent share of the general population. By contrast, the Sinhalese were vastly underrepresented. For example, they accounted for only 31 percent of the engineers hired by the government (versus their 75 percent share of the overall population). This unequal outcome had nothing to do with overt discrimination against the Sinhalese; it merely reflected the different levels and types of education achieved by the various ethnic groups. Indian Tamil plantation workers, who were less educated than both the Sinhalese and the Sri Lankan Tamils, were not hired at all for government medical and engineering positions.[11]

From Ethnic Unity to Ethnic Opportunism

Sri Lanka's independence in 1948 started auspiciously enough. Its constitution, which explicitly prohibited discrimination on the basis of ethnicity and religion, passed by a near-unanimous vote. In a speech supporting the constitution, Sri Lanka's first prime minister, D. S. Senanayake, emphatically endorsed ethnic unity:

> what we sought was not Sinhalese domination, but Ceylonese [Sri Lankan] domination.... The interests of one community are the interests of all. We are one of another, what ever race or creed.[12]

Unfortunately, colonialists had sown seeds of ethnic division in Sri Lanka long before independence. By its very essence, colonialism introduces a paradigm for stark ethnic divisions where they do not already exist. After all, it depends on distinguishing between groups—colonialists and colonized—by ethnic background and granting them different privileges and rights on that basis. Beyond that, colonialists often found it helpful to distinguish groups within the colonized population for administrative purposes. In particular, some British administrators believed that designating groups and giving them communal representation would play a useful "divide and conquer" role, making it easier to govern the population.[13] They did not go as far as the Belgian colonialists in Rwanda, instituting group preferences that sharply distinguished between groups and favored one group over another. But they set the stage for postindependence ethnic opportunists to do so.

One of these opportunists was S. W. R. D. Bandaranaike, scion of one of Sri Lanka's wealthiest families. After Senanayake's untimely death by stroke, Bandaranaike got his chance, perceiving that he could gain power by pandering to the majority Sinhalese, who resented the Tamils' disproportionate share of positions in higher education and government and felt that equal outcomes should be guaranteed. Like many ethnic opportunists, Bandaranaike was not at all representative of the people he ostensibly represented: he was Christian, educated by private English tutors, attended Oxford, and barely spoke a word of Sinhala. Privately, he was candid about his opportunism, declaring: "I'll make Arabic the official language if that'll get me into Parliament."[14] Whether or not he was sincere in rallying disaffected Sinhalese Buddhists with whom he had little in common, identity politics worked very well for him. So he launched a divisive "Sinhala only" campaign, which spurred the majority Sinhalese to elect him. After his election in 1956, Bandaranaike quickly passed the "Sinhala Only Act," which changed the official language of government from English to Sinhala.

After the act was passed, Sri Lankan students would no longer need to learn English; Sinhalese would be educated in Sinhala, and Tamils would be consigned to a separate Tamil-language education "stream." As one Sinhalese journalist wrote, this divided Sri Lanka, depriving it of its "link language"—English:

> That began a great divide that has widened over the years. Children now go to segregated schools or study in separate streams in the same school. They don't get to know other people of their own age group unless they meet them outside.[15]

As another writer put it, Sri Lankans lost "the richness of education we had as children when our schoolmates came from every background..."[16] If Sri Lankans had previously shared any asabiyah, this was the beginning of its end.

Lee Kuan Yew, Singapore's "founding father," visited Sri Lanka many times from independence until his death in 2015. He cited Sri Lanka's disastrous experience with abandoning English as motivation for his own country's insistence on English as a common, shared language—even though most people in Singapore speak other languages at home. If Singapore had followed Sri Lanka's example, he asserted, "we would have perished politically and economically..."[17] The contrast in the progress of the two countries since independence bears this out. At the end of World War II, Sri Lanka was wealthier and more democratic than Singapore. Since then, Singapore has enjoyed seven decades of peace and prosperity; Sri Lanka has suffered nearly five decades of political turmoil, violent conflict, and poverty.[18]

Beyond eliminating Sri Lanka's common "link language," the Sinhala Only Act also functioned as a de facto affirmative action program for Sinhalese. Tamils, who spoke Tamil at home and received their higher education in English, could not gain Sinhala proficiency quickly enough to meet the government requirement. So, many of them lost their jobs to Sinhalese. For example, the percentage of Tamils employed in government administrative services would drop dramatically: from 30 percent in 1956 to 5 percent in 1970; the percentage in the armed forces dropped from 40 percent to 1 percent.[19]

As has happened in many other countries, Sri Lanka's divisive ethnic policies went hand in hand with expanded government.[20] Sinhalese politicians made it clear: government would be the tool to redress perceived ethnic disparities. It would allocate more jobs and resources and that allocation would be influenced by ethnicity. As one historian writes: "a growing perception of the state as bestowing public goods selectively began to emerge, challenging previous views and breeding mistrust between ethnic communities."[21] Tamils responded to this by launching a nonviolent resistance campaign. With ethnic dividing lines now clearly drawn, mobs of Sinhalese staged anti-Tamil counterdemonstrations and then riots, culminating in the 1958 pogrom, in which hundreds—mostly Tamils—were killed.

The ethnic animus that Bandaranaike had unleashed would eventually undo him. Perhaps confirming that his ethnically divisive policies arose from ethnic opportunism rather than personal conviction, he began to make conciliatory arrangements with the Tamil leadership as soon as he had become secure in his premiership. This enraged the Sinhalese radicals whom he had originally inspired. In 1959, a cabal of disaffected Sinhalese, who felt that Bandaranaike had betrayed them, assassinated him.

Doubling Down on Socialism and Division

Shortly after Bandaranaike's assassination, his widow Sirimavo was elected prime minister. She doubled down on two of his top priorities—expansive government and affirmative action. An ardent socialist, she nationalized vast sectors of the economy: banking, media, foreign trade, transportation, and energy. The implicit message of her late husband's policies was reiterated: the government would control an increasing share of the economy, and ethnic considerations would increasingly direct that control. The results were disastrous. During her first five years in office, per capita income plunged by a staggering 13 percent.[22] Despite the country's bounteous supply of fertile tropical land, it became heavily dependent on food imports and foreign aid; people would have starved without them. Voters responded to Sirimavo's devastating mismanagement of the economy by voting her out of office.

Five years later, in 1970, Sirimavo managed to get reelected. This time around, she focused on the other part of her late husband's agenda: promoting ethnic preferences. The existing policies had already cost so many Sri Lankan Tamils their jobs that they were now underrepresented in government. However, they remained overrepresented in higher education, particularly in the sciences. For example, in 1970, they claimed over 40 percent of the places in both engineering and medicine, more than three times their share of the overall population.[23] Sirimavo and her political allies determined to address that disparity. They rewrote the constitution, removing Article 29, which prohibited discrimination based on religion and ethnicity, and therefore blocked affirmative action.[24] Then they instituted an affirmative action system that required Tamil speakers to achieve much higher test scores for university admission. For example, the required scores for admission to medical school were 250 for Tamils but only 229 for Sinhalese.[25]

This first attempt at affirmative action failed to achieve the desired outcome, with Tamils outperforming Sinhalese by so much that they still secured 35 percent of the spots in engineering and 39 percent of the spots medicine. Although these results confirmed that Tamils merited the spots they earned, the government was determined to achieve equal outcomes irrespective of merit. So, it introduced a new scheme in which the proportion of each group accepted from the applicant pool would match its share of the overall population, regardless of scores. However, even this scheme failed to completely end the disparity because more Tamils focused on science in secondary schools and therefore constituted more of the applicant pool.

The Bandaranaikes' abandonment of merit-based employment and admissions in favor of affirmative action had a predictable effect: the allocation of government jobs, resources, and higher education became a political football, hotly contested, not just between the ethnic groups but also within them. This was particularly evident in the third iteration of affirmative action, which Sirimavo's United Front coalition manipulated to benefit two of its key constituencies: Muslims and Kandyan (high country) Sinhalese.[26] This new system allocated university spots to geographical regions based on their populations; because of the geographic concentration of groups, this was effectively an ethnic quota system that helped the lower-performing Muslim and Sinhalese groups. Sri Lankan Tamils ended up losing the most spots: they were the highest-scoring group, but they had to compete for a limited number of spots within their own ranks. Muslims, who no longer had to compete against higher-scoring Sri Lankan Tamils and Low-Country Sinhalese, nearly doubled their share.[27] But the Kandyan Sinhalese, who shared their region with a large population of uneducated Indian Tamil plantation workers, gained the most; they could secure spots with the lowest scores on the island. So, ironically, a scheme ostensibly devised to equalize disparities increased them by benefitting aristocratic Kandyan Sinhalese, some of the most privileged people in Sri Lanka.[28] As one Tamil who lost his spot in engineering wrote: "They effectively claimed that the son of a Sinhalese minister in an elite Colombo school was disadvantaged vis-a-vis a Tamil tea plucker's son."[29]

This follows the pattern of many other affirmative action programs around the world: the biggest beneficiaries are typically the most privileged and politically connected individuals within the group receiving affirmative action. They are often wealthier and more privileged than many of the individuals against whom affirmative action is directed. This has been well documented in India, which has extensive data on the subgroups that benefit from its affirmative action programs.[30]

The new affirmative action schemes deepened the divides among Sri Lanka's ethnic groups, enhancing "us versus them" attitudes. This spawned riots throughout the 1970s, including a violent anti-Muslim riot in 1975 and a very deadly anti-Tamil riot in 1977. This violence was not surprising in light of a dynamic we have discussed previously: affirmative action programs do not just aggrieve the disfavored group; they also have an invidious effect on the favored group, imbuing them with a sense of insecurity and defensiveness over the benefits they receive. The favored group often justifies indefinite continuation of these benefits by claiming that the disfavored group continues to enjoy "privilege"—or by demonizing them and claiming that they behave perfidiously. Thus, the affirmative action beneficiaries are often the ones to initiate hostilities. In Rwanda, for example, it was Hutu affirmative action beneficiaries, not Tutsis, who perpetrated the violence. The situation in Sri Lanka was analogous, with Sinhalese instigating most of the initial riots.

Around the world, a common manifestation of affirmative action beneficiaries' insecurity over their benefits has been ethnic conspiracy theories. For example, theories about Chinese conspiracies have continued to circulate in Malaysia throughout its sixty-three years of affirmative action; if anything, they have worsened over time, even while any real disparities that might justify affirmative action have declined.[31] Contrast this with Thailand, which also has a disproportionately educated and wealthy Chinese minority, but no affirmative action. Thai Chinese are happily integrated with the rest of the population; ethnic conspiracy theories are unheard of.[32] Sri Lanka, with its affirmative action, followed the Malaysian example: a widely held conspiracy theory alleged that any outperformance by Tamil students was attributable to Tamil teachers illicitly rigging exam scores. This further spurred Sinhalese animus and violence toward Tamils.[33]

The timeline of the Sri Lankan conflict establishes how communal violence originated from the affirmative action policies rather than the underlying income and occupational disparity between the groups. The disparity was at its apex at the beginning of the twentieth century, when Sri Lankan Tamils constituted the majority in high-paying professions and government positions, despite their small (12 percent) share of the overall population.[34] Yet, there was no communal violence at the time or during the next half century. It was only after the introduction of affirmative action programs that ethnic violence erupted. The deadliest attacks on Tamils occurred a full decade after those programs had enabled Sinhalese to surpass Tamils in both income and education. As Thomas Sowell has observed, "it was not the disparities which led to intergroup violence but the politicizing of those disparities and the promotion of group identity politics."[35]

The lessons of the various affirmative action programs in Sri Lanka were clear to everyone: individuals' access to education and government employment would be determined by ethnic group membership rather than equal opportunity and individual merit; and political power would determine how much each group got. If you wanted your share, you needed to mobilize as a group and acquire and maintain political power at any cost. The divisive effects of these lessons would be catastrophic.

The Tamil Reaction and Civil War

Affirmative action in university admissions struck deeply at the Tamils' long-held sense that, as a group with limited resources, their best path to success was education. Tamils increasingly came to realize that they would forever be at the mercy of a system that rewarded ethnicity over merit unless they did something about it. This realization, along with the violent riots and attacks perpetrated against them, induced them to form an alphabet soup of political organizations: EROS, EPFLF, LTTE, TELO, and many others.

As is frequently the case in ethnically divided societies, the political organization with the most radical and strident positions tends to prevail. Once ethnic division is established, it is too easy to accuse moderates of being ethnic sellouts or traitors to "their own kind." In Sri Lanka, the most militant group, the Liberation Tigers of Tamil Eelam (LTTE), won out. The LTTE sought to establish an independent state (Tamil Eelam) in the north and east of the island and was ready to use violence to achieve that goal. The LTTE attacked both Sri Lankan government forces and individual Sinhalese, initiating a deadly spiral of attacks and reprisals by both sides. Both Tamils and Sinhalese committed the sort of atrocities that are tragically common in ethnic conflicts: burning people alive, torture, mass killings, and so on. Over the following thirty years, the conflict continued to fester, periodically escalating into outright civil war.

The Sri Lankan government did eventually soften some of its ethnically divisive measures. The 1978 constitution, for example, gave both Sinhala and Tamil "official and national" language status. But by then, it was too late. Tamils understood that their ability to compete fairly for jobs and education would always be at the whim of whoever held office, and the country could quickly revert to quotas and other divisive measures. Sri Lanka's experience mirrored that of so many other multiethnic societies: once ethnic division begins, it is desperately difficult to repair. Not only is there lingering rancor over past offenses, but ethnic opportunist leaders recognize they need to perpetuate the conflict to retain their power and prestige. For example, the LTTE leader, V. Prabhakaran, had acquired tremendous power and cultlike status, which he stood to lose in any peaceful reintegration of the country. In his speeches, he repeatedly condemned any Tamils who advocated reconciliation as "traitors" who "betray their own ethnic community"; the LTTE brutally executed many of these people. As one obituary put it, Prabhakaran was the leader "who refused to compromise to the end."[36] On the other side, President Mahinda Rajapaksa, whose electoral appeal depended on Sinhalese jingoism, was equally intransigent.[37]

So the conflict continued, and hundreds of thousands of people would ultimately be killed and displaced. It was not until 2009 that it finally ended—in a horrific bloodbath. The Sri Lankan army, led by Rajapaksa's brother, Gotabaya, cornered the LTTE, along with vast numbers of Tamil civilians, in a ten-square-kilometer area in Jaffna and killed forty thousand of them, including thousands of children.[38]

Secondary Effects of Ethnic Preferences

One salient lesson from the Sri Lankan experience is that ethnic preferences are not just harmful in a direct way, setting one group against another in conflict that sometimes turns violent. They also have pernicious indirect effects. In particular, when a country adopts ethnic preferences, it abandons principles of absolute meritocracy and equal opportunity; once the principles are discarded and the door is open to ethnic favoritism, it is easy to justify and accept many other sorts of favoritism. The logical and ethical steps from ethnic preferences to regional preferences, to clan preferences, and to outright nepotism are small.

When Sri Lanka became independent, its government was widely deemed one of the least corrupt in the developing world. But as ethnic preference programs were implemented and expanded, corruption increased in lockstep; it exploded under Sirimavo's government.[39] As we already saw, an affirmative action program that was ostensibly implemented to benefit disadvantaged Sinhalese was deftly contrived to benefit highly privileged Kandyan Sinhalese who lived in the Bandaranaikes' home region. Similar favoritism was applied to economic development projects and many other aspects of government.[40] The adoption of ethnic preferences had set a paradigm that pervaded the government: whoever held power could steer government resources to whomever they deemed "underserved." Today, Sri Lanka's government, which once rivaled European governments in transparency, remains highly corrupt.[41]

Summary and Conclusions

Sri Lanka's ethnic and religious groups had a very long history of tolerance and relatively peaceful coexistence. That history, along with a record of democratic and honest government, had made Sri Lanka "the best bet in Asia." However, ethnically divisive government policies quickly turned a good bet into a terrible one. By rejecting the country's shared English "link" language, the government weakened the mutual understanding and unity that its ethnic groups enjoyed. By relegating groups to different academic language tracks, it diminished asabiyah and enhanced group divisions. By implementing divisive affirmative action programs, it further deepened those divisions and pitted groups against each other. As a result, formerly inconsequential differences became lethally relevant, and an "us versus them" mindset took hold. One Sri Lankan poignantly summed it up:

> Identity was never a question for thousands of years. But now, here, for some reason it is different.... Friends that I grew up with, [messed around] with, got drunk with, now see an essential difference between us just for the fact of their ethnic identity. And there's no obvious differences at all, no matter what they say. I point to pictures in the newspapers and ask them to tell me who is Sinhalese and who is Tamil, and they simply can't tell the difference. This identity is a fiction, I tell you, but a deadly one.[42]

Sri Lanka's two majority religions, Buddhism and Hinduism, both embrace *ahimsa*—the principle of not harming any other living being—as a core belief. But even this deeply held principle was no match for the poisonous power of identity politics unleashed by policies that distinguished between groups and implemented ethnic preferences. This impelled members of both faiths to kill hundreds of thousands of people and commit unimaginable atrocities against each other.

Not only did ethnically divisive policies in Sri Lanka spur widespread violence, but they also led to both the expansion and corruption of government. As the statistics in chapter 10 show, ethnic fractionalization is highly correlated with both a government's intrusiveness and its level of corruption. This impairs economic performance and lowers living standards. Sri Lanka has been no exception to this, with an economy that has dramatically underperformed in comparison with its peers. In 1950, it was poised to outgrow Singapore. Today, after ethnically divisive and socialist policies have hamstrung Sri Lanka's economy for decades, one Singaporean, on average, makes more than seven Sri Lankans put together. Ironically, policies that were devised to elevate one group and make it better off ended up making all groups in the country vastly worse off.

Perhaps the most compelling lesson we can take from the Sri Lankan experience is that multi-ethnic societies are extremely fragile. They can easily be fractured by the divisive attitudes and policies advocated by ethnic opportunists: a single ethnic opportunist, S. W. R. D. Bandaranaike, with a cavalierly divisive election ploy, was able to initiate a gaping, deadly ethnic rift that has persisted for over half a century. Bandaranaike underestimated the depth and rancor of the rift he started, with results that were ultimately fatal for himself and hundreds of thousands of others. Unfortunately, after his death, other ethnic opportunists would assume the cause of maintaining group division: his wife, Sirimavo Bandaranaike, V. Prabhakaran, the Rajapaksas, and many others.

Fragile multiethnic societies like Sri Lanka's, once fractured, are not easily mended. As discussed in chapter 2, there is an innate human inclination to factionalism; the "us versus them" mindset is hard to overcome once it is established. Moreover, ethnic opportunists have a vested interest in perpetuating it; they derive status and political power from ongoing division and conflict. The best hope for Sri Lanka—and for all multiethnic countries—is to nurture and grow shared asabiyah and resist the siren calls of ethnic opportunists and factionalism.

9

✷

FROM COLOR BAR TO COLORBLIND IN BOTSWANA

In 1948, Ruth Williams, a twenty-five-year-old London clerk, told her parents she planned to marry a young law student. Their reaction was worse than she had expected: her father told her that she would no longer be welcome in their home if she married. Her employers' response was no better: they sacked her. When Ruth's fiancé wrote to his uncle that he intended to marry Ruth, the response was equally negative. But that was just the beginning of the young couple's troubles. Ultimately, their love affair would generate a diplomatic crisis and worldwide press furor, surpassing the union of the Duke of Windsor and Wallis Simpson as the twentieth century's most controversial marriage.[1]

The controversy arose because, two decades before *Guess Who's Coming to Dinner* hit theaters, a white woman was marrying a black man. Not just any black man, but Seretse Khama, the future king of Bechuanaland—a British protectorate in southern Africa. Like other mixed-race couples, Ruth and Seretse endured dirty looks, jeers, and discrimination whenever they went out in public. But the opposition from the British government was an even bigger problem. The British wanted to appease South Africa, whose uranium supply they desperately needed; racist

South Africa would not tolerate a mixed-race couple leading a neighboring country.[2]

It was not just white racists who opposed the marriage: Seretse's uncle Tshekedi, who was acting regent of Bechuanaland, vehemently opposed racial mixing: he once had a white man flogged for consorting with black women. He was confident that the tribe shared his feelings and would never accept a white woman. So, he and the British government colluded to prevent the marriage and to bar Seretse from leading his country after it occurred.

But, as one friend said, Ruth and Seretse's connection was "one of the greatest love stories the world has known."[3] Anyone who knew the couple at the time (or thirty years later) could tell they were absolutely, unconditionally in love with each other, and they were resolute in their desire to be together. So, when British officials persuaded the bishop of London to abort their church wedding, they got married in a civil procedure instead. Tshekedi was enraged; in his role as regent, he refused to recognize the marriage. This initiated a bitter struggle between himself, Seretse, and the British government.[4]

In Bechuanaland, major tribal issues were resolved in public gatherings called *kgotlas*. In a kgotla, every member is entitled to speak, and nobody is permitted to interrupt; decisions are reached by consensus. The kgotla tradition originated hundreds of years ago, qualifying Bechuanaland as one of the world's oldest democracies. In 1948, Tshekedi called several kgotlas to consider Seretse's marriage and future kingship. In the last of these, Tshekedi told a crowd of over nine thousand people, "If he [Seretse] brings his white wife here, I will fight him to the death." But when Tshekedi asked his supporters to rise, only nine people stood. Then Seretse spoke briefly in the gentle and persuasive manner that he was known for, calling for those who supported him and his wife to stand. Nearly all nine thousand people jumped to their feet, yelling and applauding thunderously for ten minutes straight. A British official who witnessed it wrote: "It was a stirring spectacle, a magnificent expression of public sentiment."[5]

But the British government was not moved: it ignored the will of the people of Bechuanaland and refused to recognize Seretse as leader of the country. In a shamefully deceitful ploy, the government invited Seretse back to London, ostensibly to discuss Bechuanaland's future administration. Once he was there, they reneged on their promise to allow his return and banished him from Bechuanaland for five years. They later extended that to a lifetime ban. As opposition leader Winston Churchill muttered in parliament, it was "a very disreputable transaction."[6] The people of Bechuanaland were embittered by the British government's treachery, which they knew had originated from racism. They protested and engaged in passive resistance for nearly five years while international criticism of the British government's perfidy mounted.

Finally, after leaders of Seretse's tribe sent a telegram to Queen Elizabeth, pleading for the return of their chief, the British government relented. Seretse could return, but he and Tshekedi would both have to renounce claims to the kingship. So Seretse and Ruth returned to Bechuanaland to try their hands at cattle farming. A few years later, Seretse founded the Bechuanaland Democratic Party (BDP). In 1965, he was elected prime minister of the protectorate. He successfully pushed for independence, with Bechuanaland becoming the independent nation of Botswana. In 1966, he was elected the first president of Botswana, an office he held until he died in 1980.

Founding a Colorblind Nation

The people of Botswana—the Batswana—were well acquainted with white racism. They witnessed hateful demonstrations of it in neighboring South Africa, where many of them labored as migrant workers. They also experienced it in their own country in the form of the "color bar"—the white colonialists' practice of denying black people entry to hotels, restaurants, and other establishments. Many white people also shunned Ruth and treated her shabbily because of her marriage to a black man. And, of course, there was the British government, whose deceitful and iniquitous actions against Ruth, Seretse, and the Batswana ultimately originated in racism.

Botswana's experience of colonial racism was hardly unique: many other countries that gained independence in the decades after World War II had experienced it as well. But Botswana had something those countries did not: the striking example of Ruth and Seretse. The couple was bright, charismatic, and adored by most Batswana—and they demonstrated with vivid clarity that people from vastly different backgrounds could look past ethnic and racial differences, interacting with and loving each other as individuals. They provided a stunning contrast to the racist British and South Africans who divided people into racial, ethnic, and tribal groups and accorded them different treatment on that basis. For most Batswana, it was obvious which was the better example to follow.

Perhaps from observing Ruth and Seretse's colorblind love over time, even Tshekedi changed his views on race. The former regent, who had once flogged a white man for consorting with black women and who had opposed admitting a white woman to his tribe, increasingly supported the unity of white and black people. He even accorded honorary tribal membership to several white friends. On his deathbed, he said to Seretse and his sons: "There is no such thing as race.... I want you to remember this."[7]

The Khamas' example helped inspire the Batswana with aspirations of a colorblind society and a sense of national unity that would minimize and supersede racial, tribal, and ethnic divisions. As prime minister, Seretse Khama proposed to fulfill these aspirations, declaring in a 1965 speech:

> I cannot contemplate a future for Bechuanaland with separate representations for different racial groups... We stand virtually alone in South Africa in our belief that a non-racial society can work now... I believe we have shown that people of different races and of different backgrounds... gain greatly from mutual experience and society.[8]

Unlike many other former colonies in Africa, Botswana would not just end white domination and restore black people's rights; it would strive for true equality that would ignore racial, ethnic, and tribal distinctions. The BDP election manifesto resolutely opposed any discrimination or preferences, whether negative or "affirmative":

> The Bechuanaland Democratic Party shall not allow any form of discrimination, whether political, social or economic, against any minority racial group in the country... Neither shall the laws of the country recognise any preferential considerations of a political, economic or social nature for any tribal or racial group in Bechuanaland.[9]

This philosophy would eventually be reflected in Botswana's constitution, which guarantees protection from both negative and "affirmative" discrimination based on "race, tribe, place of origin, political opinions, colour, creed or sex."[10] The Botswana government has made such an effort to be colorblind that nobody knows the country's precise racial or ethnic composition. I have requested race and ethnicity statistics from various *Statistics*

Botswana officials on multiple occasions. They always seemed puzzled why anyone would ask. Most likely, they simply do not have the numbers since the Botswana government forbids questions about race, tribe, or ethnicity on the official census. Beginning in 1971 and every ten years after that, not a single census has ever asked any of these questions. The last census to do so was under the British administration in 1964.[11]

Starting before independence, the BDP promoted the formation of a national, unifying identity—in other words, a "greater asabiyah" to unite the various tribal asabiyahs:

> The BDP stands for a gradual but sure evolution of a national state in Bechuanaland, to which the tribal groups will, while they remain in existence, take a secondary place. This is an unavoidable development, an evolutionary law to which we must yield to survive, or resist and disappear as a people... Likewise all moves towards closer inter-tribal co-operation will be encouraged, such, for instance, as the organisation of tribal and other groups into local councils, into which smaller tribal units will be absorbed for their own economic benefit, even if they retained a small measure of tribal identity.[12]

The postcolonial Botswana government carefully devised national symbols to emphasize tribal, ethnic, and racial unity. It designated the zebra as the national animal because it is one of the few large animals in the region that are free of tribal associations, and because its stripes symbolize black and white people united. The flag also features black and white stripes to represent the unified peoples of the country.

The spirit of Botswana's ethnic policy has roots in Batswana culture: one of the Batswana's most fundamental ideals is *botho*, a concept that largely overlaps with asabiyah; it denotes a sense of connectedness with others that is similar to kinship but is shared with an extended community. In keeping with this ideal, the Batswana have a long tradition of embracing and uniting diverse groups. Over the years, various groups fleeing oppression in neighboring countries have immigrated into Botswana; the Batswana have welcomed them and integrated them into the national community. For example, at the beginning of the twentieth century, members of the Herero tribe, who were fleeing German persecution in southwest Africa, were accepted by Seretse's grandfather, Khama III, and the Batswana. They ultimately became very successful, and some of their descendants number among Botswana's wealthiest citizens.[13]

The integrative tendency of Botswana society is reflected in the conflation of the terms "Batswana" and "Botswanan." Strictly speaking, "Batswana" is a plural form that denotes members of the Tswana tribe (the singular is "Motswana"), whereas the term "Botswanan" refers to citizens of Botswana. However, in common parlance, *all* citizens of Botswana, even whites, are Batswana. This promotes the sense that everybody, regardless of color, ethnicity, or subtribe, belongs to the same national tribe.

Because of Botswana's staunchly ethnicity-blind policies, the population has increasingly come to ignore racial and ethnic differences. Race and ethnicity-blindness are so ingrained that Batswana experience culture shock when they visit countries where ethnic and racial distinctions still prevail. For example, a worker at the Botswana embassy in the United States was surprised when a local friend asked him how it felt to be the only black person in the neighborhood. He answered that it never even crossed his mind: "I just didn't have that consciousness." He said the American friend was incredulous: "how can I live here and not realize it?"[14] Visitors to Botswana are inevitably impressed by the bonhomie and camaraderie they witness between black and white citizens. A visiting anthropologist's account of a border guard, who was having a bad day and acting gruffly, is typical:

> When she saw it was a Botswana passport held by a white woman, her face broke into a big smile. She greeted Charlotte, and proceeded to have a warm conversation in Setswana. Over the course of my fieldwork, I witnessed this kind of warmth between black and white citizens on countless occasions... A sense of shared citizenship, experiences, histories, and language lead black Batswana to treat their fellow patriots with great warmth.[15]

Unity and Success in Botswana

The Tswana tribe constitutes roughly 80 percent of Botswana's population. It comprises several subtribes (e.g., Bamangwato, Bafokeng, Bakwena), which were considered ethnic groups in their own right under the British protectorate.[16] It is a testimony to Botswana's efforts to foster national unity that these subgroups (which have the same language and culture) are now effectively a single group. Even if we count all the non-Tswana as distinct groups, ethnic fractionalization would already be exceptionally low for an African country. But that would still likely overstate the actual level of fractionalization. Given the long-standing policies of colorblind integration and national unity, we can surmise that many of the 20 percent who are not members of the Tswana tribe nevertheless feel they share an identity with their Batswana compatriots. That includes even whites, many of whom speak Setswana and identify strongly with their black fellow citizens. No matter how it is measured, Botswana's ethnic and racial unity sets it apart from most African nations, making it one of the continent's least fractionalized countries. This has been crucial in Botswana achieving a degree of progress and success that is unmatched in Africa.

On the eve of its independence, Botswana was the world's eighth poorest country. It had only ten kilometers of paved road and fifty people with university degrees. Botswana has little arable land and is desperately dry, so much so that the cheery (and hopeful) national motto and greeting is "Pula"—the Setswana word for rain. British experts concluded that the new nation would remain forever dependent on foreign aid, so the British government was happy to get rid of it. But the experts were wrong: for the thirty-five years after independence, Botswana had the fastest per capita growth in the entire world, outstripping even the "Asian Tiger" nations. Today, it stands out as a stunning success story—not just among African nations but among all nations. As of 2019, its per capita GDP ranks it in the upper tier of middle-income nations, surpassing countries like China and Brazil.[17]

Chapter 10 will discuss mechanisms through which ethnic unity promotes economic success. In particular, it will posit that individuals in unified societies are more likely to believe their interests are aligned with those of the rest of society. This helps diminish corruption while increasing support for public goods and fostering noncoercive, effective government. All these factors, in turn, contribute to economic growth and the quality of life. This effect has been profound in Botswana. Botswana is among the least corrupt countries in the world, outranking some OECD countries, like Italy and Spain. It excels at providing public goods, consistently ranking among the top ten in the world in measures like education spending and measles vaccinations. By most measures, it is among the most effective governments in the world. For example, it scores near the top of the Fund for Peace's annual *State Legitimacy Index* (which measures the "population's level of confidence in state institutions and processes"). It beats not only other African countries but also the United States and the United Kingdom.[18] Excelling in transparency, public goods, and effective government has propelled Botswana's development from being one of the poorest countries on the African continent to being the second wealthiest.

Economic Freedom and Success in Botswana

Ruth and Seretse Khama enjoyed their first date at London's Casino Theatre, beginning an interracial connection that inspired Botswana's people and contributed to the country's success. By coincidence, only a hundred yards from the Casino Theater was the flat where Karl Marx developed a philosophy that ultimately contributed to many other African countries' failures.[19]

Seretse was one of several future African leaders who studied in the United Kingdom around the end of World War II. His experience in the United Kingdom led him to detest preferential treatment based on ethnicity and race. He brought this abhorrence of group preferences back to Botswana, infusing his political party and the nascent nation with it. But Seretse's peers—leaders like Ghana's Nkrumah and Tanzania's Nyerere—took different lessons from their experiences in the United Kingdom: they imbibed the dogma that Marx had developed just around the corner from the Casino Theatre. They brought that dogma back to Africa, where it would be as destructive to their countries as Khama's colorblind practices were beneficial to his.

As the analysis in chapter 10 shows, ethnically divided countries that opt for intrusive, antimarket governance tend to suffer abysmal economic performance. But intrusive government does not just diminish economic growth; it also raises the stakes for ethnic competition, pitting ethnic groups against each other in a contest for the expansive spoils that the government allocates. So, when leaders like Nkrumah and Nyerere implemented variants of Marxism in their ethnically fractionalized countries, nationalizing industries and rigidly controlling commerce and the allocation of resources, the results were devastating. Most of the countries that followed this course became poorer after a decade of independence; others barely progressed. Nearly all of them suffered violent political turmoil. By contrast, countries like Cote d'Ivoire and Botswana, which opted for smaller government and free markets, did vastly better. Between 1966 and 1980, while many socialist countries lost ground, Cote d'Ivoire's per capita GDP grew by 443 percent. Botswana, which benefited from both free markets and low ethnic fractionalization, enjoyed a staggering 1,212 percent growth rate during that period. Figure 9.1 contrasts growth in Botswana and the sub-Saharan nations that chose Marxist/socialist policies.

Figure 9.1. Economic growth in Botswana and socialist sub-Saharan countries.[20]

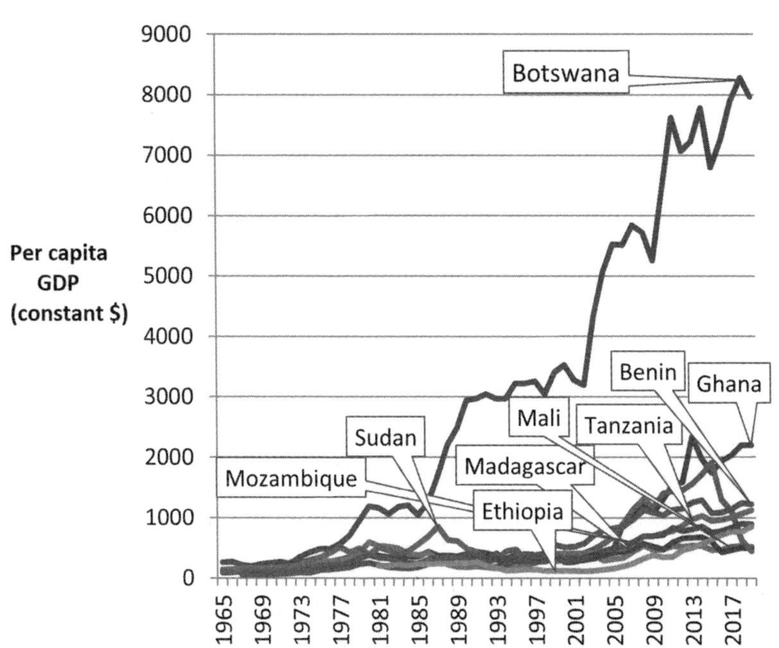

The contrast in Botswana's policies with those of the less successful African countries is striking. After independence, Botswana's government reduced spending dramatically for the first seven years; it did not return to pre-independence levels for twenty years. During that time, many other African governments ramped up spending, tightened control over their economies, and launched ambitious Soviet-style central planning initiatives. Such policies were already destructive in less fractionalized countries like North Korea and China; but the African nations' high ethnic fractionalization greatly exacerbated these malign effects. The characteristic inefficiency of big government was amplified when these ethnically divided regimes steered government resources to benefit preferred ethnic groups. For example, in Kenya, presidents Kenyatta and Moi both flagrantly funneled spending to the regions populated by their ethnic constituencies. When Moi took over, spending on roads and health in the regions dominated by his ethnic coalition nearly doubled as a percentage of the total.[21] In Ghana, Nkrumah directed his interventionist government to heavily tax cocoa exports, benefiting his Akan kinsmen at the expense the rival Ashanti, and harming the economy overall.[22] A baleful side effect of this ethnicity-based distortion of government policy was that it undermined and eroded more general standards of government integrity and transparency, legitimating a paradigm of corruption: if it is acceptable to direct policy for the benefit of an ethnic group, is it not also acceptable do so for the benefit of a clan or an individual? It is a small step to go from one to the other, a step that countless African leaders and bureaucrats took.

In Botswana, things worked very differently. Because it fostered ethnic unity, there was less incentive to adopt the sort of coercive, big-spending, antimarket government that enables one ethnic group to secure its position at the expense of others.

Moreover, the country's strong conviction against preferential ethnic policies constrained the spending and regulation that did occur. Under its National Development Plans (NDPs), the government strictly ranked projects by economic feasibility and rate of return tests. If a project did not meet the threshold, the government would not implement it, no matter which group stood to benefit. In contrast to the ethnic division in many other African countries, the idea that "we're all Batswana" and that nobody gets preferential treatment prevailed. This sense of unity and strong aversion to preferential treatment fostered a more general sense of rectitude, helping to minimize corruption. If it is unacceptable for government to favor groups, it follows that it is likewise unacceptable for it to favor individuals. As an example, one expatriate civil servant noted:

> to build the roads, from dirt to hardtop, roads were ranked according to economic return. One of the roads passed by the house of the first president [Seretse Khama]. The planners offered to build his road first, even though it did not pass the rate of return tests, but he refused and said, "I'll wait my turn," and he did.[23]

In keeping with its opposition to ethnic preferences, Botswana sought the most qualified individuals to help design and build its infrastructure, regardless of their race or origins. This contrasted starkly with many other developing countries, which insisted that specialized and prestigious positions in government (e.g., engineering and administration) could only be filled with individuals from favored ethnic groups. The result was that Botswana recruited vastly more talented individuals. Immediately after independence, this included many Europeans, but as the country became wealthier and education improved, homegrown talent took over. Comparing Botswana's government and infrastructure with those in countries that insisted on ethnic preferences is instructive. Botswana surpasses some European countries, whereas countries that observed ethnic preferences in hiring (e.g., Nigeria) are doing little better than they were when they achieved independence.

Some economists have noted the substantial contribution Botswana's natural resources (particularly diamonds) have made to its economic success. While this has been a contributing factor, it is certainly not a sufficient one, as the experience of other resource-rich African countries demonstrates. For most African countries, natural resources have been more of a curse than a blessing. Because most of these countries are ethnically fractionalized, their valuable resources, along with the overbearing governments that manage them, raise the stakes for ethnic competition and nepotism and often spur violent ethnic conflict. So, the countries with the greatest resource wealth—for example, Angola, Nigeria, and the Democratic Republic of the Congo—tend to be among the most unstable, and the most miserable. There are frequent ethnically based struggles to acquire power and to use that power to divert the resources to ethnic constituencies. By contrast, Botswana, with its strong sense of ethnic unity, has averted this problem. A feeling that "we are all one group and in it together" diminishes the desire for subgroups to seize and monopolize resources (or the government) for their own benefit. Instead, these resources can be used for the benefit of the whole society. Like the ethnically unified Nordic countries, Botswana has applied much of its resource wealth to its citizens' common benefit, investing it in public goods like infrastructure and education.

As of 2020, Botswana has the third freest economy in sub-Saharan Africa, ranking behind only Mauritius and Rwanda—two countries that have also enjoyed spectacular economic success in recent years.[24] An overall comparison of these three countries—Botswana, Mauritius, and Rwanda—with their African peers is striking. From a social and economic standpoint, they are by far the nicest places to live in Africa. In fact, they surpass several OECD countries in some quality-of-life measures. They have the least crime, the fastest-growing economies, the least corruption, the best public health systems, and so on. But economic freedom is not the only factor that distinguishes these countries. *The other key factor is that their constitutions all mandate colorblindness, categorically forbidding ethnic and racial distinctions of any kind (whether negative or "affirmative").* As in other parts of the world, this philosophy, combined with economic freedom, has achieved remarkable results.

Still Room for Improvement

Botswana's remarkable success, like that of postgenocide Rwanda, has not been flawless. In particular, the government's record is blemished by its treatment of the *Basarwa*, an indigenous group who were formerly known as *San* or Bushmen. For decades, the Botswana government attempted to relocate the approximately five thousand Basarwa living in the Central Kalahari Game Reserve, claiming that their hunting was unsustainably depleting wild game. The Basarwa, along with several international rights organizations, have credibly claimed the real motivation was diamonds (the Botswana government reserves all mineral rights in the country to itself). Several kgotlas and the Botswana courts, to their credit, have rebuked the government for its treatment of the Basarwa. But that has not saved many of them from being relocated to areas far from their ancestral homelands.

Botswana has also suffered from the HIV-AIDS epidemic, with more than 20 percent of adults infected, one of the highest rates in the world. This is probably owing more to Botswana's location than anything else; its neighbors, Eswatini and Lesotho, have even higher infection rates. Botswana's sense of asabiyah and its resultant wealth has enabled it to fight the problem better than most countries: it is one of the world leaders in distributing antiretroviral treatment, surpassing countries like the Netherlands and Norway.[25]

Summary and Conclusions

Botswana's version of asabiyah—*botho*—has deep roots in Batswana tradition. Seretse Khama and the BDP tirelessly built on the botho ideal, founding a staunchly color-blind nation that would integrate citizens from diverse backgrounds—different races, tribes, and ethnicities—and foster a shared identity and sense of cohesion among them. Few countries have gone as far as Botswana to "erase race." By nearly any measure, the results have been remarkable. To most Americans, the idea of moving to a neighborhood without ever noticing the racial background of their neighbors is an unimaginable marvel. Yet, that is the degree of colorblindness Botswana has achieved.

The national cohesion and asabiyah Botswana has cultivated have enabled it to avoid the trap of oversized, coercive, and corrupt government that so many ethnically divided African countries fell into. In contrast to these countries, Botswana has allowed free markets to function and has built an efficient national government with a degree of transparency and rectitude that many European countries can only envy. Its sense of unity has also helped Botswana reach a broad consensus on government priorities, particularly public goods. So, the country now surpasses several OECD countries in the provision of public goods like education and vaccinations. The result is that, in the span of a few decades, Botswana went from being the eighth most impoverished country in the world to becoming an upper-middle-income country, with concomitant increases in living standards. On the eve of independence, Batswana parents faced a one-in-ten chance their newborn infants would die. Now the chances are less than one in fifty. In 1965, there were fewer than fifty Batswana with university degrees and only a few more that owned cars in the entire country. Now, fifteen thousand people get university degrees every year, and there is a car for every four people.[26]

10

✷

THE SOCIAL AND ECONOMIC COSTS OF ETHNIC DIVISION

Suppose you were born in Niger. You could expect to make less in an entire year than someone from Liechtenstein makes in a single day. An American might blithely spend your entire annual income on a single weekend ski pass or a round of drinks at a Manhattan bar. As stark as that sounds, it does not fully capture how much the happenstance of birthplace affects one's life prospects. Even extremely poor people in wealthy nations tend to fare better than most people in poor nations. For example, if you were born to a family in the poorest 10 percent in Denmark, you could expect a household income six times greater than the average Egyptian's; you would also benefit from twice the years of education and an additional ten years of life expectancy.[1]

This grim contrast raises the question: how can people in a few corners of the world enjoy such prosperity and comfort while people in so many countries are so desperately poor? As anyone who has spent time in the developing world can attest, the poverty in these countries cannot be attributed to a deficit of ingenuity or work ethic. Seeing Central American mechanics fashion complex car parts out of scrap metal or African parents work seventy-hour weeks to pay for their children's after-school tutoring dispels any doubt about that. One can imagine that these people would achieve great success if they only had the opportunity to apply their skills and work ethic in the right environment. Indeed, one does not need to imagine it: immigrants from these countries tend to do very well when they come to countries like the United States. The great success of Asian immigrants in America is frequently lauded. But the impressive records of other immigrant groups are often overlooked. For example, first-generation African immigrant men make nearly as much as native-born white men, and African immigrant women make substantially more than white women. That is particularly impressive since these immigrants come from some of the poorest countries in the world and must contend with significant language difficulties and racial discrimination.

One seemingly obvious explanation for the vast disparity in living standards is that poor countries suffer from higher population density and limited natural resources. It is true that some of the poorest countries, like Haiti and Bangladesh, are densely populated and have relatively few resources. But there are numerous counterexamples that challenge this explanation. The four most densely populated countries in the world—Macau, Monaco, Singapore, and Hong Kong—all rank among the ten wealthiest. These countries are also among the poorest in resources, importing nearly everything, including essentials like food and water. At the other end of the spectrum are several countries, like Venezuela and the Democratic Republic of the Congo, that benefit from both low population densities and tremendous resource wealth but are nevertheless extremely poor.

Given the failure of the obvious explanations to account for the vastly different outcomes among nations, it is worth scrutinizing other circumstances that might explain them. When we survey the statistics, several social measures stand out. But, as we will see in this chapter, *ethnic fractionalization* (a measure of how ethnically divided a society is) is the most prominent, with a very strong and significant correlation to both income and living standards. It has powerful and intriguing relationships with a variety of other social measures, which we will also explore.

Before we embark on that exploration, it is important to note that ethnic fractionalization statistics capture group division by identification rather than origin. Countries with very diverse origins can adopt a melting pot model and thereby integrate their populations and achieve low fractionalization. For example, if we were to calculate America's ethnic fractionalization based on ethnic origin, it would be one of the most fractionalized countries in the world. But, by virtue of the melting pot, Americans whose families have been in the country for a few generations tend to identify themselves simply as American. While considering the statistics presented here, it is important to bear in mind that it is possible for people with very diverse origins and physical appearances to think of themselves as unified with a shared identity. This is something that societies from ancient Rome to Botswana have achieved.

Measuring Ethnic Fractionalization

To compare how ethnically divided countries are, we use an ethnic fractionalization (EF) measure commonly employed by economists. This measure specifies the probability that two individuals randomly chosen from the country's population will be from different groups. The more fractionalized a country is, the higher the EF number. Around the world, EF values range from roughly zero to more than 0.90.[2]

Table 10.1 Ethnic fractionalization (EF) of selected countries	
Denmark	0.16
United States	0.37
Singapore	0.41
Nigeria	0.83

Appendix B describes how EF is calculated and provides ethnic fractionalization data, as well as detailed statistical analysis of fractionalization and its correlations with a variety of economic and social statistics.

Although the United States is often described as being diverse and fractionalized, EF statistics indicate otherwise. Of the 147 countries with over two million inhabitants, seventy-nine are more fractionalized than the United States (for a complete list of EF statistics, see table B.19 in appendix B).

Given an objective numeric measure of fractionalization, such as EF, we can identify associations with other national statistics. The following sections examine EF's relationships with various social and economic measures.

Fractionalization and Violent Conflict

At the end of World War II, Christmas Islanders were so convinced ethnic conflict was inevitable that they dismantled their guns, with the Chinese residents keeping the revolvers and the Malays taking the bolts and magazines. This enabled them to maintain a defensive capability against external invaders, while avoiding the risk of mutual annihilation in the meantime.[3] Statistics suggest their fears were well-founded. The chart below groups the world's nations into thirds according to their ethnic fractionalization, indicating the number of civil wars experienced by each third between 1960 and 2020. As a group, the most fractionalized countries had six times as many civil wars as the least fractionalized.[4]

Figure 10.1. Ethnic fractionalization and civil wars.

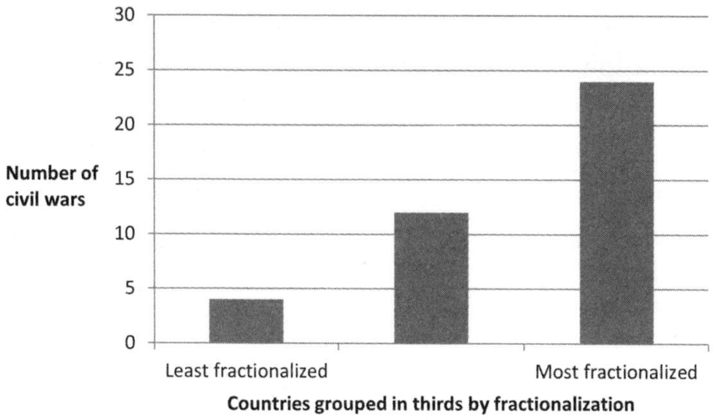

Number of civil wars
30
25
20
15
10
5
0
Least fractionalized
Most fractionalized
Countries grouped in thirds by fractionalization

This pattern applies not only to civil wars but to all types of political violence. One of the first to observe the statistical correlation was R. J. Rummel, who devoted a lifetime to the study of violent political conflict. Rummel found that over 21 percent of the variation in political violence could be directly attributed to ethnic fractionalization.[5]

Riots are also significantly correlated with ethnic fractionalization. Among countries with large urban populations, a single standard deviation increase in ethnic fractionalization is associated with a 20 percent higher occurrence of violent riots. This correlation remains statistically significant even after other socioeconomic factors are accounted for.[6]

Fractionalization, GDP, and Living Standards

As the Christmas Islanders perceived, the connection between ethnic fractionalization and violent conflict is intuitively obvious:

groups with distinct identities and differing cultural values are more likely to struggle against each other. What is less obvious is how dramatically fractionalization is linked with lower income. Figure 9.2 shows the average per capita GDP for the world's nations, grouped in thirds according to their ethnic fractionalization. The average per capita GDP of the least fractionalized countries is a staggering 4.5 times higher than that of the most fractionalized countries.

Figure 10.2. Ethnic fractionalization (EF) and per capita GDP.

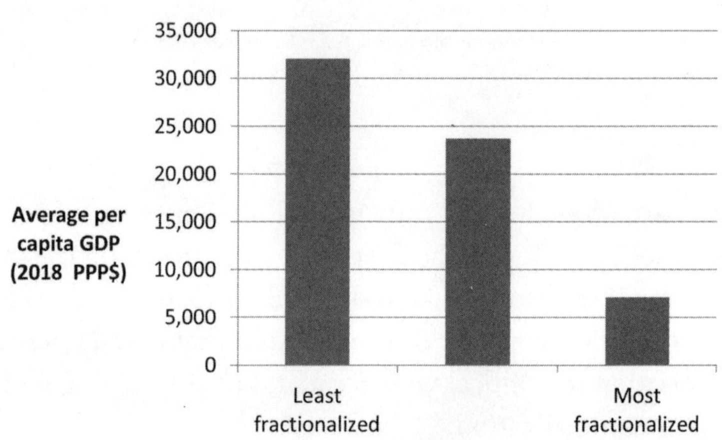

Table B.6 in appendix B details a full regression: ethnic fractionalization accounts for an incredible 36.8 percent of the variation in per capita GDP. This correlation is highly significant: the chance that it is attributable to random variation is less than one in a million. This confirms a multitude of previous studies that have found strong and highly significant correlations between fractionalization and output measures, such as GDP, productivity, and economic growth.[7] For example, one study found that every 0.10 increase in ethnic fractionalization corresponds with a 14 percent drop in income. Or, to put it in terms of actual countries:

if South Korea had Uganda's level of ethnic fractionalization, its per capita income would be $21,030 instead of $40,090.[8]

As incredible as the influence of EF on GDP is, its effect on broader measures of social well-being is even stronger. For example, the correlation with the most widely used measure of living standards, the UN Human Development Index (HDI), is strongly negative and highly significant. The level of ethnic fractionalization accounts for an astounding 40 percent of the variation in HDI levels among countries (see table B.10 in appendix B).[9] Less fractionalized countries score higher on all the HDI measures—longer life expectancies, better health, better education, and so on. For a single variable to account for 40 percent of the variation in these measures is truly remarkable.

To better understand the scale of the economic penalty associated with ethnic division, consider a simple thought experiment. Suppose that the United States could heal its ethnic division and achieve Martin Luther King Jr.'s dream that:

> little black boys and black girls will be able to join hands with little white boys and white girls as sisters and brothers.

If we could achieve that dream, uniting races in the United States would reduce ethnic fractionalization by 0.183, with potentially tremendous effects. The regression in table B.6 in appendix B indicates that a 0.183 reduction in fractionalization is associated with a massive $10,322 increase in per capita GDP.[10] Of course, the nonfinancial benefits of realizing King's dream are even more consequential.

Why Ethnic Division Is So Expensive

The connection between ethnic division and poverty is so profound that it is hard to believe. Yet numerous studies have confirmed the regressions in appendix B and failed to uncover underlying variables that might rule out a real connection. In fact, economists increasingly just assume the connection and focus instead on explaining it.[11] So how do we explain it?

An obvious starting point is ethnic violence, which exacts tremendous costs, not just in lives, but also property damage and economic disruption. The 1992 Los Angeles riots killed sixty-three people, with property damage exceeding $1.2 billion; the 2002 Gujarat riots killed over two thousand people and displaced one hundred and fifty thousand; and so on.[12] Yet, as terrible as these costs are, they account for relatively little of the overall negative effect of ethnic fractionalization on economic well-being. As table B.8 in appendix B shows, when we strip out the effects of ethnic violence, the correlation between ethnic fractionalization and per capita GDP is barely diminished. In fact, if we exclude countries with significant ethnic violence and civil wars altogether, the correlation between fractionalization and GDP remains strong and significant (see table B.9 in appendix B).

If ethnic fractionalization "causes" poor economic performance, it must do so through factors beyond violent conflict. There are several factors that are strongly associated with both ethnic fractionalization and economic performance—notably, public goods, corruption, and economic freedom. Several economists have suggested that these factors are at least part of the mechanism by which ethnic fractionalization influences economic performance.[13] The following sections will examine each of these factors.

Ethnic Fractionalization and Public Goods

Imagine being a farmer in a poor country. However hard you work, your crop ultimately depends on the rain coming at the right time. If you are lucky enough to have a good harvest, you might not get a good price for it because poor roads prevent you from getting it to the best market. Because law enforcement is limited, bad guys may extort or steal whatever money you do make. You have a hard time providing a good life for your children with that cash anyway. If they do not die at birth, they may suffer from a variety of communicable diseases because there are not any childhood vaccinations. The prospects for them improving their own lives are grim because education is limited.

Contrast that with the conditions for an American farmer. He does not worry about the timing of the rain because there is a dam and a public canal system that assure reliable water. The excellent transportation network means his crops can easily fetch the best price, even if it is a thousand miles away. An effective system of courts and law enforcement ensures that he is not swindled or robbed. His children will not get preventable diseases because nearly everyone is immunized. They can also get a good education (nearly 70 percent of young farmers have college degrees), which enables them to either become better farmers or pursue other occupations.

The differences we have just described—infrastructure, law enforcement, public health programs, and education—all constitute what economists call "public goods." Public goods play a key role in enabling people to produce more and to lead more pleasant lives; they have a very strong correlation with economic output and wealth. This correlation likely runs both ways in a virtuous circle: public goods make a country wealthier, while greater wealth enables a country to provide more public goods.

All else held equal, ethnically fractionalized countries do very poorly at providing public goods. As table B.13 in appendix B shows, ethnic fractionalization has a highly significant negative correlation with a variety of public goods. For example, a child born in a highly fractionalized country is more likely to die in childbirth and far less likely to receive essential vaccinations and a good education. If he makes it out of childhood, he is far more likely to suffer under inferior infrastructure and poor law enforcement.[14] The negative relationship between fractionalization and public goods holds not only among different countries but also among regions within countries.[15]

Why do more fractionalized societies provide fewer public goods? By definition, a public good is beyond the reach of the "invisible hand" of market forces; a society of individuals or groups acting only in their own narrow self-interest will not provide public goods. To provide public goods, a society must perceive and evaluate the costs and benefits of the public goods as shared costs and benefits; it must "internalize" them. Societies that are ethnically divided inevitably find that much more difficult to do. The most extensive study conducted on diversity and community within the United States found a consistent pattern of individuals in more diverse areas "hunkering down"—narrowly focusing on their own well-being rather than that of their communities. The study found that the more ethnically heterogeneous an area was, the lower altruism, community cooperation, and trust (even within one's own group) were. It concluded that, at least initially, "immigration and ethnic diversity tend to reduce social solidarity and social capital."[16]

Brazil, a fractionalized country with profound ethnic and racial divisions, is a good example of this; its record of providing public goods is miserable. In its infamous favelas, sewage flows in the streets; power and water supplies are often jury-rigged and unreliable; crime is rampant; and public health is abysmal. Life for predominantly black and *pardo* favela residents is as wretched as anywhere in the developing world. Beginning early in Brazil's immigrant past, individual European and Asian ethnic enclaves, which were starkly segregated, tended to provide their own public goods, while the central government provided relatively few, leaving vast numbers of freed slaves and Amerindians bereft. That tradition lives on in the *condominios fechados*, which have proliferated over the last fifty years. These gated communities, occupied by mostly lighter-skinned people, have privatized public goods—roads, power, water, police, and so on.[17] So their wealthy, influential residents have little inclination to support public goods for the broader Brazilian public.[18] Across Brazil, a few of the least fractionalized areas (e.g., Santa Catarina state) support some public goods, but more diverse and populous areas (e.g., Rio de Janeiro) support relatively few.[19] The consequences for Brazil have been substandard growth, lower living standards, and what some have called "social apartheid." With less than 3 percent of the world's population, Brazil can afford 13 percent of the world's plastic surgery.[20] Yet nobody wants to pay what is needed for honest law enforcement and adequate sanitation in the favelas.

Even if ethnic groups in a fractionalized society perceive a shared interest in providing public goods, they are more likely to disagree about the nature of the public goods. For example, they might agree that funding education is in their common interest but disagree about the content or the language of instruction, with each group desiring a curriculum that reflects its own heritage and culture. The result is that groups may be tempted to divert resources to private education and thus fail to internalize the societal costs and benefits of education.[21] For example, ethnically fractionalized Lagos, Nigeria has ten times more private schools than public.[22] By contrast, homogeneous Finland has only 3 percent of its children in private schools. Education statistics suggest this is part of a worldwide pattern: the more fractionalized a country or community is, the more it favors private over public education, and the less it funds education altogether. The bottom-line result is that fractionalized countries have vastly lower literacy rates and their students score significantly worse on international standardized tests (see table B.14 in appendix B).[23]

Ethnic Fractionalization and Corruption

Nigerian newspapers revel in tales of corruption. In one recent story, a government clerk blamed a snake for slithering into the office safe and taking $100,000 that had gone missing. In another, a top official was indicted because his apartment was overflowing with twenty million Nigerian Naira and forty-three million US dollars in purloined cash (a $1 million stack of hundreds is nearly four feet high). Nigerian corruption manifests itself in so many forms that one researcher developed a taxonomy, identifying over five hundred varieties.[24]

There is a serious side to these amusing tales: Nigeria's tremendous wealth in natural resources should make it one of the wealthiest countries in the world, yet corruption has helped make it one of the poorest. A 2016 PwC study determined that Nigeria's GDP would have been 36 percent larger if it had even modestly restrained corruption over the previous fifteen years. Over twenty-five million people who should have become middle class still languish below the poverty line because of "excess corruption."[25] Of course, Nigeria is not the only country that suffers terribly from corruption. For example, in Brazil, corruption is estimated to cost up to $51 billion annually.[26]

So why are countries like Nigeria and Brazil plagued with corruption? Is it because of lax standards of honesty embedded in African or Latin cultures? The corruption statistics compiled by international organizations provide some insight. The figure below shows the Transparency International Corruption Perception Index (CPI) ratings for several countries, along with their ethnic fractionalization levels (CPI is scaled so the least corrupt countries score highest).

Figure 10.3. Ethnic fractionalization and Corruption Perceptions Index.

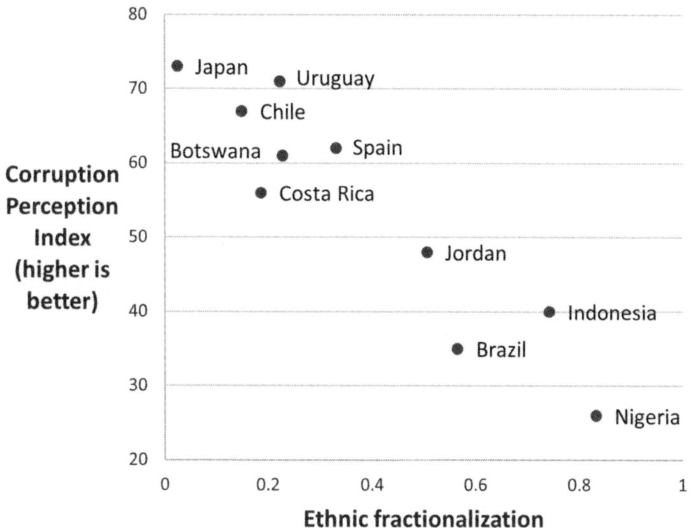

The statistics challenge the commonplace assertion that corruption only correlates with culture. Several African and Latin American countries have less corruption than many European and OECD countries. Uruguay is one of the least corrupt countries in the world, beating the United States and France by two points on the CPI scale. Botswana, Chile, and Costa Rica rank nearly as high, soundly beating Italy, Greece, and many others. Culture may have some influence on corruption levels. But what distinguishes Botswana, Chile, Costa Rica, and Uruguay from their vastly more corrupt neighbors is not culture but rather the absence of multiculturalism. With an average EF of only 0.19, they are among the least diverse countries in the world. These countries are only examples of a more general pattern: the overall correlation between corruption and ethnic fractionalization is strong and highly significant, even after other social factors are accounted for.[27] The twenty-five least corrupt countries in the world are also among the least fractionalized, with a median fractionalization score that is only half the global median.

How is ethnic fractionalization connected with corruption? In some countries, it is directly connected in the form of ethnic patronage—a practice Melanesians call *wantokism*. *Wantok*, a pidgin term derived from "one talk," refers to people who speak the same language.[28] In multiethnic governments around the world, wantokism has corrupted policy and distorted resource allocation. For example, Kenyan government outlays show that, as different ethnic groups have gained political power, they have diverted government resources to their own regions—helping their own members but harming the country as a whole.[29] Some degree of wantokism occurs in multiethnic governments around the world, including the European Union.[30]

It is likely that ethnic nepotism also has a powerful "trickle-down" effect. The ethnic competition over government resources, along with wantokism, eliminates any sense that a society is based on objective standards or true fairness. It is all about getting the most for one's own kind, a corrosive notion that undermines ideals of honesty and transparency at all levels. So, it is no surprise that countries like Nigeria, with pervasive wantokism at the group level, all have terrible corruption at the individual level as well.

Another way fractionalization may increase corruption is by discouraging governments from exposing and removing corrupt officials. Multiethnic governing coalitions, like those formed by the Ndebele and the Shona in Zimbabwe and the Malay, the

Chinese, and the Indians in Malaysia, are often fragile arrangements, which can be fractured by relatively minor disagreements. Investigating or removing a corrupt official risks antagonizing the official's ethnic group and jeopardizing the coalition. Thus, each group in a multiethnic government has an incentive to overlook corruption among the other groups. In Zimbabwe, both Ndebele and Shona officials embezzled staggering amounts and turned a blind eye to each other's activities.[31] In Malaysia, the prospect of ethnically based protest has often prevented the removal of corrupt officials. In the United States, some municipalities have refrained from removing incompetent or corrupt officials because of pressure from the officials' ethnic constituencies. This is combined with the strong inclination to keep a corrupt official in office as long as he's "one of ours."[32]

Beneath it all, ethnically fractionalized societies face the same dilemma with corruption that they do with public goods: the costs of corruption are externalities that only get internalized when people identify with, and feel an attachment to, the broader society. When they identify primarily with a constituent ethnic group, the costs remain external. Or, to put it in layman's terms: even when corruption does not directly benefit one's ethnic group, there may be a sense that it is okay because it is not hurting them—or at least not that much proportionally. If you steal from the government and your group constitutes only a fraction of the population, you are mostly stealing from people you care relatively less about. For people to refrain from stealing money when there's little chance of getting caught, they need to have a feeling of connectedness to the rest of society. In ethnically divided societies, that feeling is usually lacking. The effects are confirmed by studies that have found a strong and significant negative correlation between ethnic fractionalization and adherence to the rule of law.[33]

Ethnic Fractionalization and Economic Freedom

In just thirty-five years (1960 to 1995), the countries with the freest economies in the world—Hong Kong and Singapore—multiplied their per capita GDP by an incredible factor of fifty (an increase of roughly $23,000), despite their high population densities and lack of natural resources. By contrast, India and Myanmar, two countries with government-dominated economies, increased their per capita GDP by a paltry $500. At the end of World War II, all four countries had close to the same income. Now Hong Kong and Singapore are among the wealthiest countries in the world, while India and Myanmar are still wretchedly poor. This highlights a broader pattern across the world's economies: economic freedom, the liberty to produce and exchange goods and services free of government coercion, is very strongly correlated with economic success. Countries that rely on market forces rather than government fiat to allocate economic resources enjoy significantly higher income and economic growth.[34] The recent histories of countries like China and Vietnam, which have enjoyed skyrocketing growth rates after introducing market forces to their command economies, lend color to the statistics.

All else held equal, more fractionalized countries enjoy significantly less economic freedom (see table B.16 in appendix B). Indeed, multiethnic governments are vastly more coercive in general: of the eighty-five countries with fractionalization levels above the world median, only four have truly democratic governments.[35] Fractionalized countries are also much more likely to deny their citizens political and civil rights. There are a few possible explanations for this tendency. For example, it may be that ethnic groups in ethnically divided countries tend to use government as a tool to gain advantage over (or defend against) each other.

Whatever the explanation, the tendency of ethnically fractionalized countries to suppress economic freedom provides a strong link between fractionalization and economic output. As Figure 10.4 shows, when ethnically fractionalized countries opt for bigger, more intrusive government, the costs in foregone prosperity can be staggering.

Figure 10.4. Why economic freedom matters.

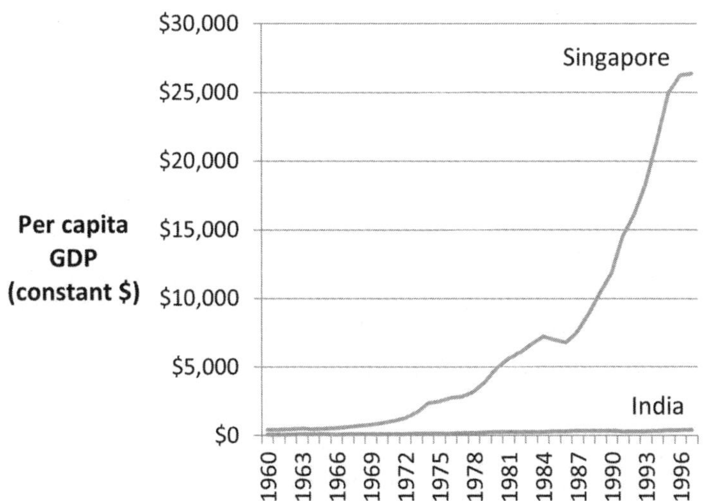

As we will see, the tragedy for ethnically divided countries is compounded: not only do they choose coercive government more often than do ethnically unified countries; doing so hurts them more. Big government is much more harmful in Nigeria than in Denmark.

Economic Freedom, Fractionalization, and GDP

Even more interesting than how fractionalization and economic freedom are correlated is how they complement each other in predicting economic performance. Figure 10.5 shows the interaction by grouping countries first by their levels of economic freedom and then by their relative levels of fractionalization. A strong advantage in either economic freedom or fractionalization tends to offset a disadvantage in the other factor. The big-government countries that do best (e.g., Tunisia and Sweden) are those with the most homogeneous populations. The multiethnic countries that do best (e.g., Switzerland and Mauritius) are those with the freest economies. With few exceptions, countries with low ethnic fractionalization and free economies are highly prosperous; highly fractionalized countries with government-dominated economies are wretchedly poor.[36]

With no other information about a country beyond its levels of ethnic fractionalization and economic freedom, one can guess its GDP and living standards with astounding accuracy. When combined, ethnic fractionalization and economic freedom levels account for a stunning 71 percent of the variation in per capita GDP and 63 percent of the variation in living standards (see table B.17 in appendix B).

Figure 10.5. Fractionalization, economic freedom, and GDP.

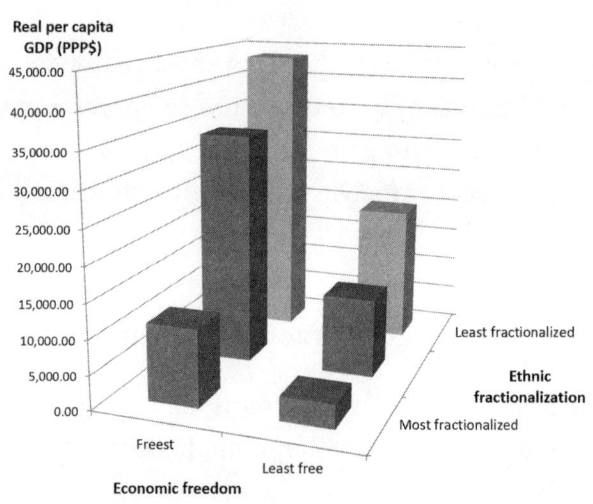

These statistics suggest that while Adam Smith's invisible hand is helpful for any country, it is absolutely critical for multiethnic countries. Intuitively, this makes sense. Big government is less of a problem when individual and national interests are closely aligned—which is more likely in less fractionalized countries. Because citizens are more likely to agree about how resources are allocated and can be assured that they are being allocated to those with whom they identify, government allocation of resources can be less contentious and more efficient, even while being more expansive. By contrast, in fractionalized countries, big government poses a tremendous challenge. In these countries, government allocation of resources is likely to be perceived as a zero-sum game. To get ahead and ensure that its interests are represented, each ethnic group has a strong incentive to secure as much government power as it can, and to maintain that power through whatever means necessary—often corruption and oppression of other groups. The more resources the government controls, the greater this incentive is. Multiethnic countries have a much better chance with a free market system in which the government distributes relatively few spoils, and the stakes for government control are not as high. Under a free market system, the desires of various groups to get ahead are channeled into productive economic enterprises rather than into controlling government and diverting its resources to themselves.

Expansive government can also harm multiethnic countries by enabling racial and ethnic discrimination. In free market economies, businesses that discriminate do so at their own expense: when they forgo lucrative sales or productive employees for noneconomic reasons like racial or ethnic discrimination, it costs them money. This is not a constraint for public officials because they are spending someone else's money. History suggests that racists tend to set aside their racism when it incurs a significant cost. For example, racist South African mining companies initially hired many black miners. It was only intrusive government measures, beginning with the 1911 Mines Work Act, that impelled them to replace black workers with whites. This pattern has been repeated in other countries, including the United States—for example, in the Jim Crow South.[37]

Free enterprise might not eliminate the malign effects of racism, but big government has the potential to make them profoundly worse. Overbearing government is a useful tool for racists: restrictive labor regulations, particularly occupational licensing and wage regulations, can be used to lock minorities and immigrants out of jobs. Of course, government-enforced ethnic preferences like those in apartheid South Africa, Malaysia, and Sri Lanka are an even more powerful tool. The cost to both the victims of those "affirmative action" policies and the countries they live in has been staggering. Malaysia's ethnic preferences have induced many of the most talented and productive citizens to leave the country. Between 2006 and 2016, nearly fifty thousand Chinese renounced their citizenship. In a recent survey, roughly half of Malaysia's Chinese and Indian citizens said they wanted to leave the country. The "brain drain" has continued to hamper Malaysia's aspirations to raise national income.[38] This problem is not confined to Malaysia: our statistical analysis confirms that the combination of ethnic fractionalization and expansive government is significantly correlated with brain drain around the world (see table B.18 in appendix B).

Fractionalization and the "Nordic Miracle"

The Nordic countries (Denmark, Finland, Iceland, Norway, and Sweden) are frequently lauded for the effectiveness of their expansive social programs and welfare safety nets. They devote large percentages of their economies to government spending but somehow manage to avoid the corruption, inefficiency, and anemic growth that is normally associated with big-government countries. As any visitor can attest, life in the Nordic countries is very pleasant, if a little cold. Proponents of "Democratic Socialism" often cite the Nordic countries as examples of its success.

Democratic Socialists overstate the scope and intrusiveness of government in the Nordic countries. These countries all rank in the top thirty on economic freedom indices. Moreover, several of them have dramatically curtailed the size of government to avert low growth. For example, between 1993 and 2007, Sweden cut government spending from more than 70 percent of GDP to less than 50 percent.[39] The Nordic countries also have the advantage of bountiful natural resources. On a per capita basis, Norway produces nearly as much oil as Saudi Arabia, and Denmark produces nearly as much as Iran. The Nordic countries top the world rankings for several other resources, like geothermal, timber, and mining. Norway's oil income has enabled it to amass a sovereign wealth fund of over $1 trillion ($200,000 per resident); just the investment income from that fund can defray a great deal of government spending even after Norway's oil income disappears.

But these factors do not go all the way to explaining how Nordic countries manage to do so well despite their relatively expansive governments. These countries excel in almost every measure of social well-being: per capita GDP, living standards, education, government transparency, and so on. Figure 10.5 suggests an explanation for this. The Nordic countries occupy the back row of the chart—that is, their ethnic fractionalization is extremely low: they are among the most homogeneous nations in the world.

Even staunch free market advocates might acknowledge that socialism can succeed in small, tightly integrated groups—for example, individual families or clans—in which externalities are internalized. Theoretically, socialism works perfectly well when every individual views the group's interests as confluent with his own. But the less a country is like a family, the less likely that is to occur and the more difficult it is to make socialism work. So, it is no surprise that less fractionalized nations (e.g., the Nordic countries) have the most success with socialist policies. Scandinavian researchers attribute their region's success to what they call "Nordic gold" —their countries' high level of "social trust" or, in other words, "asabiyah." Studies show a sharp decline of social trust in the Nordic countries following the recent surge of refugees and immigrants.[40]

One of the ironies of contemporary politics is that advocates of Democratic Socialism also tend to favor hard multiculturalism, which promotes ethnic division. Socialist policies have some chance of working in homogeneous countries. But, as figure 10.5 and the statistics in appendix B clearly show, the combination of coercive big government and ethnic division is highly correlated with extreme poverty and wretched living standards.

Is Diversity Bad?

In Western Europe and North America, the cause of "diversity" garners religious-like support. "Celebrate Diversity" flags and bumper stickers abound; most major corporations sport "chief diversity officers" and most universities have "deans of diversity." There is now an entire "diversity industry" valued in the billions.

Yet the data in appendix B suggest that ethnic diversity is strongly correlated with extensive violence, rampant corruption, poor economic growth, and abysmal living standards. A more subjective look around the world seems to confirm this. Ask anyone: "In which countries do people behave most honestly and treat each other most decently?" "In which countries are people happiest?" The answers inevitably include countries like Finland, Denmark, and Norway—some of the most homogeneous countries in the world. Table 10.2 shows a selection of the UN's "World happiness" rankings, which reflect a variety of social measures along with respondents' ratings of their own lives.

Table 10.2 "World happiness" rankings for select countries[41]

Happiness ranking	Country	Ethnic fractionalization
1	Finland	0.17
2	Denmark	0.16
3	Norway	0.18
4	Iceland	0.08
19	United States	0.37
141	Liberia	0.91

Could the diversity advocates have it all wrong? A central contention of this book is that they are not wrong—at least when it comes to the positive aspects of diversity. Throughout history, the interchange and intermingling of diverse cultures have initiated the greatest epochs of economic, technological, and artistic efflorescence. For example, the golden age of Islam was fostered by conjoining the genius of Arab, Byzantine, and Persian cultures; the Renaissance was spurred by Byzantine scholars migrating to Italy and traders bringing ideas and technology from Asia.

We cannot insouciantly ignore data that show diversity is associated with severe challenges, however; diverse societies frequently fail to support public goods, generate economic growth, and avert corruption and violence. But we must note that these challenges stem not from diversity itself but from ethnic division. The problem is not people's diverse origins but rather the invidious promotion of group distinctions and divisions and the failure to encourage unity and any sense of shared identity.

As noted earlier in this chapter, ethnic fractionalization statistics capture group division by self-identification rather than origin. Countries can influence whether groups with diverse origins will remain divided. Byzantium's Blues and Greens and the Robbers Cave experiments demonstrated that it is possible to create stark division where none formerly existed; but they also showed that people can overcome divisions that once seemed insuperable. This was confirmed in the history of Rome and the early Islamic state: embracing diversity gave those societies resilience and vigor. But they tempered that diversity with a common, shared identity that helped them avoid division and its harmful effects. For most of its history, the United States has also followed this paradigm, drawing in wildly diverse immigrants who have contributed the richness of their cultures in a fusion that has invigorated and strengthened the country. American diversity has been a great strength, one that is diminished only by disunity.

Summary and Conclusions

Avoiding violent ethnic conflict is the most obvious challenge facing multiethnic countries. However, as the data in appendix B show, there are many other serious challenges. Even the ethnically fractionalized countries that manage to avoid communal conflict tend to suffer from a host of other problems: lower living standards, poor economic infrastructure, limited political and economic freedom, pervasive corruption, oppressive government, shorter life expectancy, poor education, and so on. Statistical analyses clearly show that the more fractionalized a country is, the worse these problems are likely to be. The correlations between ethnic fractionalization and all the socioeconomic measures discussed in this chapter are amazingly robust. For most of them, the chances they are attributable to random variation are less than one in a million.

It makes sense that ethnic fractionalization and the associated lack of social cohesion influence living standards. What is surprising is how powerful the influence is—and how it becomes even more powerful when combined with measures of economic freedom. We began this chapter by observing how dramatically the happenstance of one's birthplace affects one's living standards. Our statistics show that an incredible 40 percent of that happenstance comes down to one variable: ethnic fractionalization. More incredibly, the combination of ethnic fractionalization and economic freedom explains 71 percent of the variation in per capita GDP and nearly as much of the variation in living standards. Put another way: if you had to blindly choose a country to live in, knowing only each country's level of economic freedom and ethnic fractionalization, you could confidently assure yourself of living in one of the nicest places in the world.

Although the correlations in appendix B do not conclusively prove that ethnic fractionalization "causes" lower living standards and so on, they do provide a solid basis for a working hypothesis. Ethnically fractionalized countries do worst at providing measures that require social cohesion and altruism—for example, transparent, nonoppressive government, rule of law, and public goods. The paucity of these measures, in turn, helps explain lower per capita GDP and living standards in these countries. Expansive government works poorly in multiethnic countries because it encourages the worst concomitants of interest group politics: corruption; battles over the nature and allocation of spending; coercive government; and demosclerosis. It also creates an environment that both fosters and empowers racial and ethnic discrimination.

Although the statistics paint a dire portrait of ethnic fractionalization, they also offer some hope. Among more fractionalized countries, peace and prosperity are exceedingly rare but attainable. The analysis here suggests that multiethnic countries can increase their chances for success by limiting government. While fractionalized countries may always fall short in providing public goods, they can do better by directing the productive energies of their constituent ethnic groups toward the win-win proposition of free commerce rather than the zero-sum game of contesting control of an outsized government. But the most salient solution to the vast array of problems multiethnic countries face is to diminish fractionalization by hastening the integration of disparate ethnic groups so that they share a sense of common identity. Not only does this reduce the chances of conflict; it helps a diverse society function more as a unified entity that internalizes the costs of public goods.

11

✷

CONCLUSION

Thirteen thousand years ago, two disparate groups of people settled in the Jebel Sahaba area near the northern Sudan border. Most likely, they were driven together by climate change. As the Ice Age receded, many of the food and water sources in the region disappeared, so the human population consolidated into the areas where those resources could still be found. After the groups were driven together, they did what differentiated groups who compete for resources have done throughout history: they fought each other. And, as the archaeological evidence shows, they fought frequently and savagely. More than half the skeletons excavated from the area bore fragments and injuries from stone weapons. While some of the injuries were probably fatal, many had healed, suggesting that the conflict raged for a long time. Like the modern conflicts discussed in this book, this ancient conflict involved groups trying to annihilate each other completely: victims included children under the age of five.[1] It is humanity's first recorded example of attempted ethnic cleansing.

At some point—perhaps around the same time or centuries later—other neighboring groups of humans decided that instead of trying to eradicate each other, they would meld into unified communities. This enabled them to avoid destructive intergroup conflict and it diminished the threat of attack from outsiders. As Ibn Khaldun describes it, this is how larger civilized societies emerged: groups fostered a shared sense of cohesion—of asabiyah—and became more peaceful, capable, and resilient because of it. The more broadly they extended and maintained this asabiyah, the more successful they were.

Although Ibn Khaldun may have been the first to theorize extensively about how a unifying, shared identity is essential to a successful society, the idea is as old as history. In the Bible's Tower of Babel story, it is what made mankind most powerful:

> And God said, behold, they are one people, and they all have one language . . . now nothing that they plan to do will be restricted from them.[2]

Of all the possible means to debilitate overly capable humanity, the all-knowing God chose multiculturalism. He splintered humans into diverse groups, rendering them ineffectual and incapable of shared enterprise.

The Tower of Babel theme is not limited to the Judeo-Christian tradition: it can be found in mythologies around the globe—for example, in an antedated Sumerian epic (*Enmerkar and the Lord of Aratta*), in ancient Mesoamerican legends, and in Karen and Polynesian traditions.[3] The broader theme that group division weakens a society pervades ancient classics. Homer, for example, asserted that Trojan forces were weak because of their ethnic fractionalization:

> But the clamour of the Trojan ranks was as that of many thousand ewes . . . for they had not one speech nor language, but their tongues were diverse, and they came from many different places.[4]

He contrasts the ethnically fractionalized Trojan force with the Achaeans, who also originated from different places—Sparta, Mycenae, Argos, Ithaca—but were unified like a flock of birds.[5]

Beginning in the fifth century BCE, Roman leaders like Camillus asserted that their society's success relied on integrating everyone in the Roman domain with a unifying sense of Romanitas. Social philosophers like Aelius Aristides observed that societies failing to integrate in this way were weak, with their governments distracted and impaired by internecine division. Islam, from its beginning, also focused on forming a single unified community—the ummah—that embraces peoples with very diverse origins. This focus continued with medieval historians like Ibn Khaldun and Katib Çelebi and would ultimately be advanced by modern Americans like Ralph Waldo Emerson and Israel Zangwill.

Against this millennia-spanning global backdrop, the multiculturalist supposition that ethnic fractionalization is not only acceptable but actually desirable seems eccentric and weird. If there are any cross-cultural verities—truths shared broadly by cultures around the world over time—one is that fractionalization destroys societies. Yet, 130 centuries after the Jebel Sahaba groups sought to eradicate each other because they were differentiated and pitted against each other in a competition for resources, modern multiculturalists suggest that we should maintain group preferences that differentiate people and pit them against each other in a competition for resources.

Melting Pot and Multiculturalism: Empirical Evidence

It may seem like an obvious truism that societies function better when they are unified—that dividing a community into groups is a terrible idea. Yet contemporary multiculturalists challenge that truism with their promotion of group distinctions. This book responds to that multiculturalist challenge, evaluating the melting pot and multiculturalist approaches against historical examples and statistical data.

The examples and the data are clear and compelling. Sociological experiments like the Robbers Cave study demonstrate that the mere act of identifying and distinguishing groups promotes zero-sum thinking and antagonistic behavior between them. The effect is even more profound when authorities grant privileges and preferences based on group membership rather than individual merit. The real-world evidence of this is extensive, going at least as far back as the Blues and Greens in sixth-century Byzantium. In more recent times, government support for group distinctions and preferential treatment has torn societies apart and has occasionally initiated genocide around the world, from Sri Lanka and Rwanda to the former Yugoslavia. This book has delved into only a few of these examples. There are many others—notably, the Soviet Union, India, Nigeria, and Malaysia—that have instituted group differentiation and group preferences with negative and often catastrophic results.

By contrast, melting pot societies—from ancient Rome to the early Islamic state to modern Botswana—which have sought to minimize group distinctions and forge a shared sense of identity, have typically enjoyed considerable harmony and overall success. It is no coincidence that Africa's three greatest success stories, Rwanda, Mauritius, and Botswana—countries that surpass OECD countries by many measures—all constitutionally forbid ethnic and racial discrimination, whether negative or "affirmative." Among these countries, Rwanda is a standout: with its terrible history of ethnic hatred and genocide, it has recently managed to achieve stunning success by reversing past identity politics, relentlessly suppressing group distinctions, and fostering a sense of shared national identity.

While historical case studies of multiethnic societies are instructive, the statistical data are even more compelling. They are particularly relevant for the United States, which does not face the immediate prospect of widespread ethnic violence. As chapter 10 clearly shows, ethnic violence is only one of the negative concomitants of ethnic fractionalization. Even fractionalized societies that avoid violence suffer a variety of social ills: more corruption, less democratic government, less political freedom, and diminished support for public goods like education. These societies are often also hampered by the inefficiency of ethnic spoils systems. Groups continually wrangle over the allocation of government resources, trying to assure their group gets its "fair share." The bottom-line effect is simply stunning: ethnic fractionalization "explains" 40 percent of the international variation in living standards. As a group, more fractionalized countries are vastly poorer than less fractionalized ones, with dramatically lower living standards.

These tragic statistics make intuitive sense: when a society maintains group distinctions, and particularly when it bolsters them with group preferences, people hunker down, adopting an "us versus them" outlook. Ultimately, that means citizens are less likely to make all the various civic contributions and sacrifices that people in more unified societies readily make. Why contribute to the broader community when group distinctions compel one to focus on one's own group? Group preferences also undermine universal standards of fairness; a system of preferences that offends many people's innate sense of fairness sets a paradigm for all sorts of other corruption. Sri Lanka's experience clearly demonstrates this: it went from being one of Asia's least corrupt countries to one of its most corrupt after it instituted group preferences. While the United States continues down the multiculturalist path, it might avoid Bosnia-style ethnic violence, but it may come to look progressively more like Brazil or Nigeria—countries where civic discourse is bitterly focused on group membership; ethnically concentrated gated communities abound; support for public goods is minimal; and corruption is rampant.

Past Realities and Future Pitfalls

In our survey of multiethnic countries through history and around the globe, distinct realities have emerged. Some of these realities, which are not all intuitively obvious, have particular relevance for the United States as it shifts toward multiculturalism; they are outlined below.

Social Unity Is Fragile

The Robbers Cave experiment and other sociological studies demonstrated how easily authorities can divide people into antagonistic groups. We have seen real-life examples of this around the world—for example, in the Ottoman millets, Bosnian "two schools under one roof," and Rwandan racial IDs. All of these measures enhanced group distinctions, fostering deep enmity and setting the stage for violent conflict.

America has adopted policies and attitudes that resemble these divisive measures in many ways. Although the United States does not have an official millet system, elite condemnation of "cultural appropriation" helps maintain group boundaries in much the same way. Like the millet system, the notion of cultural appropriation treats culture as a birthright. Under the millet system, individuals faced punishment for adopting the dress or manners of a millet other than their own. In contemporary America, people who adopt dress, manners, or cuisine from an ethnic group they are not born into face public condemnation for cultural appropriation.

Although America does not officially have "two schools under one roof" like Bosnia, many American universities provide separate orientation and commencement sessions for different ethnic groups, ethnic studies programs that draw participation mostly from the ethnicities being studied, and theme houses that are effectively limited to certain racial and ethnic groups.

Before the genocide in Rwanda, students had to stand up and announce their "race" on the first day of classes. Today many American schools have similar requirements. For example, Oregon's 2020 Social Science Standards call for each child to "identify the cultural characteristics of my group identity." And of course, college applicants are asked repeatedly to identify their race and ethnicity.

Ethnic Division Can Elicit Evil from Ordinary People

In researching this book, I visited many countries where extreme ethnic violence or genocide occurred. In each of these countries, I heard variations of the claim that "it wasn't bad people behaving normally; it was normal people behaving badly." In the former Yugoslavia, Rwanda, and Sri Lanka, in particular, innocent victims were murdered by neighbors, former classmates, and work colleagues. The staggering scale of low-tech slaughter required mass participation of hundreds of thousands of perpetrators —so many that these perpetrators have to be considered "normal" by virtue of the population percentage they constituted.

In all my research, I found nothing more disturbing than my interviews with Rwandan farmers who had each killed more people than serial killers like Ted Bundy. These interviews were disturbing not because these individuals were psychotic freaks like Bundy but because they were extremely ordinary. Their worlds revolved more around expectations of rainfall and market prices for their crops than pursuing some ethnic agenda. Yet, spurred by propaganda that emphasized the Tutsis' historical "privilege" and by RTLM's ethnic conspiracy theories, they took up machetes and hacked dozens of their neighbors to death.

As horrible as this is, it is not surprising. In chapter 2, we saw how official group preferences helped turn a trivial sports rivalry into murderous hatred. It takes little imagination to conceive how more tangible differences, enhanced by government recognition and preference programs, can generate even more terrible outcomes.

Divisive Ethnic Policies Make Everyone Worse Off

When I visited Rwanda, I asked Rwandans of various backgrounds whether they thought distinguishing people by race or ethnicity ever helped anyone in their country. There was complete unanimity on this point: after they got over pondering why anyone would ask such a naïve question, they made it very clear that distinguishing people by group made everyone—Hutu, Tutsi, Twa, and others—distinctly worse off. I got similar answers from Bosnians, Croatians, Kosovars, and North Macedonians. It would be risky to ask this question in Sri Lanka, but statistics provide the answer. After World War II, per capita income in Sri Lanka and Singapore was nearly identical. Sri Lanka enjoyed a tremendous advantage in natural resources. But after it abandoned its shared "link" language and adopted ethnically divisive policies, it was plagued by violent conflict and economic underperformance; today, one Singaporean earns more than seven Sri Lankans put together. All the group preferences devised to elevate Sinhalese brought down everyone in the country—Tamil, Sinhalese, and all the other groups alike.

Even if we exclude the obvious examples of countries with violent ethnic conflict, the answer is still clear. For instance, after fifty years of affirmative action, all groups in Malaysia are worse off than they might otherwise be. Ethnic Malays in Malaysia who received affirmative action for decades are much poorer than ethnic Malays in Singapore who never received it.

The United States has a terrible legacy of slavery and racism. To this day, black people and some other minority groups fare worse on every conceivable social measure: income, health, crime, and so on. Many Americans have the understandable and laudable impulse to make up for the past and to "do something about it." Yet the best motives do not always generate the best results. As experience amply demonstrates, a never-ending ethnic preference program that accentuates ethnic distinctions is likely to achieve the opposite of its intended results.

Ethnic Fractionalization and Big Government Are a Toxic Combination

The statistical analyses in chapter 10 and appendix B document how ethnic fractionalization is associated with poor social and economic outcomes. But perhaps even more strikingly, they highlight how big government compounds the negative effects of fractionalization. Highly fractionalized countries with big governments and limited economic freedom fare abysmally, always and everywhere; they are the most wretched places on Earth.

Intuitively, this makes sense: many of the negative effects of fractionalization—for example, corruption and misallocation of resources—exert themselves through government. The larger and more intrusive the government is, the more these effects are propagated. Moreover, when a country lacks a sense of cohesion and is divided into groups, the groups are likely to grapple to control as much of the government as possible. The more expansive the government is, the higher the stakes will be in this contest and the more intense and destructive it will be. Each group will use whatever government power it does acquire to press its advantage and allocate resources in its favor, causing nasty political struggles and inefficiencies that diminish overall public welfare.

Countries like Sri Lanka best exemplify this reality: its democratic tradition, pleasant climate, and abundant natural resources should have made it one of nicest places in the world. But the combination of socialism and multiculturalism has spawned terrible misallocation of resources, rampant corruption, and a wrenching, destructive contest for political power, which has made it one of the most miserable places in the world.

Unfortunately, many contemporary American elites favor precisely the policy blend of multiculturalism and big government that has proved so devastating in countries like Sri Lanka.

Group Preferences Favor Powerful Elites Over the Needy

Rwanda had decades of group preferences, first favoring Tutsis and then Hutus. Yet, the overall income difference between the two groups barely shifted during that time. The biggest gains in position and wealth accrued mostly to a tiny elite minority within each group. This pattern was duplicated in Sri Lanka: the biggest affirmative action beneficiaries were not the poor, but aristocratic Kandyan Sinhalese, many of whom were vastly wealthier than both other Sinhalese and their disfavored Tamil neighbors. The same phenomenon has occurred in other countries like India, where affirmative action beneficiaries are often richer than members of nonpreferred groups. The inescapable political reality is that an ethnic spoils system tends to favor the most politically connected elites, who can steer the spoils to themselves.

Group Preferences Are Forever

In his 1990 monograph, *Preferential Policies*, Thomas Sowell observed the tendency of group preferences to last indefinitely, noting that countries like India and Malaysia had affirmative action programs that were already decades old. Nearly all preference programs are proposed as temporary measures to address past disparities, but they quickly become perpetual entitlements. As with most government-granted entitlements, their beneficiaries tend to maintain that they are forever necessary and lobby energetically to maintain them. In India's case, group preferences have not declined, but expanded, over seven decades. In some regions, like Andhra Pradesh, half of all government jobs and university seats are now "reserved" for preferred groups. More than half the entire Indian population is eligible for some sort of group preference.[6]

Thirty years after *Preferential Policies* was published, Sowell's prediction of never-ending group preference programs has proved true. There are just two notable exceptions where these programs did actually end: the former Yugoslavia and Rwanda. In both cases, they ended with genocide.

Preferences Have Invidious Effects on Their Beneficiaries

One might expect beneficiaries of ethnic preferences to shed feelings of resentment toward the people at whose expense the benefits are granted. Yet precisely the opposite has occurred around the world. In Sri Lanka, the big Sinhalese attacks on Tamils did not begin until after group preferences were implemented and the Tamil advantages in education and government employment had already been erased. Similarly, in Rwanda, Hutus initiated the genocide only after they had enjoyed years of preferences at the Tutsis' expense. Ethnic violence tends to arise not from ethnic disparities themselves but from implementing measures to correct them. The Thai experience demonstrates this: although the Chinese minority in Thailand is wealthier and better educated than the ethnic Thai majority, there are no ethnic preference programs to eliminate this disparity. As a result, Thailand has enjoyed tremendous communal harmony between the groups.

Preferences directly foster "us versus them" attitudes. But they also indirectly poison ethnic relations by spawning "ethnic conspiracy theories." An easy and common way for the beneficiaries of preferences to perpetuate them is to concoct ethnic conspiracy theories that claim the other group is acting nefariously to maintain their privilege. The pernicious side effect of such conspiracy theories is that they demonize the other group and set the stage for violence. So, for example, Sinhalese race-baiters in Sri Lanka claimed that Tamil teachers illicitly changed standardized test scores to give Tamil students an advantage; this both bolstered support for more affirmative action and spurred attacks against the Tamils. Prior to the Rwandan genocide, RTLM radio broadcast nonstop conspiracy theories about Tutsi "cockroaches" who enjoyed unfair privileges over the Hutus. Today, ethnic conspiracy theories can be found nearly anywhere group preferences are implemented. After decades of group preferences in Malaysia, anti-Chinese conspiracy theories are more pervasive than ever, spurring attacks on the Chinese minority.

The *New York Times*'s "1619 Project" exemplifies the ethnic conspiracy theory. By presenting a tendentious, divisive history and asserting that the United States is irredeemably racist and that white Americans tenaciously maintain unfair privilege, it justifies indefinitely continuing policies that distinguish people on the basis of race. In the process, it sows dangerously corrosive ethnic division.

Ethnic Opportunists Imperil Multiethnic Societies

One common factor in the terrible ethnic conflicts discussed in this book is the "ethnic opportunist," a leader who profits from fomenting ethnic antagonism and pitting groups against each other. Some of these individuals, like Slobodan Milošević in the former Yugoslavia, may have believed in their own invidious rhetoric; others, like Kayibanda in Rwanda and Bandaranaike in Sri Lanka, cynically stoked ethnic hatred only because it advanced their own fortunes. Either way, these individuals played critical roles in dividing their societies and spurring genocide. Without their efforts, their countries might have evaded genocide and possibly avoided violent conflict altogether.

It might be too glib to suggest that some current public figures are the American counterparts of Milošević and Bandaranaike. It is true that some of these people profit enormously from promoting ethnic division. For example, one celebrity academic garners nearly $800,000 a year for speeches claiming that even "progressive white people perpetuate racial harm."[7] But the challenge for America is both subtler and more intractable than that posed by a handful of prominent ethnic opportunists. Embedded in public and private institutions across America, from government agencies to universities, to private companies, are departments and organizations with names like "Diversity, Equity, and Inclusion" (DEI). They constitute a multibillion-dollar industry, employing thousands of people. By their very profession, the people who staff these organizations are positioned as ethnic opportunists. In a unified society that values people based on the "content of their character" rather than the "color of their skin," there would be no need for DEI departments. So, those departments have a vested institutional interest in forever maintaining that our society is nowhere near that point—or perhaps that it never should be. Like most bureaucrats, DEI employees are unlikely to ever declare "mission accomplished," clear out their desks, and seek employment in more productive lines of work. Instead, they will forever maintain that there is an institutional racist conspiracy lurking around the corner. If there are no overt incidents of racism or bias, then they will conjure up "micro-aggressions" to be combated. Eventually, they might progress to nano- or pico-aggressions. But the mission will never be accomplished; the only accomplishment will be that many Americans will be taught that their fellow citizens are irredeemably racist, perpetuating group division and distrust.

Final Thoughts

After considering the terrible consequences of ethnic divisions in countries like Bosnia and Sri Lanka, it is disheartening to see Americans advance the same types of policies and rhetoric that promoted and toxified those divisions. America has a regrettable past of racial and ethnic discrimination, but if the examples in this book teach anything, it is that the solution to past segregation is not even more segregation. The answer to past racial discrimination is not even more racial discrimination. Two African countries demonstrate this best.

While it was a British protectorate, Botswana endured extensive white racism. Yet it managed to recover quickly to become one of the developing world's outstanding success stories. It achieved this not with compensatory preferences and racial payback but by completely eliminating racial and ethnic distinctions and by fostering botho, the Batswana version of asabiyah. It also followed the melting pot model, which has repeatedly demonstrated its effectiveness since the time of ancient Rome.

In proportional terms, Rwanda's genocide stands out as one of the worst racist crimes of all time. Although the genocide occurred only a few decades ago, Rwanda has managed to recover spectacularly from it. Like Botswana, Rwanda accomplished this by "erasing race" and adopting the melting pot model. Rather than instituting ethnic preferences like affirmative action, it outlawed racial and ethnic distinctions altogether. Rather than dividing people into groups, it has sought to unify them with institutions like umuganda. Rather than brooding on past injustices, it has cultivated the shared asabiyah lauded by Ibn Khaldun.

The path taken by Botswana and Rwanda lies open to America. It starts with resolute and unwavering commitments to principles like those made by Israel Zangwill in *The Melting Pot* and by the children in Rwanda's Nyange school:

> There are no groups. We are all Americans.

APPENDIX A

THE CONSTITUTION OF MEDINA

This appendix provides my translation and analysis of the Constitution of Medina. The most complete Arabic versions of the document are provided in Abu Ubayd's *Kitab al-Amwal* and Ibn Ishaq's *Sira Rasul Allah* (as redacted in Ibn Hisham's *Sira al-Nabiwiyya*).[1] Other early chroniclers and hadith compilers provide scattered fragments of it. This appendix uses Ibn Ishaq's version because it is the earliest and most complete.[2]

The constitution's language is probably the most compelling reason to consider it authentic. It contains several archaic expressions that are found only in very early Arabic sources.[3] Medieval Arab scholars were as puzzled by some of these expressions as we are today. The constitution also contains several conventions that are used in the Qur'an but are rare in documents of later provenance. For example, it uses Yathrib instead of Medina.[4] Even the modern scholars who have been most skeptical about early Islamic sources tend to recognize that the Constitution of Medina is authentic and relatively faithful to an actual historical document.

The most controversial aspect of the constitution is its inclusion of both Muslims and non-Muslims in Medina in an *ummah wahida*—a single community. The preamble and article 1 of the constitution state that the "believers and Muslims of Quraysh and Yathrib and those who followed them and joined them and fought holy war along with them" are a "single community" (ummah wahida). This community had to include the Jews since other articles of the constitution describe the Jews as joining the Muslims and fighting war alongside them (e.g., articles 24 and 38).[5] The membership of individual Jewish groups in the ummah is reiterated in articles 25–37.

Text of the Constitution

Following is a translation of the Constitution of Medina, as provided in Ibn Ishaq's *Sira*.

> Ibn Ishaq said: Muhammad, Messenger of God (SAW),[6] wrote a document between the Muhajirun [emigrants from Mecca] and the Ansar [the Medinese "helpers"], making an agreement in it with the Jews, assuring and securing them in their religion, and their property duties and rights:
>
> In the name of God, the Merciful, the Compassionate. This is a document of Muhammad, the prophet, between the believers and Muslims of Quraysh and Yathrib and those who follow them and join them and fight holy war along with them.

1. They are a unified community [*ummah wahida*] to the exclusion of others.
2. The emigrants [*Muhajirun*] of Quraysh, according to their custom, pay blood-money among themselves and ransom their captives with equity and fairness among believers.
3. Banu Awf, according to their custom, pay blood money among themselves and ransom their captives with justice and equity among believers.

4–10. Banu al-Harith, Banu Saidah, Banu Jusham, Banu an-Najjar, Banu Amr b. Awf, Banu an-Nabit, Banu al-Aws... [same as Banu Awf].

11. The believers will not abandon a person who has no tribal protection [*mufrih*] among them but will give him what is equitable in payment of ransom or blood money.

12. A believer will not ally with the client of a[nother] believer to his detriment.[7]

13. The God-fearing believers are against one who has committed injustice among them or sought to commit an act of oppression, crime, enmity, or iniquity among the believers; their hands are all against him even if he is the son of one of them.

14. A believer may not kill another believer on the behalf of an unbeliever [*kafir*] and may not help an unbeliever against a believer.

15. The protection of God is one; the neighborly protection granted by the least of them [i.e., the believers] is binding for all of them; the believers are the clients of each other to the exclusion of others.

16. Those of the Jews who follow us will receive assistance and equality; they will not be oppressed, and their enemies will not be assisted.

17. The peace of the believers is unified; a believer may not make peace without the consent of other believers in fighting in the cause of God, except in equality and justice among them.

18. In every raid undertaken with us, the raiders will take turns.[8]

19. The believers will avenge one another when one has given his blood in the cause of God.

20. The God-fearing believers are under the best and most upright guidance. A polytheist [*mushrik*] may not give

protection to a person or property of Quraysh, nor intervene in his [the Qurayshi's] favor against a believer.

21. If anyone unjustly kills a believer and there is clear evidence, he will be killed in retaliation unless the slain one's kin are satisfied with blood money. The believers are, in their entirety, against him [the killer] and nothing is permitted to them except to act against him.
22. A believer who adheres to what is in this document and believes in God and the Last Day is not permitted to help a murderer [*muhaddith*] or give him shelter.[9] He who supports or shelters him incurs the curse of God and his wrath on the Day of Resurrection, and neither repentance nor ransom will be accepted from him.
23. Whatever you differ about should be referred to God and Muhammad (SAW).
24. The Jews pay expenses with the believers as long as they wage war [together].
25. The Jews of Banu Awf are a community [*ummah*] with the believers.[10] The Jews have their religious observance [*din*] and the Muslims have theirs, [along with] themselves and their clients, except anyone who has done wrong or committed treachery; he harms only himself and the people of his house.

26–30. To the Jews of Banu an-Najjar, the Jews of Banu al-Harith, the Jews of Banu Saidah, the Jews of Banu Jusham, the Jews of Banu al-Aws... the like of what is for the Jews of Banu Awf.

31. To the Jews of Banu Thalabah the like of what is for the Jews of Banu Awf, except anyone who has done wrong or committed treachery; he harms only himself and the people of his house. Righteousness is to the detriment of treachery.
32. Jafnah, a clan of Thalabah, are like them.

33. To Banu Shutaybah the like of what is for the Jews of Banu Awf.
34. The clients of Thalabah are like them.
35. The close friends [*bitanah*] of Jews are like them.
36. No one of them [the Jews] may go out except with the permission of Muhammad (SAW), but he is not prevented from taking revenge for injuries.[11] Whoever murders [another] without warning, does so to himself and the people of his house, except if someone has wronged him. God is most accepting of this.
37. It is for the Jews to pay their expenses and the Muslims to pay their expenses. Between them is assistance against whoever attacks the people of this document. Between them is honor and friendship. Righteousness is to the detriment of treachery. No one is culpable for the treachery of his ally. Assistance goes to the wronged.
38. The Jews pay expenses with the believers as long as they wage war [together].
39. The valley of Yathrib is a sanctuary [*haram*] for the people of this document.
40. The protected neighbor is as him [the protector], as long as he does no harm or treachery.
41. No woman may be given neighborly protection, except with the permission of her people.
42. If there is, among the people of this document any dispute or disturbance from which trouble is feared, it must be referred to God and to Muhammad (SAW). God accepts what is most pious in this document.
43. Neighborly protection to the Quraysh and those who help them may not be given.
44. Among them [the Jews] is assistance against whoever attacks Yathrib.

45. If they [the Jews] are called to make peace and conclude it, they must make it and conclude it. If the believers are called similarly, they must do so except those who make war for religion. Everyone has his share from his side.
46. The Jews of al-Aws, their clients and themselves, have the same conditions as the people of this document with the pure honesty of the people of this document. Righteousness is to the detriment of treachery.
47. A guilty person brings guilt only upon himself. God accepts what is most pious in this document. This document [*kitab*] does not protect the wrongdoer or treacherous one. The one who goes out is safe and the one who stays is safe in the city, except he who commits wrongdoing or treachery. God is the protector of the honest and pious and Muhammad is the Messenger of God (SAW).

APPENDIX B

STATISTICAL ANALYSES

This appendix provides statistical data and analyses referenced in chapter 10, focusing on correlations of ethnic fractionalization and other socioeconomic measures.

Ethnic Fractionalization (EF and ELF)

Ethnic fractionalization (EF) specifies the probability that two individuals randomly chosen from a country's population will be from different ethnic groups. A high EF number indicates that a country is fractionalized; a low number indicates it is homogeneous. Mathematically, EF is defined as follows:

$$EF = 1 - \sum_{i=1}^{I} \left(\frac{n_i}{N}\right)^2, \mathrm{i} = 1, \ldots, \mathrm{I}$$

where n_i is the population of the *ith* ethnic group, N is the country's total population, and I is the total number of groups.

The EF measure used in this book is based primarily on *CIA World Factbook* data, averaging 1998–2018 numbers. The CIA dataset fails to give precise numbers for some countries or omits them entirely; so it has been supplemented with US Census

Bureau and *Encyclopedia Britannica* data. A twenty-year average is used to account for the socioeconomic effects of fractionalization being spread over time.

Ethnolinguistic fractionalization (ELF) is an alternate measure of fractionalization, calculated in the same way as EF, but based primarily on linguistic (rather than ethnic) population data. EF and ELF correlate very strongly with each other. However, EF is more useful for the study of ethnic relations because ELF does not accurately reflect the fractionalization of countries in which ethnic groups are divided along religious or racial lines. For example, ELF figures for Lebanon and Burundi are extremely low, even though both countries are clearly fractionalized, with the former divided by religion (Shi'i and Sunni Muslim; Druze; and Maronite) and the latter by historical groupings (Hutu, Tutsi, and Twa).

The table below lists some commonly used measures of ethnic and ethnolinguistic fractionalization.

Table B.1 Fractionalization measures

Measure	Description
EF (used in this book)	Calculated from averages of 1998–2018 *CIA World Factbook* ethnic data, with omissions filled with US Census Bureau and *Encyclopedia Britannica* data.[1]
Alesina EF	Compiled by Alberto Alesina et al., primarily from *Encyclopedia Britannica* (2001) and CIA (2000) ethnic statistics.[2]
Britannica EF	Calculated from *Encyclopedia Britannica* (2020) ethnic statistics.[3]
CREG EF	Compiled from the Composition of Religious and Ethnic Groups (CREG) project's (University of Illinois Champaign-Urbana) 2013 dataset of "principal ethnic groups."[4]
Easterly ELF	Originally provided in a 1997 journal article by Easterly and Levine. Their ELF index is based on an average derived from several linguistic surveys.[5]
Ethnologue ELF	Calculated as an average of 2000–2020 linguistic data provided by the Summer Institute of Language's Ethnologue project.[6]
Fearon EF	Calculated from *CIA World Factbook* data. Fearon applied judgment and several supplementary sources to determine significant ethnic groups.[7]

The table below provides Pearson correlation coefficients for the different fractionalization measures. All measures are significantly correlated, with EF showing the strongest average correlation with the other measures.

Table B.2 Correlations of fractionalization measures

	EF	Alesina EF	Britannica EF	CREG EF	Easterly ELF	Ethnologue ELF
Alesina EF	0.821*					
Britannica EF	0.898*	0.757*				
CREG EF	0.857*	0.791*	0.835*			
Easterly ELF	0.794*	0.728*	0.790*	0.842*		
Ethnologue ELF	0.734*	0.711*	0.691*	0.724*	0.865*	
Fearon EF	0.844*	0.852*	0.782*	0.810*	0.785*	0.738*

* Correlation is significant at the 0.001 level (2-tailed).

Country Selection

This book's ethnic fractionalization dataset excludes countries with populations smaller than two million because socioeconomic data is not available for many of them and because many (e.g., San Marino, Palau, and the Vatican) are only quasi-independent. Because these countries are quasi-independent and extremely small, their socioeconomic outcomes may not reflect their own policies and fractionalization levels but rather those of the countries surrounding them.

Description of the Variables

The following sections describe the variables used in the statistical analyses in this appendix. Alternate variable names are in parentheses.

Independent Variables

Table B.3 Description of independent variables

Variable	Description
Ethnic fractionalization (EF)	EF indicates the level of ethnic fractionalization within a country. It specifies the probability that two individuals randomly chosen from the country's population will be from different ethnic groups. A high EF number indicates that a country is fractionalized; a low number indicates it is homogeneous. Calculated from averages of 1998–2018 *CIA World Factbook* ethnic data, with omissions filled with US Census Bureau and *Encyclopedia Britannica* data.
Economic Freedom Index	A 2020 index compiled by the *Wall Street Journal* and the Heritage Foundation. It is based on ratings in four categories: Rule of law (property rights, government integrity, judicial effectiveness); government size (government spending, tax burden, fiscal health); regulatory efficiency (business freedom, labor freedom, monetary freedom); open markets (trade freedom, investment freedom, financial freedom). The data and methodology are available at https://www.heritage.org/index/.

Dependent Variables

Table B.4 Description of dependent variables

Variable	Description
Control of Corruption Index	A 2019 index, combining up to twenty-three different assessments and surveys on government corruption, including data from the World Bank, the Economist Intelligence Unit's *Country Risk Service*, and others. It is available at https://info.worldbank.org/governance/wgi/Home/Reports.
Corruption Perceptions Index (CPI)	A 2019 index compiled by Transparency International that scores and ranks countries based on the level of corruption in the public sector, as perceived by experts and business executives. It is a composite of thirteen surveys and assessments of corruption and is the most widely used indicator of corruption worldwide. It is available at https://www.transparency.org/en/cpi/2019/results.
Economist Democratic Government Index	A 2019 index compiled by the Economist Intelligence Unit (EIU) based on sixty indicators grouped in five different categories, measuring pluralism, civil liberties and political culture. In addition to a numeric score and a ranking, the index categorizes each country in one of four regime types: full democracies, flawed democracies, hybrid regimes and authoritarian regimes. It is published at http://www.eiu.com/.
Ethnic conflict deaths	Deaths per 10,000 population from ethnic conflicts 1960–2020, compiled primarily from the *Correlates of War Project*, published by the Inter-University Consortium for Political and Social Research, available at https://correlatesofwar.org/data-sets. Supplementary sources are noted within table B.20.
Government Integrity Index	A 2020 index from the Heritage Foundation measuring corruption, based on data from the Economist Intelligence Unit, US Department of Commerce, and Transparency International. The index is available at https://www.heritage.org/index/.

Table B.4 Description of dependent variables	
Variable	**Description**
Human Development Index (HDI)	A 2019 index from the UN Development Program that is a "summary measure of average achievement in key dimensions of human development: a long and healthy life, being knowledgeable and have a decent standard of living." It is available at http://hdr.undp.org/en/data.
Human Flight and Brain Drain Indicator	Published by the Fund for Peace, the Human Flight and Brain Drain Indicator considers the economic impact of human displacement (for economic or political reasons) and the consequences this may have on a country's development. The higher the index, the greater the human displacement. The data, from 2020, are available at https://fragilestatesindex.org/.
Human Freedom Index	A 2019 index published by the Fraser Institute, which presents the state of human freedom in the world based on a broad measure that encompasses personal, civil, and economic freedom. It is available at http://www.fraserinstitute.org/studies/human-freedom-index.
Human Rights Index	Published by the Fund for Peace, the index "looks at whether there is widespread abuse of legal, political, and social rights, including those of individuals, groups and institutions (e.g., harassment of the press, politicization of the judiciary, internal use of the military for political ends, repression of political opponents)." The data from 2020 are available at https://fragilestatesindex.org/.
Infant mortality (log of deaths per 1,000)	Infant deaths per 1,000 live births (Log). 2019 data from UN Interagency Group for Child Mortality Estimation. Data are available at https://childmortality.org/data.
Infants without measles vaccine	2018 percentage of children not receiving measles vaccines. Based on UNICEF data available at http://hdr.undp.org/en/data.
Literacy	Percentage of people ages fifteen and above who can "read and write with understanding a short, simple statement about their everyday life." 2018 data from UNESCO is available at http://uis.unesco.org/en/topic/literacy.
Mean years of school	Mean years of schooling for adults aged twenty-five. 2017–18 data from UNDP, available at http://hdr.undp.org/en/data.
Per capita GDP (log)	Per capita GDP in Purchasing Power Parity (PPP) US dollars. PPP US dollars account for lower living costs in less developed countries. The data are from the World Bank's 2018 dataset, available at https://data.worldbank.org/indicator/NY.GDP.PCAP.PP.CD.
Phone lines per 100 (log)	Fixed line phones per hundred workers, compiled in 2018 by the International Telecommunication Union (ITU). Data are available at https://www.itu.int/.
PISA scores	International math test scores for fourth-grade students in seventy-nine countries in 2018. Data are available at https://www.oecd.org/pisa/data/.
Population density	Population density (people per square kilometer of land area). 2018 data available from the World Bank at https://data.worldbank.org/indicator/EN.POP.DNST.

Table B.4 Description of dependent variables	
Variable	**Description**
Public Services Index	Published by the Fund for Peace, the Public Services Index "refers to the presence of basic state functions that serve the people. On the one hand, this may include the provision of essential services, such as health, education, water and sanitation, transport infrastructure, electricity and power, and internet and connectivity. On the other hand, it may include the state's ability to protect its citizens, such as from terrorism and violence, through perceived effective policing." The data from 2020 are available at https://fragilestatesindex.org/.
Secondary education spending (% GDP)	Current education expenditure on secondary education (as a percent of GDP), from the UNESCO 2018 dataset, available at http://uis.unesco.org/.
TIMSS math scores	Average scores from standardized math tests administered by Trends in International Math and Science in 2015 to students in forty-nine countries. Data are available at https://timssandpirls.bc.edu/.

Descriptive Statistics

The table below provides descriptive statistics for the variables described above.

Table B.5 Descriptive statistics

Variable	N	Min.	Max.	Mean	Median	SD	Type of measure
Control of Corruption Index	146	-1.80	2.21	-0.17	-0.44	1.02	Index, scaled -2.5 to 2.5. Higher values indicate less corruption
Corruption Perceptions Index (CPI)	146	9.00	87.00	42.02	37.00	19.25	Index, scaled 0–100, with higher values indicating more transparency (less corruption)
Economic freedom	141	4.20	89.40	61.61	61.60	11.95	Index, scaled, 0–100, with higher numbers indicating more economic freedom
Economist Democratic Government Index	145	1.08	9.87	5.37	5.50	2.23	Index, scaled 0–10 with higher numbers indicating more democratic government
Ethnic conflict deaths	146	0	762	17.07	0	76.64	Number per 10,000 population
Ethnic fractionalization (EF)	146	0.00	0.99	0.45	0.41	0.25	Probability, scaled from 0 to 1, with 0 indicating no fractionalization and 1 indicating complete fractionalization
Government Integrity Index	146	13.1	96.10	43.90	37.7	22.2	Index, scaled 0–100, with higher values indicating greater government integrity (less corruption)

Table B.5 Descriptive statistics

Variable	N	Min.	Max.	Mean	Median	SD	Type of measure
Human Development Index (HDI)	143	0.38	0.95	0.71	0.73	0.16	Index, scaled 0–100, with higher values indicating better human development
Human Flight and Brain Drain Indicator	144	0.70	8.90	5.33	5.65	2.04	Index, scaled 0–10, with higher numbers indicating more human flight and brain drain
Human Freedom Index	139	3.79	8.88	6.82	6.77	1.14	Index, scaled 0–10 with higher numbers indicating greater human freedom
Human Rights Index	144	0.70	9.90	5.89	6.50	2.60	Index, scaled 0–10, with higher values indicating more human rights
Infant mortality (log of deaths per 1,000)	144	0.00	4.44	2.60	2.64	1.08	Log of deaths per 1,000 live births
Infants without measles vaccine	144	1.00	63.00	12.44	7.00	13.1	Number of children per 100 under 12 months without measles vaccine
Literacy	94	22.3	99.99	81.41	88.1	19.1	% of adults above age fifteen able to read
Mean years of school	142	1.47	14.08	8.46	8.71	3.23	Arithmetic mean
Per capita GDP (log)	139	6.66	11.50	9.34	9.48	1.22	Log of real PPP-adjusted $US
Phone lines per 100 (log)	132	-6.91	4.08	1.70	2.53	2.11	Number per 100 population
PISA Scores	66	334.30	578.70	455.83	467.15	54.1	Raw test score
Population density	143	2.04	7953.00	228.56	82.24	887.21	Number of people per square kilometer
Public Services Index	145	0	10	5.40	5.40	2.80	Index, scaled 0–10, with lower values indicating better public services
Secondary education spending (% GDP)	84	0.38	4.72	1.56	1.52	0.66	% of total GDP
TIMSS math scores	46	353.00	618.00	504.04	519.50	65.57	Raw test score, scaled between 0 and 1,000, with most falling between 300 and 600

Fractionalization and Per Capita GDP

The table below shows the results of an ordinary least squares regression of Ethnic fractionalization (EF) and the log of per capita GDP.

Table B.6 Ethnic fractionalization and per capita GDP

Dependent variable	Independent variable	Constant (t)	Unstandardized coefficient (t)	Adj. R^2 (N)
Per capita GDP	EF	10.671 (63.388)*	-2.975 (-9.017)*	0.368* (139)

* Significant at the 0.001 level.

Alternate Fractionalization Measures and GDP

The strong and significant correlation between fractionalization and per capita GDP applies not only with the EF measure used in this book but with all other commonly used fractionalization measures as well.

Table B.7 Alternate fractionalization measures and per capita GDP

Dependent variable	Independent variable	Constant (t)	Unstandardized coefficient (t)	Adj. R^2 ² (N)
Per capita GDP	Alesina EF	10.542 (59.433)*	-2.623 (-7.730)*	0.299* (139)
Per capita GDP	Britannica EF	10.645 (59.978)*	-2.811 (-8.180)*	0.328* (134)
Per capita GDP	CREG EF	10.317 (53.807)*	-2.141 (-5.821)*	0.198* (132)
Per capita GDP	Easterly ELF	10.164 (69.966)*	-2.396 (-7.452)*	0.335* (132)
Per capita GDP	Ethnologue ELF	10.181 (59.054)*	-1.815 (-5.757)*	0.189* (139)
Per capita GDP	Fearon EF	10.465 (56.886)*	-2.362 (-6.990)*	0.266* (131)

* Significant at the 0.001 level.

EF, Violent Ethnic Conflict, and GDP

The table below shows partial correlations of ethnic fractionalization and per capita GDP, with the effects of ethnic conflict deaths removed.

Table B.8 Partial correlations of EF, GDP, and conflict deaths			
Dependent variable	**Independent variable**	**Variable effects removed**	**R^2 (N)**
Per capita GDP	EF	None	0.368* (137)
Per capita GDP	EF	Ethnic conflict deaths	0.354* (137)
* Significant at the 0.001 level.			

The table below shows the correlation of ethnic fractionalization and per capita GDP among countries with no civil wars and less than one death per ten thousand inhabitants in ethnic conflicts (1960–2020).

Table B.9 EF and per capita GDP in no-conflict countries				
Dependent variable	**Independent variable**	**Constant (t)**	**Unstandardized coefficient (t)**	**Adj. R^2 (N)**
Per capita GDP	EF	10.818 (54.215)*	-2.845 (-6.558)*	0.326* (87)
* Significant at the 0.001 level.				

Living Standards (HDI)

The table below shows the correlation between ethnic fractionalization and living standards, as measured by the UNDP Human Development Index (HDI).

Table B.10 Living standards (HDI) and ethnic fractionalization

Dependent variable	Independent variable	Constant (t)	Unstandardized coefficient (t)	Adj. R^2 (N)
HDI	EF	0.890 (42.308)*	-0.404 (-9.804)*	0.401* (143)

* Significant at the 0.001 level.

Living Standards (HDI) and Alternate Fractionalization Measures

Like GDP, HDI correlates strongly and significantly not only with EF, but also most other common fractionalization measures. Table B.11 shows regressions of HDI against different fractionalization measures.

Table B.11 Alternate fractionalization measures and HDI

Dependent variable	Independent variable	Constant (t)	Unstandardized coefficient (t)	Adj. R^2 (N)
HDI	Alesina EF	0.880 (40.054)*	-0.370 (-8.853)*	0.354* (143)
HDI	Britannica EF	0.884 (38.822)*	-0.376 (-8.674)*	0.347* (143)
HDI	CREG EF	0.849 (35.419)*	-0.306 (-6.647)*	0.240* (141)
HDI	Easterly ELF	0.820 (44.443)*	-0.321 (-7.873)*	0.357* (113)
HDI	Ethnologue ELF	0.836 (39.397)*	-0.273 (-7.044)*	0.255* (139)
HDI	Fearon EF	0.861 (36.996)*	-0.319 (-7.457)*	0.286* (140)

* Significant at the 0.001 level.

Fractionalization, HDI, and Underlying Variables

The table below shows the correlation of EF and HDI with the effects of various underlying variables removed. Ethnic fractionalization's influence on HDI remains robust and highly significant, even after these variables are accounted for.

Table B.12 Partial correlations of EF, HDI, and underlying variables.			
Dependent variable	**Independent variable**	**Variable effects removed**	**R^2 ² (N)**
HDI	EF	None	0.401* (143)
HDI	EF	Ethnic conflict deaths	0.396* (143)
HDI	EF	Years of independence	0.356* (143)
HDI	EF	Population density	0.399* (143)
HDI	EF	Years of independence, population density	0.349* (143)
* Significant at the 0.001 level.			

Public Goods

The table below shows the association between EF and various measures of public goods. The Public Services Index is a broad index of public goods that comprises essential services such as: health; education; water and sanitation; transport infrastructure; electricity and power; internet and connectivity. It largely subsumes the other measures listed in the table.

Note that the Public Services Index, Infants without measles vaccines, and Infant mortality variables are all scaled negatively; higher values reflect worse outcomes. Ethnic fractionalization has a strong and significant correlation with all the measures. Overall, infants in more fractionalized countries are less likely to be vaccinated and more likely to die at birth.

Table B.13 Ethnic fractionalization and public goods				
Dependent variable	**Independent variable**	**Constant (t)**	**Unstandardized coefficient (t)**	**Adj. R^2 (N)**
Public Services Index	EF	2.440 (6.354)*	6.640 (8.822)*	0.348* (144)
Infants without measles vaccine	EF	0.751 (0.387)	26.229 (6.903)*	0.246* (144)
Infant mortality per 1,000 (log)	EF	1.406 (9.725)	2.679 (9.456)*	0.382* (144)
Phone lines per 100 workers (log)	EF	3.779 (11.997)*	-4.672 (-7.556)*	0.300* (131)
* Significant at the 0.001 level.				

Ethnic Fractionalization and Education

Education is one of the largest components of public goods expenditures in many countries. The table below shows correlations of ethnic fractionalization with various education measures.

Table B.14 Ethnic fractionalization and education

Dependent variable	Independent variable	Constant (t)	Unstandardized coefficient (t)	Adj. R^2 (N)
Secondary education spending (% GDP)	EF	1.984 (14.266)*	-0.959 (-3.517)**	0.131** (83)
Mean years of school	EF	11.770 (25.771)*	-7.422 (-8.291)*	0.325* (141)
Literacy	EF	100.329 (29.280)*	-42.471 (-6.386)*	0.300* (93)
PISA scores	EF	504.429 (42.238)*	-109.080 (-4.656)*	0.241* (65)
TIMSS math scores	EF	558.602 (32.729)*	-124.446 (-3.712)**	0.218** (45)

* Significant at the 0.001 level.
** Significant at the 0.01 level.

It is important to note that the PISA and TIMSS tests are administered primarily in countries that are both wealthier and substantially less fractionalized. For example, the countries reporting TIMSS scores have a median income of roughly $41,473, versus $13,090 for all the countries in our dataset and a median EF of 0.28, versus 0.41 for the whole dataset. Because of this, these correlations understate what the correlation between EF and test scores would be if the tests were administered more broadly.

Corruption

The table below shows the association between EF and various government corruption indices. All indices are scaled so that higher values indicate greater transparency (less corruption). The correlations all indicate that fractionalization is significantly associated with lower transparency (higher corruption).

Table B.15 Ethnic fractionalization and corruption				
Dependent variable	**Independent variable**	**Constant (t)**	**Unstandardized coefficient (t)**	**Adj. R^2 (N)**
Control of Corruption Index	EF	0.589 (3.750)*	-1.705 (-5.538)*	0.170* (146)
Corruption Perceptions Index	EF	56.399 (18.925)*	-32.270 (-5.525)*	0.169* (146)
Government Integrity Index	EF	62.943 (18.927)*	-42.743 (-6.558)*	0.225* (146)
* Significant at the 0.001 level.				

Fractionalization, Political Rights, Democracy, and Economic Freedom

The table below shows the association of ethnic fractionalization and various measures of civil rights and personal and economic freedom. Note that the Human Rights Index is scaled negatively (lower values indicate greater rights); whereas all the other indices are scaled positively (lower values indicate less democracy and freedom). Thus, the regressions indicate that greater fractionalization predicts diminished human freedom, human rights, democracy, and economic freedom.

Table B.16 Ethnic fractionalization, democracy, and freedom				
Dependent variable	**Independent variable**	**Constant (t)**	**Unstandardized coefficient (t)**	**Adj. R^2 (N)**
Human Freedom Index	EF	7.730 (43.536)*	-2.033 (-5.843)*	0.194* (146)
Human Rights Index	EF	4.064 (9.909)*	4.096 (5.097)*	0.149* (146)
Economist Democratic Government Index	EF	6.863 (19.461)*	-3.349 (-4.846)*	0.135* (146)
Economic Freedom Index	EF	69.222 (35.749)*	-17.078 (-4.500)*	0.127* (146)
* Significant at the 0.001 level.				

Predicting GDP and HDI with EF and Economic Freedom

The table below shows correlations between ethnic fractionalization, economic freedom, and GDP and HDI. The Economic Freedom Index, provided by the *Wall Street Journal* and the Heritage Foundation, is a very good predictor of per capita GDP and HDI by itself. However, when EF is added to the model, the combination is an excellent predictor, explaining over 71 percent of the variation in per capita GDP and 63 percent of the variation in HDI.

Table B.17 EF, Economic freedom, GDP, and HDI

	Independent variables unstandardized coefficients (t)			
Dependent variable	Ethnic fractionalization	Economic freedom	Constant	Adjusted R^2 (N)
Per capita GDP (log)		0.078 (13.811)*	4.546 (12.845)*	0.582* (141)
Per capita GDP (log)	-1.884 (-7.845)*	0.064 (12.731)*	6.250 (17.096)*	0.712* (141)
HDI		0.009 (10.778)*	0.157 (2.996)**	0.455* (141)
HDI	-0.287 (-8.194)*	0.007 (9.339)*	0.417 (7.804)*	0.632* (141)

* Significant at the 0.001 level.
** Significant at the 0.01 level.

Ethnic Fractionalization and "Brain Drain"

The best international measure for "brain drain"—professional and talented workers leaving a country—is the Human Flight and Brain Drain Index used in the table below. Ethnic fractionalization and economic freedom are good predictors of brain drain independently; combined, they are an excellent predictor.

Table B.18 EF, economic freedom, and brain drain				
	Independent variables unstandardized coefficients (t)			
Dependent variable	Ethnic fractionalization	Economic freedom	Constant	Adjusted R^2 (N)
Human Flight and Brain Drain Index	3.767 (6.203)*		3.650 (11.777)*	0.208* (144)
Human Flight and Brain Drain Index	2.453 (4.198)*	-0.077 (-6.308)*	8.977 (10.095)*	0.382* (141)
* Significant at the 0.001 level				

Exceptions That Prove the Rule

Among the twenty countries with the highest living standards, only five are more fractionalized than the United States, which is itself less fractionalized than the average country. Because these five countries are very consistent outliers in the regressions described in this appendix—that is, because they are more prosperous, less corrupt, and less prone to communal violence than other countries with similar levels of fractionalization—they merit closer examination.

The five countries (Belgium, Canada, Spain, Switzerland, and the United Kingdom) share a few obvious characteristics: their majority groups are Western European in origin; they are democratic; they have mostly free economies; and the cultural differences among their largest ethnic groups are relatively small. Perhaps their most significant distinguishing characteristic, however, is that they all have a large degree of "ethnic federalism." In each country, the largest minority groups are concentrated in distinct regions: for example, 91 percent of French Canadians live in the province of Quebec, and most German, French, and Italian Swiss live in cantons in which their ethnicities constitute super majorities.[8] The ethnic regions in all these countries enjoy substantial political autonomy and exercise many of the powers that national governments normally reserve for themselves. For example, the Swiss cantons establish their own criteria for citizenship and naturalization and can sign treaties with foreign governments; the ethnic regions of the United Kingdom (England, Scotland, and Wales) have long had independent judiciary systems and more recently acquired their own parliaments; and the Spanish "autonomous communities" can declare their own official languages. In Belgium, Spain, and Switzerland, the autonomy of the ethnic regions is constitutionally guaranteed.[9]

Simply put, Belgium, Canada, Spain, Switzerland, and the United Kingdom are exceptions that help establish the rule. They are not so much ethnically fractionalized countries as they are confederations of homogeneous, semi-autonomous states.[10] Without taking this fact into account, the correlations of ethnic fractionalization and the various social and economic measures described in this chapter are already strong and highly significant. Taking it into consideration (for example, by treating the semi-autonomous ethnic regions as separate countries) makes these correlations even stronger. It is also noteworthy that, to the extent that these countries have curtailed the independence of their ethnic regions, they have suffered some of the problems common in other multiethnic countries. Each country has been periodically distracted by ethnic factions struggling for greater independence. ETA in Spain, Parti Québécois in Canada, Belier Party (Jura separatists) in Switzerland, and the IRA in Northern Ireland have persistently clamored for greater self-determination. When frustrated, they have occasionally turned violent.

Data Tables

The table below lists key variable values for countries with populations over two million. Variables not listed below are available at the sources listed in tables B.3 and B.4.

Table B.19 Fractionalization and dependent variable data

Country	Corruption Perception Index	Ethnic conflict deaths	Ethnic fractionalization (EF)	Human Development Index (HDI)	Per capita GDP (log)
Afghanistan	16	10.76	0.74	0.50	7.71
Albania	35	0.00	0.19	0.79	9.53
Algeria	35	18.94	0.45	0.76	9.37
Angola	26	52.65	0.75	0.57	8.87
Argentina	45	0.00	0.15	0.83	10.06
Armenia	42	0.00	0.09	0.76	9.47
Australia	77	0.00	0.16	0.94	10.84
Austria	77	0.00	0.17	0.91	10.95
Azerbaijan	30	47.28	0.17	0.75	9.58
Bangladesh	26	1.55	0.17	0.61	8.42
Belarus	45	0.00	0.33	0.82	9.87
Belgium	75	0.00	0.50	0.92	10.86
Benin	41	0.00	0.83	0.52	8.08
Bolivia	31	0.00	0.61	0.70	9.09
Bosnia and Herzegovina	36	147.27	0.64	0.77	9.61
Botswana	61	0.00	0.23	0.73	9.80
Brazil	35	0.00	0.57	0.76	9.61
Bulgaria	43	0.00	0.33	0.82	10.01
Burkina Faso	40	0.00	0.72	0.43	7.55
Burundi	19	340.03	0.63	0.42	6.66
Cambodia	20	0.06	0.13	0.58	8.36
Cameroon	25	0.00	0.84	0.56	8.21
Canada	77	0.00	0.55	0.92	10.82
Central African Republic	25	2.14	0.77	0.38	6.86
Chad	20	64.61	0.85	0.40	7.39
Chile	67	0.00	0.15	0.85	10.12
China	41	8.62	0.15	0.76	9.64
Colombia	37	5.04	0.41	0.76	9.60
Congo	19	0.00	0.73	0.61	8.12
Congo, Democratic Republic of	18	297.38	0.89	0.46	7.01
Costa Rica	56	0.00	0.19	0.79	9.89
Côte d'Ivoire	35	1.60	0.82	0.52	8.25
Croatia	47	48.93	0.27	0.84	10.24

Table B.19 Fractionalization and dependent variable data

Country	Corruption Perception Index	Ethnic conflict deaths	Ethnic fractionalization (EF)	Human Development Index (HDI)	Per capita GDP (log)
Cuba	48	0.00	0.55	0.78	
Czechia	56	0.00	0.32	0.89	10.61
Denmark	87	0.00	0.16	0.93	10.95
Dominican Republic	28	0.00	0.45	0.75	9.81
Ecuador	38	0.00	0.54	0.76	9.38
Egypt	35	0.09	0.18	0.70	9.36
El Salvador	34	0.00	0.18	0.67	9.08
Eritrea	23	0.00	0.59	0.43	7.24
Ethiopia	37	25.44	0.76	0.47	7.68
Finland	86	0.00	0.18	0.93	10.81
France	69	0.00	0.29	0.89	10.75
Gabon	31	0.00	0.82	0.70	9.62
Gambia	37	0.00	0.77	0.47	7.69
Georgia	56	35.01	0.37	0.79	9.59
Germany	80	0.00	0.20	0.94	10.91
Ghana	41	2.02	0.72	0.60	8.58
Greece	48	0.00	0.10	0.87	10.32
Guatemala	26	86.97	0.50	0.65	9.07
Guinea	29	0.81	0.72	0.47	7.85
Haiti	18	0.00	0.10	0.50	7.50
Honduras	26	0.00	0.18	0.62	8.67
Hong Kong	76	0.00	0.15	0.94	11.05
Hungary	44	0.00	0.22	0.85	10.36
India	41	0.25	0.61	0.65	8.81
Indonesia	40	11.21	0.74	0.71	9.36
Iran	26	0.04	0.67	0.80	
Iraq	20	78.06	0.40	0.69	9.30
Ireland	74	0.00	0.24	0.94	11.34
Israel	60	3.94	0.35	0.91	10.60
Italy	53	0.00	0.13	0.88	10.66
Jamaica	43	0.00	0.17	0.73	9.21
Japan	73	0.00	0.02	0.92	10.63
Jordan	48	0.00	0.51	0.72	9.22
Kazakhstan	34	0.00	0.58	0.82	10.17
Kenya	28	0.00	0.89	0.58	8.37

Table B.19 Fractionalization and dependent variable data					
Country	Corruption Perception Index	Ethnic conflict deaths	Ethnic fractionalization (EF)	Human Development Index (HDI)	Per capita GDP (log)
Korea, North	17	0.00	0.00		
Korea, South	59	0.00	0.02	0.91	10.59
Kuwait	40	0.00	0.58	0.81	10.85
Kyrgyz Republic	30	0.00	0.51	0.67	8.57
Laos	29	0.00	0.58	0.60	8.96
Lebanon	28	1.46	0.58	0.73	9.71
Lesotho	40	0.00	0.29	0.52	8.03
Liberia	28	0.00	0.91	0.47	7.34
Libya	18	0.00	0.48	0.71	9.58
Lithuania	60	0.00	0.31	0.87	10.49
Madagascar	24	0.00	0.83	0.52	7.41
Malawi	31	0.00	0.75	0.49	6.98
Malaysia	53	0.00	0.57	0.80	10.25
Mali	29	0.12	0.79	0.43	7.76
Mauritania	28	0.00	0.66	0.53	8.24
Mexico	29	0.02	0.55	0.77	9.92
Moldova	32	0.00	0.48	0.71	9.44
Mongolia	35	0.00	0.32	0.74	9.41
Morocco	41	4.16	0.25	0.68	9.06
Mozambique	26	0.00	0.36	0.45	7.19
Myanmar	29	12.85	0.58	0.58	8.52
Namibia	52	0.00	0.72	0.65	9.28
Nepal	34	0.00	0.77	0.58	8.11
Netherlands	82	0.00	0.23	0.93	10.96
New Zealand	87	0.00	0.40	0.92	10.65
Nicaragua	22	0.00	0.48	0.65	8.67
Niger	32	0.02	0.64	0.38	6.79
Nigeria	26	0.61	0.83	0.53	8.57
North Macedonia	35	0.00	0.52	0.76	9.72
Norway	84	0.00	0.18	0.95	11.12
Oman	52	0.00	0.54	0.83	10.28
Pakistan	32	0.00	0.73	0.56	8.49
Panama	36	0.00	0.51	0.80	10.37
Papua New Guinea	28	11.62	0.99	0.54	8.37
Paraguay	28	0.00	0.10	0.72	9.49
Peru	36	9.38	0.60	0.76	9.48

Table B.19 Fractionalization and dependent variable data

Country	Corruption Perception Index	Ethnic conflict deaths	Ethnic fractionalization (EF)	Human Development Index (HDI)	Per capita GDP (log)
Philippines	34	11.25	0.83	0.71	9.03
Poland	58	0.00	0.05	0.87	10.37
Portugal	62	0.00	0.09	0.85	10.44
Qatar	62	0.00	0.21	0.85	11.48
Romania	44	0.00	0.25	0.82	10.28
Russia	28	10.38	0.35	0.82	10.26
Rwanda	53	761.67	0.29	0.54	7.66
Saudi Arabia	53	0.00	0.18	0.86	10.79
Senegal	45	0.32	0.77	0.51	8.14
Serbia	39	0.00	0.30	0.80	9.78
Sierra Leone	33	13.07	0.77	0.44	7.44
Singapore	85	0.00	0.41	0.94	11.50
Slovakia	50	0.00	0.29	0.86	10.39
Slovenia	60	0.00	0.23	0.90	10.56
Somalia	9	233.21	0.20		
South Africa	44	2.42	0.37	0.71	9.47
Spain	62	0.18	0.33	0.89	10.61
Sri Lanka	38	48.92	0.42	0.78	9.49
Sudan	16	51.31	0.64	0.51	8.47
Sweden	85	0.00	0.26	0.94	10.89
Switzerland	85	0.00	0.45	0.95	11.15
Syria	13	0.00	0.42	0.55	
Taiwan	65	0.00	0.19		10.83
Tajikistan	25	10.99	0.39	0.66	8.11
Tanzania	37	0.00	0.78	0.53	8.08
Thailand	36	0.00	0.23	0.77	9.82
Togo	29	0.00	0.81	0.51	7.37
Tunisia	43	0.00	0.04	0.74	9.31
Turkey	39	3.60	0.39	0.81	10.24
Turkmenistan	19	0.00	0.33	0.71	9.63
Uganda	28	12.53	0.88	0.53	7.52
Ukraine	30	1.31	0.39	0.75	9.13
United Arab Emirates	71	0.00	0.63	0.87	11.12
United Kingdom	77	0.45	0.28	0.92	10.76
United States	69	0.01	0.37	0.92	11.05

Table B.19 Fractionalization and dependent variable data					
Country	Corruption Perception Index	Ethnic conflict deaths	Ethnic fractionalization (EF)	Human Development Index (HDI)	Per capita GDP (log)
Uruguay	71	0.00	0.22	0.81	10.00
Uzbekistan	25	0.00	0.32	0.71	8.84
Venezuela	16	0.00	0.52	0.73	
Vietnam	37	0.00	0.26	0.69	8.96
Yemen	15	0.00	0.35	0.46	
Zambia	34	0.00	0.90	0.59	8.19
Zimbabwe	24	0.00	0.47	0.56	8.12

Civil Wars and Deaths from Ethnic Conflict

Unless otherwise noted, data in the table below are from the *Correlates of War Project* published by the Inter-University Consortium for Political and Social Research.[11]

Table B.20 Civil wars and deaths from ethnic conflict			
Country	Conflicting groups	Deaths	Civil war (1960–2020)
Afghanistan	Tajiks, Uzbeks, Pashtuns	40,000	Yes
Algeria	Government, Salafis	80,000	Yes
Angola	Mbundu, Ovimbundu	162,200	Yes
Azerbaijan	Armenians, Azeris	47,000	No
Bangladesh	Government, Chittagong	25,000	No
Bosnia-Herzegovina	Serbs, Bosnian Croats, Muslims (Bosniaks)	48,953	Yes
Brazil	Amazonian Indians, non-Indian settlers	100	No
Burundi	Hutu, Tutsi	380,000[12]	Yes
Cambodia	Cambodians, Vietnamese	100	Yes
Central African Rep.	Government, Seleka	1,000	No
Chad	Anakaza, Bideyet	100,000	Yes
China	Government, (Han Chinese), Uighurs, Kazakhs (Xinjiang), Tibetans	1,200,000	No

Table B.20 Civil wars and deaths from ethnic conflict

Country	Conflicting groups	Deaths	Civil war (1960–2020)
Colombia	Government, various ethnic and political entities (FARC, ELN, EZLN)	25,000	No
Congo (Republic of)	Lari, Vili, Sundi, Kongo, Teke	3,500	Yes
Cote d'Ivoire	Muslim northern tribes (Mandinka); Christian southern tribes	4,000	Yes
Croatia	Serbs, Croats	20,000[13]	No
Democratic Republic of Congo	Hutus, various Banyarwanda, Bangilima	2,500,000[14]	Yes
Dominican Republic			Yes
Egypt	Muslim Egyptians, Copts	932[15]	No
El Salvador			Yes
Ethiopia	Government, Oromo, Eritreans	277,900	Yes
France	Right-wing attacks on immigrants of various ethnicities	50	No
Georgia	Abkhazians, Ossetians, Mkhedrioni	13,046	Yes
Germany	Right-wing attacks on Turkish and other immigrants	50	No
Ghana	Konkombas, Nunumba, Dagomba	6,000	No
Guatemala	Government, indigenous peoples	150,000	Yes
Guinea	Fulani, Malinke, Susu	1,000	No
Guinea-Bissau			Yes
India	Sikhs, Hindus, Assamese, Bodos, Tripuras, Nagas, Kashmiri Muslims, Hindus	33,376	No
Indonesia	Government, Timorese, Papuan	300,000	Yes
Iran	Government, Bahais, Kurds	300	No
Iraq	Government, Kurds, Marsh Arabs, Shiites	300,000	Yes
Israel	Government, Palestinians	3500	No
Kosovo	Serbs, Ethnic Albanians	1200	No
Laos			Yes
Lebanon	Sunni and Shiite Muslim, Druze, Christian	1,000	Yes
Liberia	Various ethnic and tribal minorities	150,000	Yes

Table B.20 Civil wars and deaths from ethnic conflict			
Country	**Conflicting groups**	**Deaths**	**Civil war (1960–2020)**
Libya			Yes
Mali	Government, Tuaregs	220	
Mauritania			Yes
Mauritius	Creole and Hindu (in minor riots in 1999)		No
Mexico	Government, Zapatistas, Indigenous peoples	200	No
Moldova	Government, Slavs	1,000	No
Morocco	Government, Sahrawi	15,000	Yes
Mozambique			Yes
Myanmar	Karen, Kachin, Mon, Rohingya, Shan	69,000	Yes
Nepal			Yes
Nicaragua			Yes
Niger	Government, Tuaregs, Mahamid	50	Yes
Nigeria	Ibo, Hausa, Fulani, Jukun, Tiv	12,000	Yes
Pakistan	Government, Baluchis, Sindhis, Bengalis, Waziri tribes	32,000	Yes
Papua New Guinea	Government, Bougainvillian	10,000[16]	Yes
Peru	Government, Sendero Luminoso, Indigenous peoples	30,000	Yes
Philippines	Government, Moros (Muslims)	120,000	Yes
Russia	Government, Ossetians, Chechens, Tajiks	150,000	No
Rwanda	Hutu, Tutsi	937,000[17]	No
Senegal	Dioula, Wolof	500	No
Sierra Leone	Government, various tribal	10,000	Yes
Somalia	Isaaqs, Ogaden, Rahawaine	350,000	Yes
South Africa	Afrikaners, Xhosa, Zulu	14,000	No
Spain	Government, Basques	853[18]	No
Sri Lanka	Tamil, Sinhalese	106,000	Yes
Sudan	Northern Arab/Muslims, Southern Nilotic, and Christian	214,500	Yes
Tajikistan	Government, Pamiris	10,000	Yes
Thailand	Government, PULO (Muslim Malay)	< 10	No

Table B.20 Civil wars and deaths from ethnic conflict

Country	Conflicting groups	Deaths	Civil war (1960–2020)
Turkey	Government, Kurds	29,657	No
Uganda	Government, Acholi, Baganda, Banyar-wanda	53,516	Yes
Ukraine	Government, ethnic Russians, Cossacks	5,826	No
United Kingdom	Government, Irish; white supremacist bombings directed at immigrants	3,000	No
USA	Various ethnic groups (in riots and other unorganized violence)	100–200	No
Yemen			Yes

NOTES

PREFACE

1 Shiva Naipaul vividly describes some killings during the pogrom. See Shiva Naipaul, *An Unfinished Journey* (London: Abacus, 1988), 111–12.

2 In addition to conflicts between Serbs and Croats in Bosnia, recent years have seen violent clashes between Mbundu and Ovimbundu in Angola; Armenians and Azeris in Azerbaijan; Bengalis and Chittagong in Bangladesh; Anakaza and Bideyet in Chad; Croats and Serbians in Croatia; Arabs, Dinka, and Nuer in Darfur; Georgians, Abkhazians, and Ossetians in Georgia; Konkombas, Nunumba, and Dagomba in Ghana; Assamese, Bodos, and Nagas in India; Javanese, Timorese, and Papuan in Indonesia; Albanians and Serbians in Kosovo; Bamar and Rohingya in Myanmar; Hausa and Igbo in Nigeria; Russian and Chechen in Russia; Hutus and Tutsis in Rwanda; and Sinhalese and Tamils in Sri Lanka—to name a few of the most violent ones. For a list of ethnic conflicts since World War II, see table B.20 in appendix B.

3 *United States 2010 Yearbook of Immigration Statistics* (Washington, DC: US Department of Homeland Security, Office of Immigration Statistics, 2010); *United States 2014 Yearbook of Immigration Statistics* (Washington, DC: Department of Homeland Security, Office of Immigration Statistics, 2014), 12.

4 Abby Budiman; Christine Tamr; Lauren Mora, *Facts on U.S. immigrants, 2018: Statistical Portrait of the Foreign-Born Population in the United States* (Washington, DC: Pew Research Center, 2020). It is based on Migration Policy Institute (MPI) tabulation of data from US Census Bureau, 2010–2015 American Community Surveys (ACS), and 1970, 1990, and 2000 Decennial Census. Immigrants are defined as people *legally* residing in the United States who were not US citizens at birth. Illegal immigrants increase the total by an estimated ten to fifteen million, though some estimates are nearly twice as high.

5 For example, in 2021, antisemitic incidents reached a forty-two-year high. See Zachary Snowdon Smith, "Antisemitic Incidents Hit 42-Year High Across U.S. in 2021, ADL Report Says," *Forbes*, April 26, 2022, https://www.forbes.com/sites/zacharysmith/2022/04/26/antisemitic-incidents-hit-42-year-high-across-us-in-2021-adl-report-says/?sh=55a05c213fab.

6 In the 1992 Los Angeles riots, for example, black and white people together accounted for less than half of both the victims and the arrests. See Paul Lieberman, "51% of Riot Arrests Were Latino, Study Says," *Los Angeles Times*, June 18, 1992, https://www.latimes.com/archives/la-xpm-1992-06-18-me-734-story.html.

7 Diane Ravitch, "Multiculturalism Yes, Particularism No," *Chronicle of Higher Education*, October 24, 1990.

1 * A BRIEF INTRODUCTION TO THE MELTING POT

1 Israel Zangwill, *The Melting-Pot: Drama in Four Acts* (New York: Macmillan, 1921), 14.

2 Later, Roosevelt wrote to Zangwill: "That particular play I shall always count among the very strong and real influences upon my thought and my life. It has been on my mind continually, and my lips often, during the last three years." Quoted from a letter dated December 11, 1912, from Zangwill to Jan Rudenyi. The letter, which is privately held, was graciously shared with the author by B. Kesselman.

3 J. Hector St. John de Crèvecoeur , *Letters from an American Farmer*, ed. Albert E. Stone (Harmondsworth: Penguin Books, 1981), 70.

4 Ralph Waldo Emerson, *Journals of Ralph Waldo Emerson*, ed. Edward Waldo Emerson and Waldo Emerson Forbes, vol. 7 (Cambridge, MA: Riverside Press, 1912), 42.

5 Gretchen Livingstone and Anna Brown, *Intermarriage in the U.S. 50 Years After Loving v. Virginia* (Washington, DC: Pew Research Center, 2017); "At Home Here," *Wall Street Journal*, July 6, 1999.

6 From the March 18, 1964 interview with Robert Penn Warren. See Garance Franke-Ruta, "Martin Luther King Jr.'s Amazing 1964 Interview With Robert Penn Warren," *Atlantic Monthly*, August 26, 2013, https://www.theatlantic.com/politics/archive/2013/08/martin-luther-king-jrs-amazing-1964-interview-with-robert-penn-warren/279014/.

7 Jimmy Carter, "Remarks on Human Rights at Notre Dame University in South Bend, Indiana," American Presidency Project, October 10, 1976, https://www.presidency.ucsb.edu/documents/remarks-human-rights-notre-dame-university-south-bend-indiana.

8 Google, "Google Books Ngram Viewer," May 25, 2022, https://books.google.com/ngrams/graph?content=multiculturalism&year_start=1960&year_end=2019&corpus=28&smoothing=3. The *Reader's Guide to Periodical Literature* did not include a topic heading for "multiculturalism" before 1988.

9 Derald Wing Sue, Christina M. Capodilupo, and Gina C Torino, "Racial Microaggressions in Everyday Life," *American Psychologist*, May–June, 2007, 276; Eugene Volokh, "UC Teaching Faculty Members Not to Criticize Race-based Affirmative Action, Call America 'Melting Pot,' and More," *Washington Post*, June 16, 2015, https://www.washingtonpost.com/news/volokh-conspiracy/wp/2015/06/16/uc-teaching-faculty-members-not-to-criticize-race-based-affirmative-action-call-america-melting-pot-and-more/.

10 William Branigin, "Immigrants Shunning Idea of Assimilation," *Washington Post*, May 25, 1998, https://www.washingtonpost.com/wp-srv/national/longterm/meltingpot/melt0525a.htm. Zangwill wrote this in the afterword of the 1916 edition of *The Melting Pot*. See Zangwill, *Melting-Pot*, 80. The brochure for US refugees is provided in: *American Council for Voluntary Agencies for Foreign Service, Guide for New Americans: An Introduction to Your New Homeland* (New York: Astoria Press, 1949), 30.

11 Roger Parloff, "Big Business Asks Supreme Court to Save Affirmative Action," *Fortune*, December 9, 2015, https://fortune.com/2015/12/09/supreme-court-affirmative-action/.

12 Independent, "New Survey Shows 2 Per Cent of Latinos Recognise Term 'Latinx' and 40 Per Cent Hate It," *Independent*, December 6, 2021, https://www.independent.co.uk/news/world/americas/us-politics/latinos-recognize-latinx-hate-it-b1970855.html.

13 The cultural fusion is most prominently symbolized in the dress of the subsequent pharaohs, who wore crowns that combined the white bowling pin design of upper Egypt with the red deshret of lower Egypt.

14 Toynbee praised Ibn Khaldun's *Muqaddimah* as "the greatest work of its kind that has yet been created by any mind in any time or place." See Arnold J. Toynbee, *A Study of History* (London: Oxford University Press, 1935), 3:322. Even Facebook founder Mark Zuckerberg has read and praised Ibn Khaldun's *Muqaddimah*.

15 Asabiyah is based on the form I verb of the root, عصب, which means to bind or tie together.

16 Heinrich Simon, *Ibn Khaldūns Wissenschaft von der Menschlichen Kultur* (Berlin: VEB Harrassowitz, 1959); T. Khemiri, „Der Asabija-Begriff in der Muqaddima des Ibn Haldun," *Der Islam* 23, no. 3 (1936): 163–88. The word predates Ibn Khaldun by at least a millennium, but Ibn Khaldun imparted his own special meaning to it. In sayings (*ahadith*) attributed to Muhammad, asabiyah connotes narrow tribal jingoism and is deprecated. See, for example Hadith no. 5121 in Imam Hafiz Abu Dawud, *Sunan Abu Dawud*, trans. Yaser Qadhi, vol. 1 (Riyadh: Maktaba Darussalam, 2008), 421. Ibn Khaldun was aware of these negative references and defends the asabiyah that he refers to as a useful and productive force.

17 Abdarrahman b. Muhammad Ibn Khaldun, *al-Muqaddimah*, ed. Ali Abdalwahid Wafi, vol. 2 (Cairo: Lajna al-Bayan al-Arabi, 1957), 434–35.

18 As Ibn Khaldun writes, "when asabiyah dies out, the nation is incapable of self-defense . . . and other nations consume it." Author's translation. Ibn Khaldun, *Muqaddimah*, 2, 441.

19 Author's translation. Ibn Khaldun, *Muqaddimah*, 2, 439–40.

2 ✻ LESSONS FROM BYZANTINE RACE RIOTS

1 From a curse tablet dated sixth century CE, now in the Hatay Archaeological Museum, Turkey.

2 Procopius, *History of The Wars, Books I and II*, trans. H. B. Dewing (New York: Macmillan, 1914), 219–21.

3 The sixth-century Byzantine chronicler, John Malalas discusses several race faction clashes and riots prior to the Nika Riot. See John Malalas, *The Chronicle of John Malalas: A Translation*, trans. Elizabeth Jeffreys, Jeffreys Michael, and Roger Scott (Melbourne: Australian Association for Byzantine Studies, 1986), 218–23. Unlike the prior clashes, the Nika riot appears to have evolved into a more general insurrection against the Byzantine government.

4 Gaius Caecilius Secundus Plinius, *Letters of Marcus Tullius Cicero and Letters of Gaius Plinius Caecilius Secundus, The Harvard Classics*, trans. William Melmoth, vol. 9 (New York: P. F. Collier & Son, 1909), 351–52.

5 For example, one prominent Primordialist, Harold Isaacs, writes: "The we-they syndrome is built in... Where there is contact or propinquity between sufficiently different groups, the normal response runs from avoidance to suspicion, to fear, to hostility, to violence." See Harold Isaacs, *Idols of the Tribe* (New York: Harper & Row, 1975), 217.

6 Anthropological fieldwork also demonstrates this. For example, in his research on Tikopia island, Raymond William Firth found a society split into starkly antagonistic groups. Each group dismissed the other as stupid and lazy, criticized their work as inferior and shoddy, and were generally hostile to them. Yet the groups were culturally indistinguishable, with the sole distinction being that one group had moved to the leeward side of the tiny, two-square-mile island, while the other occupied the windward side. This windward-leeward factionalism took precedence even over clan affiliation and all but the very closest family ties. See Raymond William Firth, *We, the Tikopia: A Sociological Study of Kinship in Primitive Polynesia* (London: Routledge, 2004), 71–75.

7 Muzafer Sherif, *The Robbers Cave Experiment: Intergroup Conflict and Cooperation* (Norman: University of Oklahoma Press, 1961).

8 For example, one Maryland school sought to educate students on discrimination by temporarily segregating blonde students. Many of the student enforcers of this mock segregation took their roles a little too seriously and began bullying and beating up blonde students. See Diane Bernard, "'No Blondes Allowed': 50 Years after a Junior High Experiment, Students Say It Had 'a Big Impact,'" *Washington Post*, December 29, 2019.

9 L. N. Diab, "A Study of Intragroup and Intergroup Relations among Experimentally Produced Small Groups," *Genetic Psychology Monographs* 82, no. 1 (1970): 49–82.

10 Henri Tajfel, "Experiments in Intergroup Discrimination," *Scientific American*, November 1, 1970, 96–102; Henri Tajfel, M. G. Billig, R. P. Bundy, and Claude Flament, "Social Categorization and Intergroup Behavior," *European Journal of Social Psychology*, April–June, 1971.

11 Procopius, *History of The Wars*, 219–21.

12 Malalas, *Chronicle of John Malalas*, 202,20.

13 Procopius, *Secret History*, trans. Richard Atwater (Chicago: P. Covici, 1927), 89, 106, 84–85.

14 Procopius, *Secret History*, 80–84.

15 D. A. Wilder, "Some Determinants of the Persuasive Power of In-Groups and Out-Groups: Organization of Information and Attribution of Independence," *Journal of Personality and Social Psychology* 59, no. 6 (1990): 1202–13. Other studies have replicated this. For example, see V. L. Allen and D. A. Wilder, "Categorization, Belief Similarity, and Intergroup Discrimination," *Journal of Personality and Social Psychology* 32, no. 6 (1975): 971–77.

16 A few scholars have tried to associate race factionalism with various social divisions, e.g., ethnicity, deme, religion, and social class. The historical evidence convincingly refutes them. Procopius, who is the principal source on the race factions at the time of the Nika Riot, tells us that the Blue-Green rivalry divided neighbors and even families; he also mentions Greens switching to the Blue side—an improbable occurrence if race factionalism had been driven by some underlying association, such as class or ethnicity. The only association of the race factions with ethnic antagonism comes from Malalas's account of the Greens of Antioch attacking Jews; some still extant hippodrome benches that have "Blues and Jews" inscribed on them also support a possible connection between the two groups. However, according to Theophanes, the Greens also included both Jews and Samaritans. See Theophanes, *Chronicle of Theophanes in Medieval Civilization*, trans. D. Munro and G. Sellerv (New York: Century, 1910), 104–7. This is confirmed by Jewish curse tablets *against* the Blues. See Ruth Shuster and Ofer Adaret, "Ancient Scroll Shows Jews Tried to Hex Chariot Races in Turkey 1,500 Years Ago," *Haaretz*, May 16, 2018, https://www.haaretz.com/archaeology/2018-05-16/ty-article-magazine/jews-tried-to-hex-chariot-races-in-turkey-1-500-years-ago/0000017f-ef64-da6f-a77f-ff6eceef0000.

17 Diab, "Study," 49–82; J. Rabbie, "The Effects of Intergroup Competition and Cooperation on Intragroup and Intergroup Relations," in *Cooperation and Helping Behavior: Theories and Research*, ed. V. Derlega and J. Grzelak (New York: Academic, 1982), 123–49.

18 Recognition of this reality dates to early evolutionary theory. In the *Descent of Man*, Darwin already speculated that natural selection could favor cooperation and altruism within groups that are much larger than families. Charles Darwin, *The Descent of Man and Selection in Relation to Sex* (New York: D. Appleton, 1909), 135. Jane Goodall found that chimpanzees often extend helping and cooperative behavior not only to kin but to completely unrelated individuals—typically when they have a "prolonged and close association." Goodall viewed this as the product of natural selection, and specifically of kin selection. Because primates use familiarity rather than more precise methods of kin recognition (e.g., pheromones), they are motivated to favor, and cooperate with, familiar individuals even when they are not actual kin. From a kin selection standpoint, it's safest for an individual primate to presume another familiar individual is related (false positives are better than false negatives) and cooperate with them. See Jane Goodall, *The Chimpanzees of Gombe: Patterns of Behavior* (Cambridge, MA: Harvard University Press, 1986), 380.

3 ✶ THE ROMAN MELTING POT

1 Tranquillus Gaius Suetonius, *The Twelve Caesars*, trans. Robert Graves (London: Penguin, 1979), 176–77.

2 Although the gladiatorial occupation was manifestly hazardous, there are numerous inscriptions and other references to retired gladiators. For example, one inscription refers to a collegium of retired gladiators in Ancyra.

See *Inscriptiones Latinae Selectae.*, ed. Hermann Dessau, 3 vols. (Berlin: Weidmann, 1955), 7559. Suetonius mentions Tiberius hiring retired gladiators. See Suetonius, *Twelve Caesars*, 117. By contrast, Diocletian was the only emperor (out of approximately ninety) who retired voluntarily and died peaceably.

3 This more complete version of Claudius's speech comes from Tacitus. See Publius Cornelius Tacitus, *The Annals of Imperial Rome*, trans. Michael Grant (London: Penguin, 1996), 243–44. The text of the bronze tablet now in the Museum of Gallo-Roman Civilization in Lyon varies slightly from Tacitus's version. For example, the wording differs, and it includes raucous interruptions from senators in attendance. But the overall thesis is the same. See *ILS*, 212.

4 Marcus Tullius Cicero, *The Orations of Marcus Tullius Cicero*, trans. C. D. Yonge (London: George Bell & Sons, 1891), 325.

5 Aelius Aristides, "The Ruling Power: A Study of the Roman Empire in the Second Century after Christ through the Roman Oration of Aelius Aristides," *Transactions of the American Philosophical Society* 43, no.4 (1953): 901–2.

6 Publius Cornelius Tacitus, *Rome and Italy: Books VI–X of The History of Rome from its Foundation*, trans. Betty Radice (London: Penguin Books, 1982), 177. This was not just boasting or propaganda on the Romans' part. Outsiders also noted Rome's liberal granting of citizenship. For example, in the third century BCE, Philip V of Macedon wrote a letter citing the Romans' readiness to grant citizenship, even to former slaves. See M. M. Austin, *The Hellenistic World from Alexander to the Roman Conquest: A Selection of Ancient Sources in Translation* (Cambridge: Cambridge University Press, 1981), 118.

7 For example, one edict that grants full citizenship to the local duovirs, aediles, and quaestors (*ILS*, 6088). Over time, consuls and emperors added ways for individuals with Latin rights to attain full citizenship. For example, *Institutes of Roman Law by Gaius* specifies that Latins who built ships to import corn, constructed a large house in Rome, or worked as millers for three years earned full citizenship. See Gaius, *Institutes of Roman Law By Gaius* (Oxford: Clarendon Press, 1904), 1:32–34.

8 Veterans received "diplomas" of wood or bronze that documented their service and detailed the citizenship rights granted. Many of these are still extant. See, for example, *ILS*, 9054 or the diploma depicted in figure 3.1. This also applied to sailors in Rome's navy (cf. *ILS*, 1986). There are numerous examples of auxiliaries receiving citizenship for superior performance before they completed their service: see, for example, *Corpus Inscriptionum Latinarum* (Berlin: Berlin-Brandenburgische Akadamie der Wissenschaften, 2001), 16.160. There are also instances of entire units receiving citizenship before they had retired.

9 Titus Livius, *The Rise of Rome: Books 1–5*, trans. T. J. Luce (Oxford: Oxford University Press, 1998), 37.

10 Sextus Frontinus gives an extensive list of the ruses Hannibal employed in the second Punic war. See Sextus Julius Frontinus, *The Strategems*, trans. Charles E. Bennet (Cambridge, MA: Harvard University Press, 1925), 101–3.

See also Polybius, *The Rise of the Roman Empire*, trans. Ian Scott-Kilvert and F. W. Walbank (London: Penguin, 1979), 259–60.

11 Polybius, *Rise of the Roman Empire*, 252–57: "For until this moment, even though the Romans had been defeated in two battles, not a single Italian city had gone over to the Carthaginians: all had kept faith with Rome, although some of them were suffering severely." The citizens of Gerunium, for example, rejected Hannibal's repeated overtures for an alliance, and ultimately sacrificed their lives. See Polybius, *Rise of the Roman Empire*, 261.

12 Polybius, *Rise of the Roman Empire*, 476.

13 "Now that [the Gauls] have assimilated our customs and culture and married into our families, let them bring in their gold and wealth [and become senators]" (Tacitus, *Annals* 243–44).

14 See book 60, section 17 of Dio's history: Cassius Dio, *Dio's Roman History: In Nine Volumes*, trans. Earnest Cary and Herbert Baldwin (Cambridge, MA: Harvard University Press, 1914–27), 7:412.

15 A provincial with a dubious claim to citizenship could secure it by joining a legion. Also, when legionaries were desperately needed, Roman leaders sometimes enrolled entire groups of noncitizens. For example, Julius Caesar recruited a legion in Transalpine Gaul with the Gallic name "Alauda." He made all Alauda legionnaires full Roman citizens. See Suetonius, *Twelve Caesars*, 23.

16 Fragment of a bronze diploma dated 89 CE, from the author's collection. It was granted by Domitian to a veteran who served in Moesia (now Bulgaria).

17 Yann Le Bohec, *The Imperial Roman Army* (New York: Routledge, 1994), 89.

18 Cassius Dio is the principal source on Quietus. See book 68, section 18 of his history: Dio, *Roman History*, 8:396–97.

19 Aristides, "Ruling Power," 903.

20 Lindley Richard Dean, "A Study of the Cognomina of Soldiers in the Roman Legions" (PhD diss., Princeton University, 1916), 13.

21 See, for example, *CIL*, 7.506. Also see Tertullian, *Apology*, trans. Gerald H. Rendall (Cambridge, MA: Harvard University Press, 1977), 83–85.

22 *CIL*, 2.4147. There are numerous epitaphs honoring soldiers with extremely long terms of service, sometimes forty years or more. For example, see *CIL*, 8.217. Serving in many different regions was quite common. One inscription describes an Anatolian who served in twenty-three different provinces. *L'Annee Epigraphique*, (Paris: Presses Universitaires de France, 1997), 777.

23 The Res Gestae Divi Augusti ("The Deeds of the Divine Augustus") is an inscription celebrating Augustus' accomplishments. The most complete version is furnished by the Monumentum Ancyranum in Ankara, Turkey. Many other inscriptions scattered across Europe, the Middle East, and North Africa document individual settled veterans. See Theodor Mommsen, *Res Gestae Divi Augusti* (Berlin: Weidmann, 1865), 3, 16, 28.

24 Gaius Plinius Secundus, *The Natural History of Pliny*, trans. John Bostock and Herny Thomas Riley, vol. 1, 3.6 (London: George Bell, 1893), 181.

25 Seneca's comments are from his *Apocolocyntosis*. See Lucius Annaeus Seneca, *Satyricon & Apocolocyntosis*, trans. Michael Heseltine and W. H. D. Rouse (Cambridge, MA: Harvard University Press, 1961). Augustus decreed that Romans must wear togas to be admitted to the forum and law courts. See Suetonius, *Twelve Caesars*, 77.

26 Tacitus, Agricola's son-in-law, writes the following: "He was also attentive to provide a liberal education for the sons of their chieftains... and his attempts were attended with such success, that they who lately disdained to make use of the Roman language, were now ambitious of becoming eloquent. Hence the Roman habit began to be held in honor, and the toga was frequently worn." See Cornelius Tacitus, *The Germany and the Agricola of Tacitus: The Oxford Translation Revised with Notes* (Chicago: C. M. Barnes, 1897), 114.

27 Some notable examples of such city charters are the Tablet of Heraclea and the Charters of Urso, Salpensa, and Malaca. See *ILS*, 6085, 87, 88, 98.

28 Claudius Rutilius Namatianus, *Rutilii Claudii Namatiani De reditu suo libri duo*, trans. Charles Haines Keene (London: G. Bell, 1907), 118.

29 Claudius Claudianus, *Claudian*, trans. Maurice Platnauer, vol. 2 (London: W. Heinemann, G. P. Putnam Sons, 1922), 54–55.

30 Strabo, for example, noted how Romans were much more dedicated to the construction of infrastructure such as roads and aqueducts than the Greeks. See Strabo, *The Geography of Strabo*, trans. Horace Leonard Jones (Cambridge, MA: Harvard University Press, 1923), 406.

31 For example, see the speeches "Against Eubulides" and "Against Naeara" by Demosthenes: *Demosthenes, Speeches 50–59*, trans. Victor Bers (Austin: University of Texas Press, 2003).

32 For example, one inscription is from a Parthian who was captured when he was a boy but was eventually made a citizen (*ILS*, 1980). Gaius's *Institutes* even allow citizenship for emancipated slaves provided they have not taken up arms against Rome or been convicted of criminal charges (see Gaius, *Institutes*, 1.13–19).

33 Marcellinus only enumerates the number of fighting men (fifteen thousand); whereas Eunapius puts the total number of refugees at two hundred thousand. See Ammianus Marcellinus, *The Later Roman Empire*, trans. Walter Hamilton (London: Penguin Books, 1986), 416–17. Eunapius was presumably alluding to the dragon's teeth in the legend of Cadmus. He inaccurately uses the term "Scythian" to refer to the Goths. See Eunapius et al., *The Fragmentary Classicising Historians of the Later Roman Empire Eunapius, Olympiodorus, Priscus and Malchus*, trans. R. C. Blockley, vol. 2 (London: Francis Cairns Publications, 1983), 61–63.

34 Procopius attributes these words to Totila. Because Procopius accompanied the general Belisarius to Italy, it is conceivable that he had firsthand accounts of Totila's words and actions. Procopius, *Procopius, History of The Wars, Books VII (continued) and VIII*, trans. H. B. Dewing (Cambridge, MA: Harvard Univ. Press, 1962), 367.

35 Unlike Procopius, who was present for some of the conflicts he chronicles, Jordanes was writing roughly a hundred years after Attila's death. It seems

improbable that he would have an accurate account of Attila's words. However, if these words were not actually spoken by a barbarian, they at least reflected Roman observers' perceptions of their own weaknesses. Jordanes, *Jordanes, The Origin and Deeds of the Goths*, trans. Charles C. Mierow (PhD diss., Princeton University, 1908), 63.

36 See Libanius's funeral oration for the emperor Julian in Libanius and Gregory Nazianzen, *Julian the Emperor: Containing Gregory Nazianzen's Two Invectives And Libanius' Monody With Julian's Extant Theosophical Works*, trans. C. W. King (London: George Bell And Sons, 1888), 146.

37 Synesius, *The Essays and Hymns of Synesius of Cyrene, Including the Address to the Emperor Arcadius and the Political Speeches*, trans. Augustine FitzGerald (London: Oxford University Press, 1930), 1091–92.

38 Synesius, *Essays and Hymns*, 1093. As noted above, the toga had tremendous symbolic significance for the Romans. For example, the emperor Augustus required all Roman citizens to wear it in the forum. Suetonius, *Twelve Caesars*, 77.

39 "When Rufinus had concerted these infamous devices, he discovered that Alaric became seditious and disobedient to the laws, for he was displeased that he was not entrusted with the command of some other military forces besides the Barbarians . . ."
Zosimus, *The History of Count Zosimus, Sometime Advocate and Chancellor of the Roman Empire: Complete in One Volume* (London: J. Davis, 1814), 133.

40 Zosimus, *History*, 165.

4 * THE MULTICULTURALIST MEXICA

1 The Spanish accounts are from Cortes and one of his soldiers, Bernal Diaz. See Hernán Cortes, *Cortes: Five Letters 1519–1526*, trans. J. Bayard Morris (London: Routledge, 1928), 218; Bernal del Castillo Diaz, *The Discovery and Conquest of Mexico*, trans. Genaro Garcia (New York: Farrar, Straus & Cudahy, 1956). For the Aztec account, see the Florentine Codex in *Conquest of New Spain: 1585 Revision*, trans. S. L. Cline (Salt Lake City: University of Utah Press, 1989), 130.

2 Diaz, *Discovery and Conquest*, 321.

3 According to Cortes's secretary and biographer, Francisco Lopez de Gómara, Cortes grew up a sickly child, becoming a troublemaker as a young adult. His parents were undoubtedly relieved that he achieved the relatively modest status of notary. See Francisco Lopez de Gómara, *Cortes: The Life of the Conqueror by His Secretary*, trans. Lesley Byrd Simpson (Berkeley: University of California Press, 1964), 7–8.

4 Cortes's soldier Bernal Díaz Del Castillo wrote the following: "It was stated that he had reigned for seventeen years and was the best king they ever had in Mexico, and that he had personally triumphed in three wars against countries he had subjugated." See Diaz, *Discovery and Conquest*, 294.

5 Diaz asserts that Montezuma could field one hundred and fifty thousand, though some estimates were as high as four hundred thousand. See Diaz, *Discovery and Conquest*, 56.

6 It is also notable that the Nahua translator Malintzin probably did not speak Spanish at this point, so Montezuma's speech underwent a double translation from Nahua to Mayan to Spanish. So, nuances of Montezuma's flowery language might have been lost or misinterpreted. Only later second and thirdhand versions of the initial encounter suggest that Montezuma made obeisance to Cortes as a deity. These sources had motives for portraying events this way. Surviving members of the Aztec elite wanted to blame Montezuma's foolishness for their loss to the Spanish. Europeans, like Gómara, confident in their cultural superiority, probably fantasized that superstitious natives worshipped them as gods.

7 Encisco Y Valdivia shipwrecked near the coast in 1511. Several survivors were either killed and eaten, or enslaved. Cortes's Mayan translator, Geronimo de Aguilar, was one of two survivors. There were also two exploratory visits by Cordoba and Grijalva (in 1517 and 1518). Both men were attacked. See Juan de Grijalva, *The Discovery of New Spain in 1518*, trans. Henry R. Wagner (Berkeley: Cortes Society, 1942), 73.

8 Diaz, *Discovery and Conquest*, 77.

9 According to the Florentine Codex, Montezuma even attempted to blockade the roads to Tenochtitlan. See *Conquest of New Spain*, 64. If anything, Montezuma considered himself the superior being. According to Cortes, attendants pushed him away when he tried to embrace the Aztec king. See Cortes, *Five Letters*, 69; Diaz, *Discovery and Conquest*, 193.

10 Cortes lists the following in the siege of Tenochtitlan: "40 horse, 550 foot, including 80 crossbowmen and musketeers and eight or nine field guns, but very little powder" (Cortes, *Five Letters*, 137). This was probably the peak strength Cortes's force achieved since it included the combined resources of his and Narvaez's force before the subsequent losses. The Florentine Codex describes the Aztec tactics for avoiding projectiles: "when we Mexicans had learned to judge how the shots from the guns and bolts from the crossbows would fall, none of us ever ran a direct course. We would zig-zag from one side to the other" (*Conquest of New Spain*, 67).

11 Whatever the crossbow's effectiveness, Cortes never had more than a combined total of eighty crossbows and arquebuses. The longbow was still widely used in Europe as late as the 1600s, because, in the hands of a skilled bowman, it was superior to the crossbow and the arquebus. The Aztecs had many skilled bowmen, who were trained to hunt with bows since early childhood. See Hans Delbrück, *History of the Art of War: Within the Framework of Political History*, trans. Walter J. Renfroe (Westport, CT: Greenwood Press, 1985), 39–40. See also Trevor Nevitt Dupuy, *The Evolution of Weapons and Warfare* (New York: Da Capo Press, 1984), 97.

12 The "Anonymous Conquistador, a companion of Hernan Cortes" describes the cotton armor of the Aztecs as being "two fingers thick" and capable of deflecting arrows. See *Narrative of Some Things of New Spain and of the Great City of Temestitan, Mexico: Documents and Narratives Concerning the Discovery and Conquest of Latin America*, trans. Marshall Howard, vol. 1 (New York: Cortes Society, 1969), 21–22.

13 The Aztecs did not use captured Spanish swords as swords, but instead worked the blades into javelin tips, suggesting that they did not think the Spanish swords were superior to their own maquahuitl. The maquahuitl was a long wooden club, similar to a cricket bat, with sharp obsidian blades embedded in it. The obsidian blades can hold a sharper edge than tempered steel. See *Narrative of Some Things*, 1, 23.

14 Cortes's secretary and biographer, López de Gomara, who was not present during the conquest of Mexico, makes the claim that the Aztecs viewed horses as divine centaurs. This was typical of Gomara, who liked to think the Aztecs were awed by the godlike presence of his countrymen. See de Gómara, *Cortes: The Life*, 46. By contrast, in the Florentine Codex, the Aztecs describe the horses as deer. Diaz notes that the Aztecs killed and ate the horses they captured. See Diaz, *Discovery and Conquest*, 352.

15 *Obras históricas, publicadas y anotadas por Alfredo Chavero, Historia Chichimeca* (Mexico City: Oficina tip. de la Secretaria de fomento, 1892), 205–7.

16 The Aztecs quickly learned to use pikes against the Spanish horses and scattered cobbles in pathways and courtyards to impede them. They also submerged pikes in Lake Texcoco, allowing their own small canoes to pass, but skewering the deeper-hulled Spanish brigantines.

17 In flower wars (*xochiyaoyotl*), the Mexica attempted to disable their opponents, typically by cutting their hamstrings. Spanish accounts of their battles with the Aztecs never mention this tactic. Instead, they describe the Aztecs' heavy use of lethal projectile weapons (arrows, spears, and rocks), which are best suited for killing at a distance, not for taking live captives. Of Diaz's numerous battle accounts, only a few describe the sort of hand-to-hand attacks in which captives might be taken; the vast majority describes massive assaults with projectile weapons. Díaz describes only one incident in which the Aztecs clearly planned to take a captive: when they tried to take Cortes. See Diaz, *Discovery and Conquest*, 380.

18 Extant Aztec codices exquisitely depict the tribute the Aztecs extracted from the provinces: textiles, chilies, precious stones, feathers, and shields. For example, see *Codex Mendoza* (Tenochtitlan, 1541), 17V.

19 See the Durán Codex in Diego Durán, *The History of the Indies of New Spain*, Civilization of the American Indian Series 210, trans. Doris Heyden (Norman: University of Oklahoma Press, 1994), 236–37. Like Guaxaca, Alauiztla and Oztoman were depopulated before being colonized. See Durán, *History*, 210, 344.

20 Shirley Brice Heath, *Telling Tongues: Language Policy in Mexico, Colony and Nation* (New York: Teachers College Press, 1972), 3.

21 See Durán, *History*, 210, 232.

22 Diaz, *Discovery and Conquest*, 122.

23 For example, see the *Codex Chimalpopoca*, which has been translated by John Bierhorst in *The Codex Chimalpopoca: History and Mythology of the Aztecs*, trans. John Bierhorst (Tucson: University of Arizona Press, 1992), 158–60.

24 Diaz, *Discovery and Conquest*, 157.

25 Describing the Aztecs' fractionalization to the Spanish emperor, he quoted the Bible: "Every kingdom divided against itself is brought to desolation" (Cortes, *Five Letters*, 53).

26 After leaving Cholula for Tenochtitlan, Cortes claimed to have "over four thousand" native allies accompanying him.

27 Cortes wrote: "Your Majesty can well imagine... what the defenders of the city would feel on seeing themselves attacked by those whom they thought to be their vassals and friends . . ." See Cortes, *Five Letters*, 180–81.

28 Cortes, *Five Letters*, 209.

29 Diaz, Discovery and Conquest, 366–67.

30 Cortes, *Five Letters*, 224. Cortes estimated the allies killed fifteen thousand fleeing Aztecs in a single day. See Cortes, *Five Letters*, 227.

5 * ISLAM, FROM MELTING POT TO MILLET

1 By the reign of Sultan Hisham ibn Abd al-Malik, roughly a hundred years after the beginning of the Islamic era, the Islamic domain had expanded to 13.2 million square kilometers.

2 Ironically, anti-Muslim polemicists find common cause with eighth- and ninth-century Muslim historians and quote them extensively, while ignoring seventh-century Christian sources that depict a more tolerant Islam. For example, Robert Spencer celebrates the historian Ibn Ishaq as a "pious Muslim," who presents a "devastating refutation of the whitewashed, peaceful Muhammad of PC myth." See Robert Spencer, *The Politically Incorrect Guide to Islam (and the Crusades)* (Washington, DC: Regnery, 2005), 16.

3 For example, both Arab and Byzantine sources (al-Tabari and Theophanes) describe the early Islamic siege of Constantinople (674–78 CE).

4 See book 15 of Johan bar Penkaye's *Rish Melle*, translated in Sebastian P. Brock, "North Mesopotamia in the Late 7th Century: Book XV of John Bar Penkāyê's 'Riš Mellē,'" *Jerusalem Studies in Arabic and Islam* 9 (1987): 57.

5 Syriac speakers referred to the early invaders as *Mhaggraye* or *Tayyaye* (Arabs); Greek speakers called them *Agarenoi* or *Sarakenoi.* One of the earliest non-Islamic sources (the *Doctrina Jacobi Nuper Baptizati*) does not refer to Muslim invaders, but to forces of "Saracens and Jews." A translation of this fascinating document can be found at *Teaching of Jacob Newly Baptized*, trans. Andrew S. Jacobs, accessed July 18, 2022, http://andrewjacobs.org/translations/doctrina.html. Substantial Christian forces fought alongside Muslims at least until the end of the second Islamic civil war. The Christian Taghlib tribe, for example, fought on behalf of Muslim leaders, marching into battle bearing crosses. The al-Jarajimah, who were also Christian, fought alongside Muslim forces and were exempt from poll taxes. See Ahmad ibn-Jabir al-Baladhuri, *The Origins of the Islamic State: Being a Translation from the Arabic of the Kitab Futuh Al-Buldan*, trans. Philip Hitti, vol. 1 (New York: Columbia University Press, 1916), 249.

6 According to Ibn Khallikan's thirteenth-century biographical sketch, Khalid al-Qasri constructed a church in Iraq around 730 CE. See Ibn Khallikan, *Kitab Wafayat al-Ayan (Ibn Khallikan's Biographical Dictionary)*, trans. William MacGuckin Slane, vol. 1 (Paris: Oriental Translation Fund of Great Britain and Ireland, 1842), 485.

7 For example, the Kathisma Church, the ruins of which lie neglected by the side of Israel's Highway 60, was shared by Christians and Muslims. In other locations, such as Amman, mosques were colocated in complexes with churches. See figure 14 in Alastair Northedge and C.-M. Bennett, *Studies on Roman and Islamic 'Ammān: The Excavations of Mrs. C-M Bennett and Other Investigations* (Oxford: Oxford University Press, 1992).

8 Maayan Cohen and Deborah Cvikel, "Ma-agan Mikhael B, Israel: A Preliminary Report of a Late Byzantine–Early Islamic Period Shipwreck," *International Journal of Nautical Archaeology* 48, no. 1 (November 20, 2018): https://onlinelibrary.wiley.com/doi/10.1111/1095-9270.12331; Ariel David, "Shipwreck Off Israeli Coast Changes What We Know About the Early Islamic Period," *Haaretz*, March 30, 2022, https://www.haaretz.com/israel-news/2022-03-30/ty-article-magazine/shipwreck-changes-what-we-know-about-the-early-islamic-period/00000180-5bb7-d615-a9bf-dff7aa9b0000.

9 The eighth-century historian, al-Kalbi, lists a vast array of idols, along with the tribes that worshipped them. The decision to raid another tribe often involved the gods directly; it was based on a sortilege ritual using the idols. See Hisham al-Kalbi, *The Book of Idols*, trans. Nabih Amin Faris (Princeton, NJ: Princeton University Press, 1952), 35, 47. Pre-Islamic poetry is replete with exultant accounts of one tribe's depredations on another. See, for example, Zuhair's poem in *Mu'allaqat (Die Sieben Mu'allakat)* (Berlin: W. Speman, 1891), 52–54.

10 Qur'an 49:11–13 (translation mine).

11 Author's translation of a hadith (saying attributed to Muhammad). Aḥmad ibn Muhammad Ibn Hanbal, *al-Musnad wa-bi-hāmishihi kitāb Muntakhab kanz al-'ummāl fī sunan al-aqwāl wa-al-af'āl lil-Muttaqī al-Hindī.*, vol. 6 (Cairo: al-Maṭba'ah al-Maymanīyah, 1895), Hadith no. 23489. "Red" likely refers to lighter skin, though some hadith scholars have suggested "black" refers to Arabs and "red" to Persians and other non-Arabs.

12 Coins from the author's collection. The left coin bears a menorah, along with an Arabic legend that likely reads "there is no god but Allah." The reverse (not shown) reads "Muhammad is the Messenger of God" in Arabic. Some scholars have tried to dismiss the menorahs on similar coins as inverted images of mosque domes. However, this rare specimen clearly shows a three-prong base, typical of menorah images of the time. See Dan Barag, "The Islamic Candlestick Coins of Jerusalem," *Israel Numismatic Journal* 10 (1988–89). The center coin mimics a Byzantine design with a ruler bearing a cross and globus cruciger. For other examples, see Clive Foss, *Arab-Byzantine Coins* (Washington, DC: Dumbarton Oaks, 2008), 46–47. The coin on the right depicts a Zoroastrian fire temple; the obverse (not shown) depicts the

Muslim governor of Basra in the image of an infidel Sasanian monarch. Most of the text on the obverse is Pahlavi. However, the exergue bears an Arabic *bismillah* ("in the name of Allah") legend.

13 This was most likely a deliberate policy choice. They already had to change the pre-Islamic dies to add Arabic text and dates, so it would have been a simple matter to replace the images at the same time. Yet they chose not to. In any case, coins were not the only place early Muslims stamped "infidel" religious symbols. For example, when the Islamic government rebuilt the Hammat Gader baths near the Sea of Galilee, it added an inscription that credits Mu'awiya's governor with construction of the baths; the inscription bears a cross.

14 Translation in Michael Philip Penn, *When Christians First Met Muslims: A sourcebook of the Earliest Syriac Writings on Islam* (Oakland: University of California Press, 2015), 36. Johan Bar Penkaye, a Christian monk, similarly wrote that God had "prepared them [the Arabs] beforehand to hold Christians in great honour." See the translation provided in Brock, "North Mesopotamia in the Late 7th Century," 57.

15 The Armenian chronicler Sebeos notes that Mu'awiya hired a Jewish governor. See Sebeos, *The Armenian History attributed to Sebeos*, ed. James Howard-Johnson, trans. Robert W. Thomson (Liverpool: Liverpool University Press), 102–3. He also employed thousands of Christian fighters. See Sebeos, *Armenian History*, 154.

16 Qur'an 2:256.

17 Qur'an 2:62 (author's translation). Qur'an 3:199 repeats this theme. The phrase, "[who] believe in God and the Last Day," appears over a hundred times in the Qur'an, mostly to identify those whom God favors. Significantly, it is a formulation that implicitly includes followers of all the contemporary monotheistic faiths. Another pair of verses (Qur'an 7:157–58) claim that Muhammad is foretold in the Torah and the Gospel and that he is "Messenger of God to *you all*." Early scholars disagreed about who the "Sabians" were. Several Muslim leaders used the category to justify tolerance of members of non-Abrahamic faiths.

18 This view of early Islam was first proposed by Professor Fred Donner. See Fred M. Donner, *Muhammad and the Believers: at the Origins of Islam* (Cambridge, MA: Harvard University Press, 2012); Fred M. Donner, "From Believers to Muslims: Confessional Self-Identity in the Early Islamic Community," *Al-Abhath* (2003): 9–53.

19 The document is regarded as authentic by even the most skeptical Western historians.

20 Qur'an 41:34. See also Qur'an 24:22, Qur'an 5:49, and Qur'an, 42:39.

21 The Banu Umayya, for example, harshly persecuted the early Muslims in Mecca. However, after Muhammad conquered Mecca, he forgave them; they joined him and ultimately furnished more of early Islam's caliphs than any other lineage.

22 Even eighth- and ninth-century Muslim historians, who emphasize the role of Muslim piety in the Islamic conquests, provide many accounts of Christians and Jews aiding and abetting Muslim forces against the Byzantines. For example, the ninth-century historian Baladhuri describes how both Christians and Jews of Hims vowed to hold the city for the Islamic state against the Byzantines: "no governor of Heraclius shall enter the city of Hims unless we are first vanquished and exhausted." See al-Baladhuri, *The Origins of the Islamic State*, 1:211.

23 The Abbasid government was still minting coins bearing both Pahlavi and Arabic writing—as well as Zoroastrian fire temples—150 years into the Islamic era, which suggests these Persians' cultural sensibilities were accommodated, if not integrated.

24 Al-Jahiz, whose name means "goggle-eyed," was a scholar's scholar. He wrote over a hundred books and was killed when a stack of books in his personal library fell on him.

25 Al-Jahiz, *The Life and Works of Jahiz: Transl. of Selected Texts*, ed. D. M. Hawke, trans. Charles Pellat (Berkeley: University of California Press, 1969), 92. The "affected orator" had spoken positively of the army's diversity, saying that it was good the groups could work together. However, the mere acknowledgment of ethnic difference was unacceptable to al-Jahiz's correspondent. Al-Jahiz did write a book lauding the virtues of black people over those of white people (*Kitab Fakhr as-Sudan ala al-Bidan*), but it had a tongue-in-cheek, satirical tone. It can be read as a parody of the *Shu'ubiyya* movement, which sought to maintain distinct cultural identities for individual groups, particularly Persians.

26 See Fred McGraw Donner, *The Early Islamic Conqeusts* (Princeton, NJ: Princeton University Press, 1981), 258.

27 In Persia, in particular, Islam faced cultural backlash from the Shu'ubiyya movement, which sought to keep the Persian language and culture from being overwhelmed by the Arabic influence.

28 The historians al-Tabari and al-Waqidi had Persian roots; Abu Ubayd was Greek; and al-Bukhari came from Uzbekistan.

29 Robert G Hoyland, *In God's Path: The Arab Conquests and the Creation of an Islamic Empire* (Oxford: Oxford University Press, 2015), 162–63, 206.

30 Umayyad dirham from the author's collection. The verses in the center of the coin are from Qur'an 112:1–3.

31 Other verses on the Dome of the Rock include "Praise be to God, who did not take a son" and "Do not say three" (i.e., do not invoke the Trinity).

32 See Linda T. Darling, *Revenue-Raising and Legitimacy: Tax Collection and Finance Administration in the Ottoman Empire, 1560–1660* (Leiden: E. J. Brill, 1996), 27; Oded Peri, "The Muslim Waqf and the Collection of Jizya in Late Eighteenth-Century Jerusalem," in *Ottoman Palestine, 1800–1914: Studies in Economic and Social history*, ed. Gad Gilbar (Leiden: E. J. Brill, 1990), 287. It may also have stemmed from rulers believing they were more secure

with a "divide and conquer" approach that segregated the population into contingents that had competing interests and were separately dependent on them for their status.

33 Many of the sartorial and other restrictions were outlined in the so-called "Pact of Umar." A copy of this pact is provided in Abu Bakr Ahmad Ibn Muhammad Al-Khallal, *Ahl al-Milah wa al-Ridah wa al-Zanadiqah wa Tarik kkal-Salah was al-Fara'd Min Kitab al-Jame*, vol. 2 (Riyadh: Maktabet al-Ma'arif lil Nasher was al-Tawzi, 1996), 94. Another is in Abu Bakr Muhammad ibn al-Walid Al-Turtushi, *Siraj al-Muluk* (Alexandria: al-Matba a al Wataniya, 1872), 229–30. However, both date from several centuries after the pact was allegedly written and are of dubious provenance. Regardless of its authenticity, this pact either reflected or directed the policies of many Muslim rulers toward their non-Muslim subjects for a thousand years. We can see "Pact of Umar" restrictions on dhimmi dress in Ottoman firmans, for example. See Ahmet Refik, *On altıncı asırda İstanbul hayatı: 1553–1591* (Istanbul: Devlet Basımevi, 1935), 50–51.

34 For example, one Christian, Abu Umar ibn Gundislavus, became vizier, the highest nonhereditary office. A Jew, Hasdai bin Shaprut, was the caliph's physician, unofficial vizier, and foreign affairs minister. Many other Jews attained prestigious bureaucratic and diplomatic posts.

35 Juan Gil, *Corpus scriptorum Muzarabicorum* (Madrid: Instituto Antonio de Nebrija, 1973), 270–315.

36 Jahangir, *The Tuzuk-i-Jahangiri*, ed. Alexander Rogers, trans. Henry Beveridge, vol. 1 (Delhi: Munshiram Manoharlal, 1968), 37–38.

37 Angus Maddison, *The World Economy: Historical Statistics* (Paris: OECD Publishing, 2003), 259.

38 Kritovoulos, *History of Mehmed the Conqueror*, trans. Charles T. Riggs (Princeton, NJ: Princeton University Press, 1954), 94–95. Another contemporary account is provided by George Sphrantzes, *The Fall of the Byzantine Empire: A Chronicle by George Sphrantzes*, trans. Marios Philippides (Amherst: University of Massachusetts Press, 1980), 134. Sphrantzes takes a more negative view of Mehmed, but confirms the "millet" arrangement.

39 Author's photograph of the original document, which is kept in a remote mountain monastery in Fojnica, Bosnia. In part, it reads: "Let nobody attack, insult, or endanger their life or their property, or the property of their church..."

40 The "millet system" originated as a patchwork of *firmans* (decrees), *ahdnames* (pacts), and official practices with various groups. The term is newer than the concept it represents, but it is not quite the neologism or "myth" that Braude suggests. See Benjamin Braude, "Foundation Myths of the Millet System," in *Christians and Jews in the Ottoman Empire: The Functioning of a Plural Society* (London: Holmes & Meier Publishers, Ltd., 1982), 69–88. For example, there are references to Armenian and Orthodox millets in 1746 CE and 1756 CE firmans. Ahmet Refik, *Hicri on ikinci asırda İstanbul hayatı: 1100–1200* (Istanbul: Devlet Matbaasi, 1930), 160–63, 83–84, 205–6. Earlier

Ottoman administrations also used terms like *ta'ife* and *cemaat* to refer to groups with millet-like status, so Braude's argument is about little more than semantics. Documents like the Ahdname of Milodraž and narrative accounts like Kritovolous's establish that the Ottomans implemented a set of policies that we now associate with the term "millet." Whether the term was actually used at the time, is an inconsequential point.

41 Although Kurds were an ethnic group within the Muslim community, they were granted millet-like status through an array of agreements and declarations by various Sultans. See Latif Tas, "The Myth of the Ottoman Millet System: Its Treatment of Kurds and a Discussion of Territorial and Non-Territorial Autonomy," *International Journal on Minority and Group Rights* 21, 4 (October 2014): 497–526. Kemal Karpat asserts that the Ottoman government recognized both Kurds and Turkmen as millets. See Kemal Karpat, "Millets and Nationality: The Roots of the Incongruity of Nation and State in the Post-Ottoman Era," in *Christians and Jews in the Ottoman Empire: The Functioning of a Plural Society* (London: Holmes & Meier Publishers, Ltd., 1982), 149. In the nineteenth century, the millet conception acquired an increasingly ethnonational flavor, with the term evolving to mean "nation."

42 Quer, for instance, praises Ottoman multiculturalism as an example for modern governments. Giovanni M. Quer, "De-Territorializing Minority Rights in Europe: A Look Eastward," *Journal of Ethnopolitics and Minority Issues in Europe* 12, no. 1 (2013): 76–98.

43 In 1492, when Jews were expelled from Spain, Sultan Bayezid II sent his navy to evacuate them to the Ottoman Empire, famously ridiculing the Spanish monarchs: "Can such a king be called wise and intelligent, one who impoverishes his country and enriches my kingdom?" Although he treated Jews far better than did the Europeans, Bayezid was one of the less tolerant Ottoman sultans.

44 As Voltaire wrote: "The Sultan governs in peace twenty million people of different religions… The empire is full of Jacobites, Nestorians, and Monothelites; it contains Copts, Christians of St. John, Jews and Hindoos. The annals of Turkey do not record any revolt instigated by any of these religions." See Voltaire, *Toleration and Other Essays, Translated with an Introduction by Joseph McCabe* (New York: Knickerboker Press, 1912), 23.

45 A number of these were brought into the Sultan's service through the devşirme, in which Christian youths were recruited (often forcibly), converted to Islam, and then trained for service. The practice ended during the seventeenth century.

46 In the words of a sixteenth-century Italian trained to serve the Sultan, the goal was to produce a "warrior statesman and loyal Muslim who at the same time should be a man of letters and polished speech, profound courtesy and honest morals." See Halil İnalcık, *The Ottoman Empire : the Classical Age 1300–1600* (London: Phoenix Press, 2000), 78–79.

47 As Sultan Murad IV decreed: "They are to be treated with contempt, made submissive, and humbled in their clothes, and styles of dress… do not

allow them to mount a horse, wear sable fur, sable fur caps, satin, and silk velvet... Do not allow infidels and Jews to go about in Muslim manner and garment." The English translation here is from Marc David Baer, "Honored by the Glory of Islam: The Ottoman State, Non-Muslims, and Conversion to Islam in Late Seventeenth-Century Istanbul and Rumelia" (PhD diss., University of Chicago, 2001), 153–54. Even Muslims could not ignore the dress restrictions. William Eton, an eighteenth-century traveler, recounts an Ottoman judge caning a Muslim for wearing a turban that might be mistaken for that of an "infidel." See William Eton, *A Survey of the Turkish Empire* (London: T. Cadell, Jr. and W. Davies, 1798), 34–35.

48 Non-Muslims were not allowed to live anywhere near mosques. See Refik, *On altıncı asırda İstanbul hayatı*, 14–15, 52. Beyond that, the various millets were mostly confined to distinct sectors, which are still evident in larger cities. Ottoman defters show that small towns were likewise segregated. See Halil İnalcık, "Ottoman Methods of Conquest," in *The Ottoman Empire: Conquest, Organiization and Economy* (London: Varirorum Reprints, 1978), 126–27.

49 Ogier Ghiselin De Busbecq, *The Life and Letters of Ogier Ghiselin de Busbecq*, trans. Charles Thornton Forster and F. H. Blackburne Daniell (London: C. Kegan Paul, 1881).

50 Samuel Greene Wheeler Benjamin, *The Turk and the Greek: Or, Creeds, Races, Society, and Scenery in Turkey* (New York: Hurd and Houghton, 1867), 31.

51 Istimalet can be translated as "inclining to" or "attracting."

52 Examples of the tax exemptions are in the Kanun of the Vlachs of Herzegovina. See Ahmet Akgündüz, *Osmanlı Kanunnâmeleri ve Hukukî Tahlilleri*, vol. 2 (Istanbul Araştırmaları Vakfı: Osmanlı Araştırmaları Vakfı, 1990), 409–12; Halil İnalcık, *Fatih devri üzerinde tetkikler ve vesikalar* (Ankara: Türk Tarih Kurumu Basımevi, 1954), 156–57. For further discussion of istimalet policies, see the following sources: Halil İnalcık, "The Status of the Greek Orthodox Patriarch Under the Ottomans," *Turcica* 21–22 (1991): 196–97; Branislav Đurđev, *Uloga crkve u starijoj istoriji srpskog naroda* (Sarajevo: Svjetlost, 1964), 122; and İstimalet in İslâm Ansiklopedisi İslâm. Ansiklopedisi (Istanbul: Maarif Matbaasi, 1993).

53 Sir Charles Eliot, *Turkey in Europe* (London: E. Arnold, 1980), 82.

54 Population estimates before the nineteenth century are imprecise. But it is likely Muslims did not become a majority until at least the sixteenth century. An 1831 census confirms a persistently large non-Muslim population: non-Muslims constituted 17 percent of the population in Anatolia and 63 percent in Rumelia. See Stanford J. Shaw, "The Ottoman Census System and Population, 1831–1914," *International Journal of Middle East Studies* 9, no. 3 (October 1978): 326. The Ottoman government resembled some earlier Muslim regimes in this regard. Muslims were a small minority for all ninety years of the Umayyad dynasty and all three hundred years of the Mughal reign.

55 Edmund Spencer, *Travels in European Turkey, in 1850*, vol. 1 (London: Colburn, 1851), 130–31. The early American traveler, Samuel Benjamin,

wrote a similar, ominous assessment: "The body politic is too much like Nebuchadnezzar's dream, composed of materials so incoherent that a blow could resolve it into a confused mess of antagonistic elements." See Benjamin, *The Turk and the Greek*, 32. Around this time, there were two prominent instances in which Christians went after Jews: the Damascus affair and the Rhodes blood libel (both in 1840).

56 Vasileios Meichanetsidis, "The Genocide of the Greeks of the Ottoman Empire 1913–1923: A Comprehensive Overview," *Genocide Studies International* (Spring 2015): 104–73; Benny Morris and Dror Ze'evi, *The Thirty-Year Genocide: Turkey's Destruction of Its Christian Minorities, 1894–1924* (Cambridge, MA: Harvard University Press, 2019), 467. The killings during the 1820s and World War I were preceded by a 1770 mass killing in Smyrna, witnessed by Baron de Tott. See François Baron de Tott, *Memoirs of Baron de Tott*, vol. 1 (London: G. G. J. and J. Robinson, 1786), 237.

57 After a century, the numbers of Armenians murdered and deported remain controversial. Claiming that the event *was* a genocide is illegal in Turkey; claiming that it *was not* is illegal in France.

6 ✻ THE BALKANS—MILLET, MULTICULTURALISM, AND MURDER

1 Al Kamen, "NATO Going for Green Eggs on Its Face," *Washington Post*, February 9, 2000, https://www.washingtonpost.com/wp-srv/WPcap/2000-02/09/032r-020900-idx.html; Dr. Seuss, *The Sneetches and Other Stories* (New York: Random House, 1961).

2 E. Bosch and F Calafell et al., "Paternal and Maternal Lineages in the Balkans Show a Homogeneous Landscape over Linguistic Barriers, Except for the Isolated Aromuns," *Annals of Human Genetics* 70, no. 4 (August 2006): 459–87.

3 The differences among these languages are less than those between British and American English. Slovenian and Macedonian, however, are also South Slavic languages (like Serbo-Croatian) but they are not mutually intelligible.

4 By contrast, 36 percent of Americans and 89 percent of Nigerians attend services weekly. *The Age Gap in Religion Around the World*, Pew Research (2018), 64–67.

5 For example, Slovenia's Commission on Concealed Mass Graves recently documented a mass grave with fifteen thousand victims, exposed during highway construction. "Forgotten Victims: Slovenian Mass Grave Could Be Europe's Killing Fields," *Spiegel International*, August 21, 2007, https://www.spiegel.de/international/europe/forgotten-victims-slovenian-mass-grave-could-be-europe-s-killing-fields-a-501058.html.

6 The Ustaše sought an improbable alliance between Catholic Croats and Muslim Bosniaks (who they asserted were "Muslim Croats") against the Orthodox Serbs. The numbers of "cleansed" Serbs are still disputed: they range as high as six hundred thousand killed and three hundred thousand deported. Large numbers of Roma and Jews were also killed.

7 Author's translations from the memoir of Plenipotentiary General von Horstenau. Edmund Glaise von Horstenau, *Ein General im Zwielicht: die Erinnerungen Edmund Glaises von Horstenau*, ed. Peter Broucek, vol. 3 (Vienna: Böhlau Verlag, 1988), 167–68. The concentration camp he described (Jasenovac) was known as the "Auschwitz of the Balkans."

8 Some Balkan people, attracted by the Islamic faith (or by the perquisites of being Muslim under the Ottomans) converted to Islam rather than remain in millets; conversion was most prevalent in Bosnia, Kosovo, and Albania. Roughly a quarter of Bosnians had converted by the sixteenth century. See Vera Kržišnik-Bukić, *Bosanska identiteta med preteklostjo in príhodnostjo* (Ljubljana: Institut za narodnostna vprašanja, 1996), 22.

9 Sir Heny Blount, *A Voyage into the Levant: a Breife Relation of a Iourney, Lately Performed by Master H. B.* (London: I. L. for Andrew Crooke, 1636), 109.

10 Originally, the millets were a religious conception. But on a regional level, they increasingly defined (or were defined by) ethnic boundaries. This was reflected in the establishment of regional Orthodox millets, e.g., the Serbian and Bulgarian millets. Perhaps in reaction to the spread of nationalism in Europe, people in the Balkans increasingly tended to conflate religion and ethnicity. For example, Bosnian Muslims (Bosniaks) and Albanians were often referred to as "Turks," even when they had neither Turkish ancestry nor the ability to speak Turkish. Similarly, Catholics, irrespective of their origins, were deemed Croats and Orthodox were deemed Serbs. See Rade Petrović, *Nacionalno pitanje u Dalmaciji u xix stoljeću: (Narodna stranka i nacionalno pitanje 1860–1880)* (Sarajevo: Svjetlost, 1968), 366.

11 Spencer, *Travels in European Turkey*, 1, 96. Fifty years later, a journalist recounted an anecdote illustrating how factionalism had made even simple law enforcement difficult and dangerous when different groups were involved. He describes the killing of a Bulgarian by an Albanian in Macedonia. Although the Albanian's guilt was clear, the Ottoman authorities could not bring him to justice because his community would not cooperate, even after many of them were jailed: "To punish a simple outbreak of private passion in which no political element was involved he [the Ottoman prefect] had to mobilise the whole armed force of his district, and even then he failed" (H. N. Brailsford, *Macedonia: Its Races and Their Future* [London: Methuen, 1904], 32).

12 The group outlined the new country in the *Corfu Declaration*, the original text of which is provided by Charles F. Horne, ed., *The Great Events of the Great War*, vol. 7 (New York: National Alumni, printed by J. J. Little & Ives, 1920), 23–25.

13 While the Ustaše sought to cleanse their territories of Serbs, the Četniks, a collection of Serbian paramilitaries, attempted to cleanse theirs of Bosniaks and Croats. Although the Četniks sometimes fought against the Nazis, they also collaborated with them, particularly when it served their underlying goal, which was to form a greater Serbia, free of non-Serbs. The Četniks ultimately killed an estimated sixty thousand Bosniaks and Croats.

14 Even today, numbers of deaths are widely disputed. Total deaths in Yugoslavia have been estimated at one million. The Croatian-dominated Nezavisna Drava Hrvatska (NDH) genocide of the Serbs accounted for roughly three hundred and fifty thousand; Četnik killings, sixty thousand; and the Bleiburg repatriations, two hundred thousand. See Vladimir Geiger, "Human Losses of Croats in World War II and the Immediate Post-War Period Caused by the Chetniks (Yugoslav Army in the Fatherland) and the Partizans (People's Liberation Army and the Partizan Detachment of Yugoslavia/Yugoslav Army) and the Yugoslav Communi," *Review of Croatian history* 8, no. 1 (2012): 77–121.

15 The ethnic breakdown of the Partisan force very closely approximated that of the entire country. See Sabrina P. Ramet, *The Three Yugoslavias: State-Building and Legitimation, 1918–2005* (Bloomington: Indiana University Press, 2006), 153.

16 Ivo Banac, "Political Change and National Diversity," *Daedalus* 119, no. 1 (Winter 1990): 152.

17 John R. Lampe, *Yugoslavia as History: Twice There Was a Country* (Cambridge: Cambridge University Press, 2000), 236–37.

18 Nikola Bakovic, "No One Here is Afraid of Blisters or Work," *Hungarian Historical Review* 4, no. 1 (2015): 30.

19 In one example, a commander recounts how a young man whose father had been killed by the Ustaše overcame his loathing for Croats by working together with them in the youth brigades. See Bakovic, "No One Here is Afraid," 49.

20 As Marx and Engels put it, "the working men have no country…National differences and antagonisms between peoples are vanishing gradually from day to day." See Karl Marx and Friedrich Engels, *Manifesto of the Communist Party* (New York: Rand School of Social Science, 1919), 36.

21 Terry Martin, *The Affirmative Action Empire: Nations and Nationalism in the Soviet Union, 1923–1939* (Ithaca, NY: Cornell University Press, 2001).

22 *Soviet Culture and Power: A History in Documents, 1917–1953*, ed. Katerina Clark and Evgeny Dobrenko (New Haven, CT: Yale University Press, 2007), 61–62.

23 As Terry Martin puts it, "the nationality line on Soviet passports became one of the single most import factors in reinforcing the belief, and the social fact, that national identity was primordial and inherited" (Martin, *The Affirmative Action Empire*, 449).

24 Martin, *The Affirmative Action Empire*, 311. The divisive effects of the Soviet "Affirmative Action" program were evident in the Soviet military, as a Rand report from the 1980s noted: "Racism is the dominant feature of the relationship between Slavs and non-white non-Slavs . . ." See Alexander Alexiev and S. Engders Wimbush, *The Ethnic Factor in the Soviet Armed Forces* (Santa Monica, CA: Rand Corporation, 1983), 9. Even after the fall of the Soviet Union, violent ethnic conflicts have lingered in Soviet successor states: among Kyrgyz and Uzbeks in Kyrgyzstan; Ossetians and Abkhazia in Georgia; and so on.

25 Banac suggests that Tito may also have been motivated by concerns about Serbian domination of Yugoslavism but cites no evidence to support this view. See Banac, "Political Change and National Diversity," 153.

26 These rights are outlined in articles 171 and 246–48 of the 1974 Yugoslav constitution. Cf. *The Constitution of the Socialist Federal Republic of Yugoslavia*, ed. Dragoljub Durovic, trans. Marko Pavicic (Ljubljana: Dopisn Delavska Universza, 1974). The constitution distinguishes among *republics (republike)*, i.e., geographically defined political entities like Croatia and Bosnia, which can host multiple ethnicities; *nations (narodi)*, i.e., ethnic groups such as Serbs and Slovenes which can be distributed across republics; and *nationalities* (*narodnosti)*, i.e., members of nationalities like Albanians, whose native countries border on Yugoslavia.

27 Aleksandar Pavković, "Multiculturalism as a Prelude to State Fragmentation: The Case of Yugoslavia," *Journal of Southern Europe and the Balkans* (2001): 138.

28 See, for example, Article 242 of the 1974 Yugoslav constitution, which establishes quotas for the YPA officer corps. For a broader discussion of the nationality key policy, see Thomas S. Szayna and Michele Zanini, "The Yugoslav Respective Case," in *Identifying Potential Ethnic Conflict: Application of a Process Model* (Santa Monica, CA: Rand, 2000).

29 Some non-Albanian Muslims also responded by declaring they were Albanian to take advantage of the ethnic preferences. See Trivo Indjich, "Affirmative Action: The Yugoslav Case," *Il Politico* 48, no. 3 (1983): 547–48.

30 In his famous Kosovo Polje speech, Milošević declared, "We are again in battles and are facing battles. They are not armed, but that has not yet been ruled out." The original text of the speech is provided in "Govor Slobodana Miloševića na Gazimestanu 1989. godine," *Pecat*, June 30, 2011, http://www.pecat.co.rs/2011/06/govor-slobodana-milosevica-na-gazimestanu-1989-godine/.

31 In 2020, the World Jewish Congress asked the Croatian government to cancel a mass honoring the Ustaše (who murdered thousands of Jews and Roma in addition to Serbs).

32 Xhorxhina Bami, "Kosovo's Bosniaks, Struggling to Survive Between Albanians and Serbs," *Balkan Insight*, September 8, 2020, https://balkaninsight.com/2020/09/08/kosovos-bosniaks-struggling-to-survive-between-albanians-and-serbs/.

33 For example, see *Robert D Kaplan, Balkan Ghosts: A Journey through History* (New York: Picador, 2005).

7 * ETHNIC IDENTITY CARDS AND GENOCIDE IN RWANDA

1 James Munyaneza, "Tribute to Massacred Nyange Students," *New Times*, January 30, 2009, https://www.newtimes.co.rw/section/read/6924.

2 Eugène Kwibuka, "A Tribute to Our Heroes," *New Times*, February 1, 2018, https://www.newtimes.co.rw/section/read/228793; John Rucyahana, *The*

Bishop of Rwanda: Finding Forgiveness Amidst a Pile of Bones (Nashville, TN: Thomas Nelson, 2008), 200. Some children escaped; but six died and several others were seriously injured. "Nothing Can Stop the Nyange School Massacre Survivor Who Defied Killers," *East African*, January 17, 2014, https://www.theeastafrican.co.ke/tea/rwanda-today/news/nothing-can-stop-the-nyange-school-massacre-survivor-who-defied-killers--1321988.

3 In 2002, The Rwandan government claimed that 1,074,017 (out of roughly seven million) Rwandans were killed. See *Dénombrement Des Victimes Du Genocide: Rapport Final* (Kigali: Ministère de L'Administration Locale de L'Information et des Affaires Sociales, 2002). However, there are both higher and lower estimates. Rwandans are still discovering mass graves twenty-five years later. See Ignatius Ssuuna, "Days before 26th Anniversary of Country's Genocide, Rwanda Finds Mass Grave That Could Contain 30,000 Bodies," *USA Today*, April 5, 2020, https://www.usatoday.com/story/news/world/2020/04/05/rwanda-finds-genocide-grave-could-contain-30-000-bodies/2951851001/.

4 For example, one genocidaire I interviewed described killing his neighbor and five family members with a panga (machete).

5 Jeffrey Drope and Neil Schluger, eds., *The Tobacco Atlas*, 6th ed. (Atlanta: American Cancer Society, 2018).

6 One DNA study found a slightly higher incidence of Nilotic paternal lineages among Tutsis, but overall differences are minimal. J. R Luis et al., "The Levant versus the Horn of Africa: Evidence for Bidirectional Corridors," *American Journal of Human Genetics* 74, no. 3 (2004): 536.

7 For example, see Jean Hatzfeld, *Machete Season: The Killers in Rwanda Speak; A Report* (New York: Farrar, Straus and Giroux, 2005), 114.

8 The Kinyarwanda terms are *icyihuture* ("Tutsification") and *gucupira* ("Hutufication"). See Gerard Prunier, *The Rwanda Crisis: History of a Genocide* (New York: Columbia University Press, 1995), 13–14, 26. There is a particularly notable instance of a Twa being elevated to Tutsi status and founding a prominent Tutsi lineage. José Kagabo and Vincent Mudandagizi, "Complainte des gens de l'argile: Les Twa du Rwanda," *Cahiers d'Études africaines* (1974): 78–79.

9 Patient Kanyamachumbi, *Société, culture et pouvoir politique en Afrique interlacustre: Hutu et Tutsi de l'ancien Rwanda* (London: Viking, 1995), 120–21.

10 Prunier, *The Rwanda Crisis*, 39.

11 This was in keeping with the "Hamitic hypothesis," a racist theory with a long history. English explorer John Speke was the first to apply it to Rwandans. See John Hanning Speke, *The Discovery of the Source of the Nile* (London: Andrews UK, 1901), chapter 9. See also Edith R. Sanders, "The Hamitic Hyopthesis: Its Origin and Functions in Time Perspecive," *Journal of African History* 10, no. 4 (October 1969): 521–32.

12 Another Belgian priest wrote that Tutsis were "superb humans" with a fine combination of Aryan and Semitic traits. See Mahmood Mamdani, *When*

Victims Became Killers (Princeton, NJ: Princeton University Press, 2001), 87–88.

13 Curiously, the ID cards have the term "ubwoko" before Hutu, Tutsi, and Twa. The term translates as "clan" rather than "race" and denotes a category that consistently crosses Hutu, Tutsi, and Twa lines. It was almost as if the Belgians tacitly acknowledged that the racial distinction was a fraud. Historians disagree how Belgians determined one's "race." Some have claimed administrators identified anyone with more than ten cows as a Tutsi. However, this implies an improbably large cattle population.

14 Prunier, *The Rwanda Crisis*, 26–27; Mamdani, *When Victims Became Killers*, 89–90.

15 If this latter view had ever been held before in Rwanda it was only a very, very long time ago. In the twentieth century, it was both novel and dangerous. Two years before the genocide, one Hutu leader suggested killing Tutsis and throwing their bodies in the river to float back to "their country of origin, Ethiopia." This was recounted in a court case: Leon Mugasera v. The [Canadian] Minster of Citizenship and Immigration, A-316-01 and A-317-01 (September 8, 2003). Retrieved from http://www.law.utoronto.ca/documents/Mackin/mugesera.pdf . This was grimly prophetic: during the genocide, so many corpses would float into Lake Victoria that the locals stopped fishing there.

16 Guy Logiest, *Mission au Rwanda* (Brussels: Didier Hatier, 1988), 135. The Belgian governor Jean-Paul Harroy wrote a self-serving account that exemplified the Belgian administration's attitudes at this point, with Harroy fancying himself the "great pioneer of the Rwandan popular revolution." See Jean-Paul Harroy, *Rwanda: [de la féodalité à la démocratie 1955–1962]; souvenirs d'un compagnon de la marche du Rwanda vers la démocratie et l'indépendance* (Brussels: Académie der sciences d'outre-mer, 1984).

17 Philippe Leurquin, *Le niveau de vie des populations rurales du Ruanda-Urundi* (Louvain: Institut de recherches économiques et sociales, 1960), 203.

18 The full text of the 1957 document, titled "*Manifeste des Bahutu: Note sur l'aspect social du problème racial indigène au Rwanda*," is reproduced in F. Nkundabagenzi, *Rwanda Politque, 1958–1960* (Brussels: Centre de Recherche et d'Information Socio-Politiques, 1961), 20–29.

19 Elisabeth King, *From Classrooms to Conflict in Rwanda* (Cambridge: Cambridge University Pres, 2014), 82–83.

20 New students were also required to stand up in class and identify their "race"; if they did not know it, they were sent home to ask their parents. See Hatzfeld, *Machete Season*, 217; Omar McDoom, *Rwanda's Ordinary Killers: Interpreting Popular Participation in the Rwandan Genocide* (London: Destin Development Studies Institute, 2005), 17, 19.

21 King, *From Classrooms to Conflict*, 71.

22 Author's interviews with genocidaires in the Bugasera district in 2019. Jean Hatzfeld encountered similar responses in his interviews. Cf. Hatzfeld, *Machete Season*, 219–20.

23 "Malaysia's identity politics has triggered a competition among political parties, non-government organisations, and political elites to be the biggest champion of Malay rights and special privileges . . ." See Amy Chew, "Malaysia's Dangerous Racial and Religious Trajectory," *Interpreter*, September 25, 2019, https://www.lowyinstitute.org/the-interpreter/malaysia-s-dangerous-racial-and-religious-trajectory. Members of these organizations have spread myths about ethnic Chinese burning Malaysian flags and trying to take over.

24 Responsibility for the assassination is still disputed. Hutu extremists and the French government (at least initially) blamed the RPF. The RPF resolutely denied responsibility, noting that the missiles that downed the plane were launched from government-controlled territory. If Hutu extremists weren't responsible, they were surprisingly well prepared for the event. They had stockpiled and distributed tens of thousands of machetes (in a country where most rural households already possessed one) and trained the *Interahamwe* militia, which was steeped in ethnic hatred for Tutsis.

25 This claim is advanced by Omar McDoom, who has conducted extensive surveys of genocidaires over twenty years. There were roughly 1.7 million Hutu males aged 15–64 and one million victims; since the genocidaires were predominantly male, the arithmetic requires high numbers of both killers and victims per killer. See Chris Arnot, "What Caused the Genocide in Rwanda?" *Guardian*, November 30, 2010, https://www.theguardian.com/education/2010/nov/30/rwanda-genocide-research; Scott Straus, "How Many Perpetrators Were There in the Rwandan Genocide? An Estimate," *Journal of Genocide Research* 6, no. 1 (2004): 90, 94.

26 "Rwanda Genocide: Catholic Church Sorry for Role of Priests and Nuns in Killings," *Guardian*, November 20, 2016, https://www.theguardian.com/world/2016/nov/21/rwanda-genocide-catholic-church-sorry-for-role-of-priests-and-nuns-in-killings.

27 Hatzfeld, *Machete Season*, 214, 24.

28 See, for example, the RTLM broadcast transcript: "May 16–17 Radio Broadcast Transcript," UN International Criminal Tribunal for Rwanda, http://migs.concordia.ca/links/RwandanRadioTrascripts_RTLM.htm. This broadcast has chilling interviews with several captured children who were allegedly spies. During the genocide, RTLM broadcast useful information for genocidaires: where Tutsis were hiding; which Hutus might be helping them; and admonitions to avoid laughing while killing Tutsis in front of international aid workers. One study found that areas with RTLM coverage had significantly more killings and attributed 10 percent of all killings to RTLM's influence. David Yanagizawa-Drott, "Propaganda and Conflict: Evidence from the Rwandan Genocide," *Quarterly Journal of Economics* 129, no. 4(2014): https://live.hks.harvard.edu/publications/propaganda-and-conflict-evidence-rwandan-genocide. See also Brittnea Roozen and Hillary C. Shulman, "Tuning in to the RTLM: Tracking the Evolution of Language Alongside the Rwandan Genocide Using Social Identity Theory," *Journal of Language and Social Psychology* 33, no. 2 (2014): 165–82.

29 From an interview with a genocidaire. See Omar Shahabudin McDoom, "Predicting Violence within Genocide: A Model of Elite Competition," *Political Geography* 42 (September 2014): 19.

30 McDoom, "Predicting Violence," 41.

31 UNDP, "Human Development Index (HDI)," United Nations Development Programme, May 20, 2022, https://hdr.undp.org/data-center/human-development-index.

32 Because they became such a menace after the genocide, nearly all the dogs were killed by the RPF and UNAMIR. To this day, one rarely sees dogs in Rwanda.

33 "Community Service for Tens of Thousands of Genocidaires," *New Humanitarian*, September 21, 2006, https://www.thenewhumanitarian.org/report/61143/rwanda-community-service-tens-thousands-genocidaires.

34 Rwanda's Constitution of 2003 with Amendments through 2015, 10.2, art. 37, art. 57.

35 The Rwanda Reconciliation Barometer is published by Rwanda's National Unity and Reconciliation Commission (NURC). It is an annual assessment of the status of reconciliation in Rwanda, which includes extensive surveys of over ten thousand private households and respondents in institutional households. *Rwanda Reconciliation Barometer* (Kigali: NURC, 2015), 19. https://www.nurc.gov.rw/fileadmin/Documents/Others/RWANDA_RECONCILIATION_BAROMETER_2020.pdf

36 James Karuhanga, "Rwanda's Commitment to Peacekeeping Remains Intact 15 Years On," *New Times*, July 4, 2019, https://www.newtimes.co.rw/news/rwandas-commitment-peacekeeping-remains-intact-15-years. Rwandan UN troops have proudly introduced the umuganda tradition to countries they have been stationed in, where it has been very well received. Following on umuganda's success, the Rwandan government recently introduced "car-free" days. For two Sunday mornings each month, many roads are closed and driving motorized vehicles is discouraged across the country. The roads are taken over by huge crowds of cyclists and joggers. This event also has a festive air with some groups sporting curious matching outfits. Although it happens twice a month, the press frequently covers it, usually with photos of famous people participating alongside everyone else. Like umuganda, this event has become a unifying force and a source of national pride.

37 Heritage Foundation statistics only go back to 1997. See "Heritage Foundation," Index of Economic Freedom, accessed July 19, 2022, https://www.heritage.org/index/. The Fraser Institute rates Rwanda lower than Botswana and Uganda, ranking it number 56 in the world (in 2017). See "Economic Freedom," Fraser Institute, accessed July 19, 2022, https://www.fraserinstitute.org/economic-freedom.

38 In constant Rwandan francs, per capita GDP was 282,000 in 1960, but only 336,000 in 1993 on the eve of the genocide. See "GDP Per Capita (Constant LCU)—Rwanda," World Bank, accessed July 19, 2022, https://data.worldbank.org/indicator/NY.GDP.PCAP.KN?locations=RW.

39 "GDP (Constant 2010 US$)—Rwanda," World Bank, accessed July 19, 2022, https://data.worldbank.org/indicator/NY.GDP.MKTP.KD?locations=RW.

40 "Life Expectancy at Birth, Total (Years)—Rwanda," World Bank, accessed July 19, 2022, https://data.worldbank.org/indicator/SP.DYN.LE00.IN?locations=RW. The poverty information is from the *CIA World Factbook*, CIA.gov, accessed July 19, 2022, https://www.cia.gov/the-world-factbook/.

41 General Romeo Dallaire made these comments in a September 2020 Aegis Trust webcast that I participated in. See Aegis Trust, "From Hate to Humanity: Lessons from Rwanda," September 6, 2020, https://www.hatetohumanity.aegistrust.org/. In a subsequent session of the same webcast series, British investigative journalist and genocide expert Linda Melvern called Rusesabagina "the eyes and ears of Hutu Power in the hotel." See "From Hate to Humanity: Lessons from Rwanda," September 13, 2020. One survivor of the Hotel des Milles Collines (the hotel portrayed in *Hotel Rwanda*) has written a book recounting Rusesabagina's opportunistic behavior during the genocide and his support for "Hutu Power" terrorist organizations. See Edouard Kayihura, *Inside the Hotel Rwanda: The Surprising True Story…and Why it Matters Today* (Dallas: BenBella Books, 2014).

42 For comparison, US soldiers, along with some Dachau internees, killed nearly the entire guard contingent at the camp after they had surrendered. See Daniel Bates, "Revealed: American Doctor's First-Hand Account of How He Saw Dachau's SS Guards Being Tortured and Shot Dead by GIs in 'Cold Blood' Because They 'So Had It Coming,'" *Daily Mail*, May 20, 2015, https://www.dailymail.co.uk/news/article-3088025/How-American-doctor-witnessed-Dachau-s-SS-guards-tortured-shot-dead-GIs-cold-blood-coming.html.

43 *The Human Freedom Index 2018* (Washington, DC: Cato Institute, 2018).

44 *Rwanda Reconciliation Barometer.*

8 * FROM SERENDIPITY TO CALAMITY IN SRI LANKA

1 *Sri Pada* is one of several Sri Lankan shrines that have been shared by different religions. There are other mosques (such as the Dewatagaha mosque in Colombo) and burial sites around the country that attracted worshippers from multiple faiths.

2 Muhammad Ibn Battuta, *Ibn Battuta: Travels in Asia and Africa, 1325–1354* (London: Routledge & Sons, 1929), 254–56. In the thirteenth century, Marco Polo also marveled at Sri Lanka's pacifism, writing that the inhabitants were so lacking in combative spirit that if they ever had need of soldiers, they had to hire them from other countries. See Marco Polo, *The Travels of Marco Polo the Complete Yule-Cordier Edition*, trans. Henry Yule, vol. 2 (New York: Dover Publications, 1993), 314. In the fifteenth century, the Chinese explorer, Zheng He, also visited Sri Pada. Perhaps taking a cue from the locals, he made offerings to not only Allah, but also Buddha and the Hindu god Vishnu. Zheng He left a record of his offerings on a stone tablet (the Galle Trilingual Inscription, dated 1409), which is kept in the Colombo National Museum.

3 "Both King and People do generally like the *Christian* Religion better than their own: and respect and honour the Christians...;" (Robert Knox, *An Historical Relation Of the Island Ceylon, in the East-Indies* [London: Richard Chiswell, 1681], 83–85, 43). Knox was likely the inspiration for Defoe's *Robinson Crusoe.*

4 John Gimlette, *Elephant Complex: Travels in Sri Lanka* (New York: Alfred A. Knopf, 2016), 235–36.

5 Sir Andrew Caldecott, *Great Britain, Colonial Office, Correspondence Relating to the Constitution Of Ceylon* (London: His Majesty's Stationary Office, 1938), 81 Gimlette, *Elephant Complex*, 275. A 1951 World Bank report lauded the lack of communal conflict and the way "disputes are settled without physical violence." See *The Economic Development of Ceylon: Report of a Mission Organised by the International Bank for Reconstruction and Development* (Baltimore: Johns Hopkins University Press, 1953). A solitary communal riot did occur in 1915, but an official investigation noted that the riot was initiated by migrant Muslims from Malabar. It contrasted them with the local Muslims who "learnt in the course of centuries the necessity of living in peace with their Sinhalese fellow subjects and being tolerant to their religious observances. . . ." See P. Ramanathan, *Riots and Martial Law in Ceylon, 1915* (London: St. Martin's Press, 1916).

6 Lacille de Silva, "Parliament Spreads Deceitfulness Not Democracy—Why?" *Colombo Telegraph*, January 31, 2019, https://www.colombotelegraph.com/index.php/parliament-spreads-deceitfulness-not-democracy-why/.

7 Naipaul, *An Unfinished Journey*, 111.

8 Gautam Kumar Kshatriya, "Genetic Affinities of Sri Lankan Populations," *Human Biology* 67, no. 6 (1995): 864.

9 Naipaul, *An Unfinished Journey*, 112. William Borders, "Strife in Sri Lanka Abates, But the Tensions Persist," *New York Times*, August 30, 1977, https://www.nytimes.com/1977/08/30/archives/strife-in-sri-lanka-abates-but-the-tensions-persist-tensions-and.html.

10 K. M. de Silva, "Affirmative Action Policies: The Sri Lankan Experience," *Ethnic Studies Report* 15, no, 2 (July 1997): 278–79.

11 Burghers and Europeans, who spoke English and were generally more educated, like the Sri Lankan Tamils, also held outsized proportions of government employment.

12 Lukman Harees, "Independence Not An Accident: Inspiring Examples From Then Muslim Leaders," *Colombo Telegraph*, February 1, 2016, https://www.colombotelegraph.com/index.php/independence-not-an-accident-inspiring-examples-from-then-muslim-leaders/. Senanayake's profession of communal amity was marred by his support for the Ceylon Citizenship Act, which effectively blocked many Indian Tamils from citizenship. He did nevertheless advocate a secular state and a shared sense of nationhood that embraced the country's constituent groups. The fact that G. G. Ponnambalam, one of the most prominent and ardent advocates of Tamil rights, joined his cabinet, speaks to Senanayake's transethnic appeal. See K. M. de Silva, "Sri Lanka's

First Decade of Independence: Phase II in the Transfer of Power," *Verfassung und Recht in Übersee / Law and Politics in Africa, Asia and Latin America* 8, nos. 3/4 (1975): 333–35; K. M. de Silva, *A History of Sri Lanka* (New York: Penguin Books, 2005), 608.

13 In particular, the British governor, Sir William Manning, opposed the Ceylon National Congress, which emphasized national unity. He undermined the organization by encouraging various groups to seek communal representation. See de Silva, *A History of Sri Lanka*, 484–88. As an end to British rule was being contemplated, the Donoughmore Commission and the colonial office's Soulbury report took a different view. They acknowledged that communal representation and division, which made Sir Lanka more manageable as a colony, would make it perilously unstable as an independent country. See *Ceylon: Report on the Commission of Constitutional Reform* (London: His Majesty's Stationery Office, 1945), 7.

14 Sachithanandam Sathananthan, "How We Came To This Pass—II," *Colombo Telegraph*, June 27, 2019, https://www.colombotelegraph.com/index.php/how-we-came-to-this-pass-ii/. He also remarked (in English, ironically): "I have never found anything to excite the people quite the way this language issue does." See Gordon Weiss, *The Cage: The Fight for Sri Lanka and the Last Days of the Tamil Tigers* (New York: Bellevue Literary Press, 2012), 32.

15 Barbara Crossette, "Sri Lankans Lament Loss of a Linguistic Bridge," *New York Times*, June 11, 1986, https://www.nytimes.com/1986/06/11/world/sri-lankans-lament-loss-of-a-linguistic-bridge.html.

16 Crossette, "Sri Lankans Lament Loss."

17 "Excerpts from an Interview with Lee Kuan Yew," *New York Times*, August 29, 2007, https://www.nytimes.com/2007/08/29/world/asia/29iht-lee-excerpts.html.

18 After World War II, Singapore was in a much worse state than Sri Lanka. Today, Singapore outranks the United States on the UN's Human Development Index, while Sri Lanka trails behind Albania and Iran.

19 "Linguistic Slights Spur Ethnic Division in Sri Lanka," *Economist*, March 2, 2017, https://www.economist.com/asia/2017/03/02/linguistic-slights-spur-ethnic-division-in-sri-lanka.

20 Bandaranaike got as far as nationalizing the ports and buses before he was assassinated; the rest would be left up to his wife.

21 Nira Wickramasinghe, "Democracy and Entitlements in Sri Lanka: The 1970s Crisis over University Admission," *South Asian History and Culture* 3, no. 1 (January 2012): 82.

22 Irving B. Kravis, Alan Heston, and Robert Summers, *World Product and Income: International Comparisons of Real Gross Product* (Baltimore: Johns Hopkins University Press, 1982), 15. During Sirimavo's second tenure (1970–77), it averaged less than 1 percent growth a year. For the whole period (1960–78) the average GDP growth rate was a dismal negative 1.2 percent. See Surjit S. Bhalla and Paul Glewwe, "Growth and Equity in Developing

Countries: A Reinterpretation of the Sri Lankan Experience," *World Bank Economic Review*, September, 1986, 51–52.

23 Wickramasinghe, "Democracy and Entitlements in Sri Lanka," 84.

24 K. M. de Silva, "Sri Lanka (Ceylon) The New Republican Constitution," *Verfassung und Recht in Übersee / Law and Politics in Africa, Asia and Latin* 5, no. 3 (1972): 241.

25 Wickramasinghe, "Democracy and Entitlements in Sri Lanka," 85.

26 Wickramasinghe, "Democracy and Entitlements in Sri Lanka," 86. Sirimavo, like her husband, came from a wealthy Kandyan Sinhalese family. Her education minister, Badiuddin Mahmud, was a Muslim who exerted a strong influence in her administration.

27 The number of Muslims in science faculties doubled between 1970 and 1975. Wickramasinghe, "Democracy and Entitlements in Sri Lanka," 86.

28 De Silva, "Affirmative Action Policies." This new arrangement angered not only Tamils, but also Low-Country Sinhalese.

29 S. Ratnajeevan H. Hoole, "Tamils Were Still Shut Out," *Sri Lanka Guardian*, February 24, 2008, http://www.srilankaguardian.org/2008/02/tamils-were-still-shut-out.html.

30 Thomas Sowell, *Affirmative Action around the World: An Empirical Study* (New Haven, CT: Yale University Press, 2004), 34, 186–87.

31 For example, see Holly Reeves, "Mahathir Hits New Low: Blaming the Chinese for Poor Politics Is a Coward's Way," *ASEAN Today*, January 18, 2017, https://www.aseantoday.com/2017/01/mahathir-hits-new-low-blaming-the-chinese-for-poor-politics-is-a-cowards-way/; "That's Not a Chinese Malaysian Burning the Jalur Gemilang, it's a Filipino Cop . . . from 2013!" *Star*, August 23, 2019, https://www.thestar.com.my/news/true-or-not/2019/08/23/thats-not-a-chinese-malaysian-burning-the-jalur-gemilang-its-a-filipino-cop--from-2013; Amy Chew, "In Malaysia, Fake News of Chinese Nationals Getting Citizenship Stokes Racial Tensions," *This Week In Asia*, September 10, 2019, https://www.scmp.com/week-asia/people/article/3026427/malaysia-fake-news-chinese-nationals-getting-citizenship-stokes.

32 Nirmal Ghosh, "Little Distinction between Ethnic Thai and Chinese amid Close Ties," *Straits Times*, February 19, 2015, https://www.straitstimes.com/asia/se-asia/little-distinction-between-ethnic-thai-and-chinese-amid-close-ties.

33 De Silva, "Affirmative Action Policies: The Sri Lankan Experience," 256.

34 English-speaking Burghers enjoyed an even more outsized share of jobs. Their overrepresentation peaked early in the 1900s. See Wickramasinghe, "Democracy and Entitlements in Sri Lanka," 90.

35 Sowell, *Affirmative Action around the World*, 92.

36 Veluppillai Prabhakaran, "Reflections of the Leader—Quotes by Veluppillai Pirapakaran," trans. Peter Schalk and Alvappillai Velupillai, Tamilnation.org, acccessed July 19, 2022, https://tamilnation.org/books/eelam/schalk_reflections_of_a_leader; Peter Wonacott, "A Notorious Terrorist Who

Refused to Compromise to the End," *Wall Street Journal*, May 19, 2009, https://www.wsj.com/articles/SB124269099109232581.

37 "LTTE Can Be Dealt Only Militarily, Says Rajapakṣa," *Economic Times*, November 14, 2008, https://economictimes.indiatimes.com/news/politics-and-nation/ltte-can-be-dealt-only-militarily-says-rajapaksa/articleshow/3710647.cms.

38 "Sri Lanka: Bring Up the Bodies," *Economist*, March 8, 2014, https://www.economist.com/asia/2014/03/08/bring-up-the-bodies. Former UN spokesperson Gordon Weiss, who was an eyewitness, provides the most thorough and balanced account of this final bloodbath in *The Cage: The Fight for Sri Lanka and the Last Days of the Tamil Tigers.*

39 "Sri Lanka Investigating Regime Ousted in 1977," *New York Times*, August 2, 1978, https://www.nytimes.com/1978/08/02/archives/sri-lanka-investigating-regime-ousted-in-1977.html.

40 Rajesh Venugopal, *Nationalism, Development and Ethnic Conflict in Sri Lanka* (Cambridge: Cambridge University Press, 2018), 13–14; Benedikt Korf, "Dining with Devils? Ethnographic Enquiries into the Conflict–Development Nexus in Sri Lanka," *Oxford Development Studies* 34, no. 1 (August 2006): 49–51.

41 Sri Lanka ranks in the bottom half of the world in most measures. See Transparency International, *Global Corruption Report (2018)* (Berlin: Transparency International, 2019).

42 William McGowan, *Only Man is Vile: The Tragedy of Sri Lanka* (London: Pan Books, 1993), 105.

9 ∗ FROM COLOR BAR TO COLORBLIND IN BOTSWANA

1 The 2016 film, *A United Kingdom*, dramatizes the story of Ruth and Seretse and demonstrates how it continues to capture public interest even seventy years later.

2 This was a particularly sensitive issue for South Africa because it was about to institute its infamous apartheid policy. The sensitivity was enhanced because Bechuanaland's capital was not located in Bechuanaland itself, but across the border in Mafeking, South Africa. The capital was moved to Gaborone, Botswana in 1965.

3 The friend was Tanzanian leader Julius Nyerere. "Ruth Khama: A London Secretary Who Became Part of One of the World's Greatest Love Stories," *Herald*, May 26, 2002, https://www.heraldscotland.com/news/11961889.ruth-khama-a-london-secretary-who-became-part-of-one-of-the-worlds-greatest-love-stories/.

4 Mary Benson, *Tshekedi Khama* (London: Faber & Faber, 1960), 179.

5 Susan Williams, *Colour Bar: The Triumph of Seretse Khama and his Nation* (London: Penguin Books, 2016), 74.

6 472 Parl. Deb. H.C. (5h ser.) 1950 col 295, https://hansard.parliament.uk/Commons/1950-03-08/debates/20e135b2-50e4-46e1-bf01-e6e5153e85a2/Triba

lChiefBechuanaland(Recognition)#contribution-53a9518d-9a14-44d8-ba9d-f782b27833a8.

7 The moving first-hand account of Tshekedi's death is from Mary Benson, Tshekedi's friend and secretary. Benson, *Tshekedi Khama*, 303.

8 "Bechuanaland's Future, Non-Racial Democracy," *Fordham Ram*, October 29, 1965. https://www.library.fordham.edu/digital/item/collection/RAM/id/8914

9 Bechuanaland Democratic Party, *B.D.P. Election Manifesto* (Gaberone: Bechuanaland Democratic Party, 1965).

10 See article 15 of the Botswana constitution, "Botswana's Constitution of 1966 with Amendments through 2005," https://www.constituteproject.org/constitution/Botswana_2016.pdf?lang=en.

11 *Population and Housing Census 2011 Administrative and Technical Report* (Gaborone: Statistics Botswana, 2016), 57.

12 *B.D.P. Election Manifesto.*

13 In the first genocide of the twentieth century, German colonialists killed over 80 percent of the Herero. See Frank Robert Vivelo, "The Entry of the Herero into Botswana," *Botswana Notes and Records* 8 (1976); Bammaruru Bahumi Kebonang, "The History of the Herero In Mahalapye, Central District: 1922–1984," *Botswana Notes and Records* 21 (1989).

14 Owen Ullmann, "As U.S. Marks Black History Month, Botswana Offers a Valuable Lesson about Racial Harmony" *USA Today*, February 1, 2019, https://www.usatoday.com/story/news/world/2019/01/31/botswana-offers-u-s-valuable-lesson-achieving-racial-harmony/2731108002/.

15 Catie Gressier, *At Home in the Okavango: White Batswana Narratives of Emplacement and Belonging* (Oxford: Berghahn Books, 2015), 75.

16 J. Clark Leith, *Why Botswana Prospered* (Montreal: McGill-Queen's University Press, 2005), 28–30.

17 Daron Acemoglu, Simon Johnson, and James A Robinson, "An African Success Story: Botswana," in *In Search of Prosperity: Analytic Narratives on Economic Growth*, ed. Dani Rodrik (Princeton, NJ: Princeton University Press, 2003), 80. See also "Databank World Development Indicators: Popular Indicators," World Bank, accesseed July 19, 2022, https://databank.worldbank.org/source/world-development-indicators; Festus Mogae, "How We Created and African Success Story," *New African*, April, 2005, 32–33.

18 "Government Expenditure on Education, Total (% of GDP)," World Bank, accessed July 19, 2022, https://data.worldbank.org/indicator/SE.XPD.TOTL.GD.ZS. . See also " Global Data (2020)," Fragile States Index, accessed July 19, 2022, https://fragilestatesindex.org/data/.

19 The Casino Theatre is now called the Prince Edward Theatre. Marx lived in two different houses on Dean Street, just around the corner. He and Friedrich Engels wrote the *Communist Manifesto* in 1847, exactly one hundred years before Ruth and Seretse's first date.

20 "GDP Per Capita (Current US$)," World Bank, accessed July 19, 2022, https://data.worldbank.org/indicator/NY.GDP.PCAP.CD.

21 Joel D. Barkan and Michael Chege, "Decentralising the State: District Focus and the Politics of Reallocation in Kenya," *Journal of Modern African Studies* (1989): 448–50.

22 William Easterly and Ross Levine, "Africa's Growth Tragedy: Policies and Ethnic Divisions," *Quarterly Journal of Economics* (November 1997): 1217–18.

23 Scott A. Beaulier, *Look Botswana, No Hands! Why Botswana's Government Should Let the Economy Steer Itself* (Fairfax, VA: Mercatus Center, George Mason University, 2013), 5–6. For more examples, see Marian L. Tupy, "Botswana and Zimbabwe: A Tale of Two Countries," *American*, May 14, 2008.

24 Heritage Foundation, "Index of Economic Freedom," accessed July 20, 2022, https://www.heritage.org/index/.

25 World Health. Organization, "Estimated Antiretroviral Therapy Coverage among People Living with HIV (%)," Global Heath Observatory, October 11, 2021, https://www.who.int/data/gho/data/indicators/indicator-details/GHO/estimated-antiretroviral-therapy-coverage-among-people-living-with-hiv-(-).

26 *Tertiary Education Statistics 2018* (Gaborone: Human Resource Development Council of Botswana, 2018), 25. Over 10 percent of private cars are either BMWs, Land Rovers, Lexuses, or Mercedeses. See *Transport & Infrastructure Statistics Report 2019* (Gaborone: Botswana Minsitry of Transport and Communications, 2020), 1, 50.

10 * THE SOCIAL AND ECONOMIC COSTS OF ETHNIC DIVISION

1 Denmark and Egypt are far from the extremes; their per capita GDPs rank sixteenth and ninety-fourth, respectively, out of 188 countries.

2 For the calculation of the ethnic fractionalization index and comparisons of different fractionalization measures, see "Ethnic Fractionalization (EF and ELF)" in appendix B.

3 Donald Horowitz, *Ethnic Groups in Conflict* (Berkeley: University of California Press, 1985), 563.

4 Other studies have documented the correlation of fractionalization and civil wars. See, for example, Ibrahim Elbadawi and Nicholas Sambanis, "How Much War Will We See? " *Journal of Conflict Resolution* 46, no. 3 (June 2002). Some have suggested that the relationship is curvilinear with the probability of civil war rising with fractionalization at lower levels but then flattening at higher levels. See Joan Esteban, "Polarization, Fractionalization, and Conflict," *Journal of Peace Research* 45, no. 2 (2008). Others have noted that civil wars correlate somewhat better with ethnic polarization than ethnic fractionalization: the odds of war are highest when the population is close to evenly divided. See Jose Montalvo and Marta Reynal-Querol, "Ethnic Polarization, Potential Conflict, and Civil Wars," *American Economic Review* 95 No. 3 (2005). This is perhaps implicit in the definition of civil war: when many groups are fighting, it is anarchy rather than war.

5 Rummel used a dataset of 140 countries over fifty years. To determine whether the connection was direct, he applied factor analysis to strip out the effects of a wide variety of underlying social and economic factors. See R. J. Rummel, "Is Collective Violence Correlated with Social Pluralism," *Journal of Peace Research* 34 (May 1997). More recent studies have confirmed the connection between fractionalization and political violence. See, for example, Hilde Bakkan, Tor Jakobsen, and Jo Jakobsen, "Unpacking Ethnicity: Exploring the Underlying Mechanisms Linking Ethnic Fractionalization and Civil Conflict, Peace and Conflict," *Journal of Peace Psychology* 22, no. 4 (2016).

6 The correlation was significant at the 5 percent level. The study found that fractionalization is most strongly correlated with riots "when individuals from different ethnic groups live together in close quarters" and concluded that ethnic heterogeneity is a "central component" in explaining the occurrence of riots. See Denise DiPasquale, "The L.A. Riot and the Economics of Urban Unrest," *Journal of Urban Economics* 43 (1998).

7 In their seminal and groundbreaking study, Easterly and Levine found "a movement from complete [ethnic] heterogeneity to complete homogeneity...is associated with an income increase of 3.8 times." See Easterly and Levine, "Africa's Growth Tragedy," 1239. Several other studies have proposed alternate fractionalization measures but have still confirmed Easterly and Levine's results. See, for example, Daniel Posner, "Measuring Fractionalization in Africa," *American Journal of Political Science* 48, no. 4 (October 2004). Some studies have correlated differences in fractionalization with economic growth over time. See, for example, Natalka Patsiurko, "Measuring Cultural Diversity: Ethnic, Linguistic and Religious Fractionalization in the OECD," *Ethnic and Racial Studies* 35, no. 2 (2012).

8 South Korea has a per capita Gross National Income (GNI) of $40,090 and an EF of 0.0020 (Alesina's measure); Uganda has a GNI of $1,970 and EF of 0.9302. See Alberto Alesina et al., "Fractionalization," *Journal of Economic Growth* 8, no. 2 (2003): 167.

9 The F-statistic for the regression is 96.1; the p-value is 1.265E-17. As table B.11 in appendix B shows, the correlation is not dependent on the particular ethnic fractionalization index used here; alternate fractionalization indices also have highly significantly negative correlations with living standards.

10 This is based on the regression in table B.6 in appendix B. A per capita increase of $10,322 is somewhat smaller than what Alesina's model predicts (a 14 percent increase for each 0.10 decrease in fractionalization). See Alesina et al., "Fractionalization."

11 See, for example, Elissaios Papyrakis and Pak Hung Mo, "Fractionalization, Polarization, and Economic Growth: Identifying the Transmission Channels," *Economic Inquiry* 52, no. 3 (2014).

12 "The 10 most-costly riots in the U.S.," *Chicago Tribune*, November 26, 2014, https://www.chicagotribune.com/chi-insurance-civil-unrest-riots-bix-gfx-20141126-htmlstory.html; "Timeline of the Riots in Modi's

Gujarat," *New York Times*, August 19, 2015, https://www.nytimes.com/interactive/2014/04/06/world/asia/modi-gujarat-riots-timeline.html.

13 Easterly and Levine, "Africa's Growth Tragedy"; Alesina et al., "Fractionalization."

14 Many other studies have found significant negative correlations between fractionalization and the provision of public goods, even when other factors, such as income, are accounted for. See, for example, Rafael LaPorta et al., "The Quality of Government," *Journal of Law, Economics and Organization* 15, no. 1 (1999); Alberto Alesina, "Public Goods and Ethnic Diversity: Evidence from Deforestation in Indonesia," *Economica* 86, no. 341 (2019); Easterly and Levine, "Africa's Growth Tragedy"; Mwangi S. Kimenyi, "Ethnicity, Governance and the Provision of Public Goods," *Journal of African Economies* 15, suppl. 1(2006).

15 One study, which covered several thousand US cities and counties, found that the provision of public goods is "inversely related to... ethnic fragmentation, even after controlling for other socioeconomic and demographic determinants" See Alberto Alesina, Reza Baqir, and William Easterly, "Public Goods and Ethnic Divisions," *Quarterly Journal of Economics* 114, no. 4 (November 1999): 1243.

16 Robert D. Putnam, "E Pluribus Unum: Diversity and Community in the Twenty-first Century," *Scandinavian Political Studies* 30, no. 2 (2007).

17 Teresa P. R. Caldeira, *City of Walls: Crime, Segregation, and Citizenship in Sao Paulo* (Berkeley: University of California Press, 2000), 256–91. Most Brazilian gated communities differ from those in the United States, featuring high, barbed wired-topped walls and private security guards armed with machineguns. See Thayana Marques Araujo Ayoobi, "A Tale of Modern Segregation in High-end Brazilian Gated-Communities," *Globe Post*, May 25, 2018, https://theglobepost.com/2018/05/25/brazil-modern-segregation/.

18 Overall government spending in Brazil is fairly high for a middle-income country. However, that spending has been directed toward wealthier recipients, leaving public goods, particularly in poor areas, underfunded. See World Bank, *Brazil Public Spending on Social Programs: Issues and Options* (New York: World Bank, 1988).

19 Santa Catarina ranks first in virtually every category: low infant mortality, education, life expectancy, and so on. In 2018, Santa Catarina devoted 14 percent of its budget to education, whereas Rio de Janeiro devoted only 8 percent. See "Boost Open Budgets Portal," World Bank, accessed July 19, 2022, http://boost.worldbank.org/. See also Pedro Henrique Soares Leivas and Anderson Moreira Aristides Dos Santos, "Horizontal Inequality and Ethnic Diversity in Brazil," *Oxford Development Studies* (2018): 348–62.

20 Jonathan Watts, "Why Brazil Loves Nip and Tuck, As Told by Country's Plastic Surgery 'Maestro,'" *Guardian*, September 14, 2014, https://www.theguardian.com/world/2014/sep/24/brazil-loves-nip-tuck-plastic-surgeon-ivo-pitanguy.

21 Estelle James conducted a study of educational spending in fifty countries and found that cultural heterogeneity is "the most important explanatory factor" in the percentage of private school spending. See Estelle James, "Why Do Different Countries Choose a Different Public-Private Mix of Educational Services?" *Journal of Human Resources* 28, no. 3 (Summer 1993); Estelle James, "The Public/Private Division of Responsibility for Education: An International Comparison," *Economics of Education Review* 6, no. 1 (1987).

22 "Low-Cost Private Schools," *Economist*, August 1, 2015.

23 Others found a strong negative correlation between ethnic fractionalization and both school spending and quality. See Edward Miguel and Mary Kay Gugerty, "Ethnic Diversity, Social Sanctions, and Public Goods," *Journal of Public Economics* 89, 11–12 (2005).

24 Nurith Aizenman, "A New 'Taxonomy Of Corruption' In Nigeria Finds 500 Different Kinds," npr.org, August 28, 2018, https://www.npr.org/sections/goatsandsoda/2018/08/28/641245377/a-new-taxonomy-of-corruption-in-nigeria-finds-500-different-kinds.

25 PricewaterhouseCoopers, *Impact of Corruption*, PricewaterhouseCoopers (2016). The study found that Nigeria only needed to reduce corruption to Malaysia's levels. Malaysia is itself fairly corrupt, with a 53 rating on Transparency International's CPI scale. See also "The $20-Billion Hole in Africa's Largest Economy," *Economist*, February 2, 2016, https://www.economist.com/middle-east-and-africa/2016/02/02/the-20-billion-hole-in-africas-largest-economy. Paolo Mauro and others have conducted broader studies connecting corruption and low growth. See Paolo Mauro, "Corruption and Growth," *Quarterly Journal of Economics* 110, no. 3 (1995); Paolo Mauro, *The Effects of Corruption on Growth, Investment, and Government Expenditure*, International Monetary Fund Working Paper no. 96/98 (September 1996).

26 "Relatório Corrupção: custos econômicos e propostas de combate," Federação das Indústrias do Estado de São Paulo, March 2010. A single scandal (known as *lava jato*, or "car wash") cost the country multiple billions, enough to educate "17 million children." Ed Davey, "Enough to Educate 17 Million Children: The True Cost of Brazil's Car Wash Scandal," *New Statesman*, March 23, 2018, https://www.newstatesman.com/world/americas/south-america/2018/03/enough-educate-17-million-children-true-cost-brazil-s-car-wash-scandal.

27 See figure 10.3. The correlation of EF to corruption is significant at the 0.1 percent level. These results confirm earlier studies by Paolo Mauro, who used Country Risk Services corruption statistics. Mauro found that ethnic fractionalization is "highly correlated" with corruption, significant at the one percent level. See Mauro, "Corruption and Growth," 693. Other studies have confirmed Mauro's findings. See, for example, LaPorta et al., "The Quality of Government."

28 Peter Larmour, "Corruption and Governance in the South Pacific," paper presented at the Pacific Islands Political Studies Association, Palau, 1996; M.

Monsell-Davis, "Urban Exchange: Safety-Net or Disincentive? Wantoks and Relatives in the Urban Pacific," *Canberra Anthropology* 16, no. 2 (1993).

29 Easterly and Levine, "Africa's Growth Tragedy," 1216–17.

30 For example, the *Economist* notes that in Nigeria members of the ethnic majority in each state "dominate the administration and hand out the best jobs and contracts to each other." See "Survey: Nigeria," *Economist*, August 21, 1994. The history of the European Commission (EC) government demonstrates that corruption is not just a function of culturally based standards of honesty. Individual European countries are some of the least corrupt in the world; if that were a sufficient condition for combined government probity, the EC would also be relatively corruption-free. But the EC, unlike the constituent national governments, embraces a highly fractionalized population and suffers from the corresponding level of corruption. From its very inception it has allowed misallocation and embezzlement totaling many billions. See, for example, "Corruption Scandal Jolts European Union," *Boston Globe*, March 14, 1999; David Brooks, "The New Europe—Farce; Brussels Sprouts a Scandal," *Weekly Standard*, March 29, 1999.

31 "Rolling Thunder," *The Sunday Times*, February 28, 1999.

32 "Racial Politics in Buffalo," *Wall Street Journal*, April 8, 1999.

33 Michael Touchton, "Dangers of diversity: Ethnic Fractionalization and the Rule of Law," *Economics, Management, and Financial Markets* 1 (2013).

34 A regression of real per capita GDP and the Economic Freedom Index yields a strong and highly significant correlation. See table B.17 in appendix B.

35 This is based on the ratings of the Economist Intelligence Unit. *Democracy Index 2019: A Year of Democratic Setbacks and Popular Protest, Economist Intelligence Unit*, 2019. Two of the four fully democratic countries—Switzerland and Canada—have EF numbers that overstate their actual fractionalization. See "Exceptions that Prove the Rule" in appendix B. An earlier study found that a one percent change in ethnic fractionalization corresponds with a 0.14 increase in the likelihood that a state will be less democratic. See Philippe Aghion, Alberto Alesina, and Francesco Trebbi, "Endogenous Political Institutions," *Quarterly Journal of Economics* 119, no. 2 (2004).

36 Somalia could be considered a possible exception, with its relatively low ethnolinguistic fractionalization. However, if we account for the fact that Somali clans are effectively ethnic groups, fractionalization is quite high. Moreover, neither of the organizations that publish economic freedom indexes rate Somalia; if we consider that the warlords are effectively the government, the economy could also be described as "government-dominated."

37 Walter E. Williams, *South Africa's War against Capitalism* (New York: Praeger, 1989).

38 Tashny Sukumaran, "What's Causing Malaysia's Ethnic Chinese Brain Drain?" *This Week in Asia*, May 20, 2017, https://www.scmp.com/week-asia/politics/article/2095012/whats-causing-malaysias-ethnic-chinese-brain-drain.

39 "Sweden Government Spending to GDP," Trading Economics, accessed July 19, 2022, https://tradingeconomics.com/sweden/government-spending-to-gdp.

40 *Trust—The Nordic Gold* (Copenhagen: Nordic Council of Ministers, 2017). Recent studies show a sharp decline in social trust in the Nordic countries following the recent surge of refugees and immigrants. See, for example, Karl Mc Shane, "Getting Used to Diversity? Immigration and Trust in Sweden," *Economics Bulletin* 37, no. 3 (2017).

41 "World Happiness Report," 2019. The EF number for Iceland is from Alesina's dataset. See Alesina et al., "Fractionalization."

11 * CONCLUSION

1 Isabelle Crevecoeur et al., "New Insights on Interpersonal Violence in the Late Pleistocene Based on the Nile Valley Cemetery of Jebel Sahaba," *Scientific Reports*, May 27, 2021. Some remains from the site are on display at the British Museum.

2 The Hebrew *am achad* (עַם אֶחָד) is translated here as "one people," though "one community" is perhaps a more faithful rendering.

3 S. N. Kramer, "The 'Babel of Tongues': A Sumerian Version," *Journal of the American Oriental Society* 88 (1968).

4 Homer, *The Illiad of Homer*, trans. Samuel Butler (London: Longmans, Green, 1898), 62.

5 Homer, *Illiad*, 40.

6 "Andhra Pradesh 50 Percent Reservation to BCs, SCs, STs and Minorities in all the Nominated Posts," act no. 24 of 2019. The Indian Supreme court caps "reservations" at 50 percent, but many regions have instituted reservations that reach this cap. G Ananthakrishnan, "Supreme Court Throws out Maratha Quota Law, Cites 50% Reservation Cap," *Indian Express*, May 6, 2021, https://indianexpress.com/article/india/supreme-court-quashes-maharashtra-law-granting-reservation-to-maratha-community-7302656/.

7 Christopher Eberhart, "Anti-Racist Author DOUBLES Speaking Fees as America Goes Woke: 'White Fragility' Writer Robin DiAngelo Charges an Average of $14,000 Per Speech and Makes '$728K a year,'" *Daily Mail*, July 2, 2021, https://www.dailymail.co.uk/news/article-9749517/An-anti-racist-author-Robin-DiAngelo-makes-728K-year-speaking-engagements.html.

APPENDIX A * THE CONSTITUTION OF MEDINA

1 Al-Qazim Ibn Sallam Abu 'Ubayd, *Kitab al Amwal*, ed. Muhammad Khalil Harras (Cairo: Maktaba al-Kulliyat al-Azhariyah, 1968); 'Abd al-Malik Ibn Hisham, *as-Sira al-Nabiwiyya (Das Leben Muhammed's nach...bearbeittet von...Ibn Hisham)*, ed. Ferdinand Wüstenfeld (Göttingen: Dieterischen Buchhandlung, 1859–60).

2 My translation uses Ibn Hisham's recension in as-Sira al-Nabiwiyya. I have adopted some phrases from Wellhausen, Wensinck, Watt, Guillaume, and

Lecker. See Julius Wellhausen, *Skizzen und Vorarbeiten: Medina vor dem Islam* (Berlin: Reimer, 1889), 67–73; A. J. Wensinck, *Muhammad and the Jews of Medina*, trans. W. Behn (Freiburg im Breisgau: K. Schwarz, 1975), 52–61; Muhammad Ibn Ishaq, *The Life of Muhammad: A Translation of Ishaq's Sirat Rasul Allah*, trans. A. Guillaume (Karachi: Oxford University Press, 1967), 231–33; Michael Lecker, *The "Constitution of Medina": Muhammad's First Legal Document* (Princeton, NJ: Darwin Press, 2004). The numbering used in this appendix follows Wensinck's.

3 For example, *'atabata* ("to kill unjustly"), *mufrih* ("person who has no tribal protection"), and *bitanah* ("close friends"). The term بطانة appears in Qur'an 3:118. Ibn Hisham claims that a mufrih is a person who has a large debt and a large family—an interpretation that does not fit well in the context of the constitution. The dictionary definitions for some these terms refer back to the constitution itself. For example, see Lane's definition of مفرح in Edward William Lane, *An Arabic-English Lexicon* (London: Williams and Norgate, 1877), 2362.

4 The word "Medina" appears once, in article 47. However, in the context of that article it denotes "city" in the general sense rather than the specific city of Yathrib. So, Guillaume's assertion that the line was a later addition is unfounded.

5 Other chroniclers were clear about the inclusion of Jews, including the large Jewish tribes. See, for example, Muhammad b. Umar al-Waqidi, *Kitab al-Maghazi*, ed. Marsden Jones (Oxford: Oxford University Press, 1966), 1:176.

6 SAW is an abbreviation for *salla Allahu alayhi wa sallam*, a customary salutation that Muslims utter after Muhammad's name.

7 Client (*mawali*) is used in the sense of a client-patron relationship.

8 In his notes, Ibn Hisham suggests this article required raiders to share camels or horses when there were not enough to go around.

9 The word *muhaddith* literally means "innovator." In Islam, innovation has negative associations, suggesting impiety. However, the preceding articles focus on protection and blood-money. So Lecker's translation of muhaddith as "murderer" makes the most sense in this context.

10 Abu Ubayd's version of this article has "community of the believers" (*ummah min al-mu'mineen*) in place of Ibn Ishaq's "community with the believers" (*ummah ma'a al-mu'mineen*). One variant manuscript has the word *amana* instead of *ummah*. Based on that, Michael Lecker provides an alternate translation: "The Jews of Banu Awf are secure from the believers." However, Ibn Ishaq is the earlier (and more reliable) transmitter, and we already know from article 1 that the Jews in the document are included in the *ummah*.

11 The antecedent for "them" is not entirely clear in this article. Wensinck thinks it is "the people of this document." However, in articles 37, 39, and 46, the constitution clearly specifies "people of this document" when it refers to them. Moreover, the articles before and after this article deal with Jews. So "the Jews" is the most likely antecedent.

APPENDIX B * STATISTICAL ANALYSES

1 *CIA World Factbook*, (La Vergne, TN: Skyhorse Publishing, 2019); "History of Burundi," in *Encyclopedia Britannica* (Chicago: Encyclopedia Britannica, 2020).

2 Alesina et al., "Fractionalization," 155–94.

3 "History of Burundi."

4 "Ethnic Groups Data," 2020.

5 Easterly and Levine, "Africa's Growth Tragedy." The data come from the following sources: S. I. Bruk and V. S. Apenchenko, eds., *Atlas Narodov Mira* (Moscow: USSR Academy of Sciences, 1964); Janet Roberts, "Sociocultural Change and Communication Problems," in *Study of the Role of Second Languages in Asia, Africa, and Latin America*, ed. Frank A. Rice (Washington, DC: Center for Applied Linguistics of the Modern Language Association of America, 1964); Siegfried H. Muller, *The World's Living Languages: Basic Facts of Their Structure, Kinship, Location, and Number of Speakers* (New York: Ungar, 1964).

6 "Ethnologue: Languages of the World," in *Ethnologue Project*, ed. Raymond G. Gordon, and Barbara F. Grimes (Dallas: SIL International, 2020).

7 James D. Fearon, "Ethnic and Cultural Diversity by Country," *Journal of Economic Growth* 8 (2003): 195–222. Fearon relied on data from Scarritt and Mozaffer. See James Scarritt and Shaheen Mozaffar, "The Specification of Ethnic Cleavages and Ethnopolitical Groups for the Analysis of Democratic Competition in Contemporary Africa," *Nationalism and Ethnic Politics* 5, no. 1 (1999). He used other sources to judge which groups were significant.

8 Minority populations are similarly concentrated in the other countries: in Belgium, Dutch-speaking Flemish are concentrated in Flanders and French-speaking Walloons are concentrated in Wallonia (only the capital, Brussels, is substantially mixed); in Spain, most Basques and Catalans live in the Pais Vasco and Catalonia, respectively; in the United Kingdom, Scots, Welsh, and Irish are concentrated in Scotland, Wales, and Northern Ireland.

9 The Belgian Constitution establishes individual "community governments" for the language groups (i.e., Flemish, Walloon, and German). Various articles of the constitution grant specific powers to the community governments. For example, article 127 grants them control over education and cultural issues. Spain's republican government initially granted autonomy to its ethnic regions. This autonomy was abrogated by General Franco, but then subsequently restored under the constitution of 1978. Article 1 of the constitution of 1978 establishes "autonomous communities" (e.g., the Pais Vasco and Catalonia), which it grants a large degree of self-government. Article 3 grants the autonomous communities the right to designate their own official languages. The Swiss constitution grants many of the prerogatives of sovereignty to the individual cantons: Article 9 allows the cantons to sign their own foreign treaties and article 44 delegates determination of citizenship and naturalization to the cantons. Articles 3 and 5 describe the overall relationship between the national government and the cantons.

10 For example, the EF value for Quebec province by itself would be a relatively low 0.20 (compared to the 0.55 figure for all of Canada).

11 "Resort to War: 1816–2007," Correlates of War Project, updated April 6, 2020, https://correlatesofwar.org/data-sets.

12 Roland Anthony Oliver and Michael Crowder, *The Cambridge Encyclopedia of Africa* (Cambridge: Cambridge University Press, 1981), s.v. "History of Burundi."

13 "Presidents Apologise over Croatian War," *BBC News*, September 10, 2003, http://news.bbc.co.uk/2/hi/europe/3095774.stm.

14 "Death Toll from Congo at 2.5 Million," *Chicago Tribune*, May 2, 2001, https://www.chicagotribune.com/news/ct-xpm-2001-05-02-0105020274-story.html; "Congo Leader's Poor Precedent," *Christian Science Monitor*, December 17, 1997, https://www.csmonitor.com/1997/1217/121797.opin.opin.2.html.

15 *The Weeks of Killing: State Violence, Communal Fighting and Sectarian Attacks in the Summer of 2013* (Cairo: Egyptian Initiative for Personal Rights, 2014).

16 *20 Years on, Bougainville Families Haunted by Missing*, Radio New Zealand International, Auckland, 2015.

17 "Rwanda Census Puts Genocide Death Toll at 937,000," *Reuters News*, April 14, 2014.

18 "ETA's Bloody History: 853 Killings in 60 Years," Associated Press, updated May 2, 2018.

INDEX